Youth

Key Concepts
Published

Youth

Gill Jones

polity

First published in 2009 by Polity Press

Polity Press
65 Bridge Street
Cambridge CB2 1UR, UK

Polity Press
350 Main Street
Malden, MA 02148, USA

ISBN-13: 978-0-7456-4094-5
ISBN-13: 978-0-7456-4095-2 (pb)

A catalogue record for this book is available from the British Library.

Typeset in 10.5 on 12 pt Sabon
by SNP Best-set Typesetter Ltd., Hong Kong
Printed and bound in Great Britain by MPG Books Ltd, Bodmin, Cornwall

The publisher has used its best endeavours to ensure that the URLs for
external websites referred to in this book are correct and active at the time of
going to press. However, the publisher has no responsibility for the websites
and can make no guarantee that a site will remain live or that the content is
or will remain appropriate.

Every effort has been made to trace all copyright holders, but if any have been
inadvertently overlooked the publishers will be pleased to include any
necessary credits in any subsequent reprint or edition.

For further information on Polity, visit our website: www.polity.co.uk

Contents

Acknowledgements

I am indebted to all those who have helped me over the years gradually develop the ideas in this book. The list is long, but includes the colleagues and clients I worked with when I was a social worker in London and Auckland in the 1970s, who showed me how individuals, families and communities function in the face of adversity; the colleagues I have worked with as a social scientist since, in Surrey, London, Edinburgh, Cambridge and Keele, who have in various ways helped me formulate an understanding of the social world; the wider network of friends who have always provided a sounding board for ideas; and not least the young people and parents who took part in the various research projects which have framed my understanding of youth in late modernity and reminded me what it is like to be young.

1
What is 'Youth'?

What's in a word?

'Youth is just a word,' according to Pierre Bourdieu, who subsequently goes a long way towards showing how and why this is not the case. As he indicates (1978), 'youth' has been an evolving concept, layered upon layers with values which reflect contemporary moral, political and social concerns. 'Youth' is a social construction with social meanings and it is the task of the sociology of youth to understand how and why these have developed. This book is about the changing approaches to youth as a theoretical concept, and the ways in which these have been applied in practice, including to young people.

The terminology of youth has developed over time, and its etymology throws some light on the problems of current English usage. According to the Oxford English Dictionary (SOED, 1983) 'youth', meaning the period between childhood and adulthood, is Old English (as are the terms 'child' and 'childhood'), while the adjective 'youthful' dates from 1561. The terminology of youth is somewhat restricted compared with that of childhood and leads to confusion. Firstly, whereas 'childlike' and 'childish' can be used to distinguish between positive and negative attributes respectively, there are no corresponding terms 'youthlike' and 'youthish' which might have similarly distinguished between positive and negative attributes of young people. Instead, 'youthful' serves confusingly to describe both. 'Youthfulness' thus conveys qualities, such as strength, beauty, idealism and energy, which are seen as desirable and coveted by older age groups, but on the other hand is also associated with 'inferior' characteristics of inexperience, lack of wisdom, hot-headedness, experimentation, naivety, greenness, and lack of maturity and sense. For the nineteenth-century composer Richard Wagner, youth represented heroic German nationalism in the romantic tradition of *Sturm und Drang*;[1] indeed Philippe Ariès (1962) has suggested that Wagner's Siegfried was 'the first typical adolescent of modern times'. On the other hand, indicating that youth is not simply a product of industrialization, one of Shakespeare's characters complained about young people (he specified those aged between 16 and 23) 'wronging the ancientry', while around 2,400 years ago Socrates commented that they 'scoff at authority and lack respect for their elders'.[2] So, youth is to be celebrated and deplored, and young people depicted as both heroes and villains.

Secondly, the word 'youth' is often used to denote both a person (in the same way as 'child' or 'adult') and a part of the life course (in the same way as 'childhood' and 'adulthood'). The expression 'youthhood' is now obsolete but, had it persisted, might have prevented this conflation. Although the concept of youth is still upheld as an ideal, once the term is applied to young people it becomes laden with negative meanings and, when it surfaces in its plural form of 'youths' (when, thanks to the media, 'hoodies' come to mind), tends also to be male-specific. I therefore use the term 'youth' in the sense of 'youthhood' to describe the part of the life course between childhood and adulthood (though the difficulties with this application will also become apparent), and also for succinctness as an adjective (such as in 'youth policy' or 'youth unemployment'), but never as a term for young people.

From his readings of French texts, Philippe Ariès (1962) argues that the states of childhood and youth did not exist in the Middle Ages since children were absorbed into the adult world at an early age. From later texts, Ariès identifies seven ages of life – *childhood* (from birth to age seven), *pueri-*

tia (from seven until fourteen), *adolescence* (from 14 until – variously – 21, 28 or older), *youth* (then the central age in the lifespan, lasting until 45 or 50), *senectitude*, and finally two stages of *old age*. These seven stages were linked to the planets and represented an attempt at the scientific understanding of biological destiny. Youth was at this time associated with the ability to be self-sufficient and responsible for others, in a very different construction from that of the present day. Over time, childhood and youth gradually became separated out from adulthood, largely through education, but this was only among the upper class. By the seventeenth century, childhood had become associated with dependence, so that childhood could only be left by leaving the state of dependence (Ariès, 1962), but this still only related to the upper classes. The terminology of childhood (such as 'lad' or 'boy') was applied to many working-class adults who were still in dependent situations, such as servants and apprentices. It was not until the nineteenth century, when child protection laws began to prohibit child employment and education was extended, that working-class childhood came to be distinguished from dependent adulthood. Ariès thus sees current understandings of childhood and youth as the product of industrialization. Youth is also, in other respects, the product of social and educational reforms, mainly during the twentieth century and mainly as a result of the development of welfare capitalism, in Britain at least. It is policy legislation above all else which defines life stages mainly by age, and designs provision accordingly, because age is amenable to measurement.

Pierre Bourdieu reminds us that the apparently arbitrary age divisions in societies reflect power relations and result from forms of manipulation. This does not only apply to youth. He argues that both youth and old age are socially constructed in the conflict (*lutte*) between the young and the old (Bourdieu, 1978). Thus, arguably, both current negative media representations of young people and moral panics over them represent manipulations by older and more powerful age generations. Intergenerational power relations may therefore be the key to understanding youth. To talk about young people as though they were a social unit, with common interests, strengths and weaknesses at a biologically defined age, is itself an obvious manipulation. The constructions of 'youth' during the modern age say as much about the builders as about their subjects, and the way that the concept of youth has been used clearly relates very closely to historical conditions and the social concerns of the time.

This chapter is about the rise and fall of the concept of youth within a more general story about the building and dismantling of grand narratives. Its theme is to examine the various ways in which young people have been seen to fit structurally with the wider society: by stage in life course, age, generation, social class, gender or as individuals. It begins to address further questions – how to understand the changing 'social context', and the relationship between 'youth', young people and the 'whole', and how and why constructions of youth vary by time and space, historically, cross-nationally and cross-culturally. Youth in late modernity is not the same as youth at the height of modernity, or youth in pre-industrial times. In order to facilitate cross-national variation without resorting to an evolutionary approach, we need to consider how wider social trends, such as empire-building, industrialization and urbanization in the eighteenth and nineteenth centuries, or the creation of welfare states, new technologies and globalization in the twentieth and twenty-first centuries, have affected constructions of youth and the experiences of young people in some countries and could affect them in others.

Key themes

Emerging from this narrative are some key themes which have formed the focus of academic debates over the decades. These have often been posited at first as either/or dualities, though, as the debates progress or collapse, it often seems that there was some right on both sides, depending on the circumstances. Sometimes it seems that the dualities are to be associated with the modern age, when such constructions were common, rather than with late modernity when many commentators reject them as inappropriate, outmoded or untenable. Debates include the following:

1   The *science versus nature* debate was the main thrust of the eighteenth-century Enlightenment, with its emphasis on rationality and epistemology rather than on the acceptance of fate. The shift from the dominance of myth and tradition to that of scientific knowledge marked the beginning of the age of modernity. Education was seen as the means of freeing young people from the traditional beliefs otherwise instilled in them by their parents.

2   The *biology versus culture* (and *nature versus nurture*) debates shifted the focus from youth as biologically determined to the study of the impact of social and cultural contexts on young people's experiences of youth. Early psychology was based on individual development and it was only later that the significance of the social and cultural context came to be recognized. The debate has been re-awakened with advances in new genetics, which once again suggest that some physical and psychological conditions are genetically inherited, and that the social is not always paramount. But there is still a tension between the two: at the most basic level, youth is biologically determined, but even this is changing, with earlier puberty, later childbearing and greater longevity.

3   The *age generation or social class* debate, between functionalists and subcultural theorists during the 1960s and 1970s, was over which was the more significant variable for understanding young people's social locations. The challenge became to reconcile the two, and to incorporate other structural factors into a more pluralist approach to youth. Current explanations of social inequality in youth suggest that it is important to understand both the structural and the cultural elements.

4   The *conflict versus consensus* debate, in the context of social continuity and change, posited ideas of generational conflict against ideas of generational conformity. The question was whether young people are socialized to accept the normative consensus or whether it might be part of the role of new generations to challenge and possibly resist it. The question therefore is whether the emphasis should be on effective socialization and social control, or whether challenges to social norms are needed, especially in circumstances where the norms reflect the ideology of a dominant and possibly corrupt power.

5 *Structure versus agency*, the big and long-standing debate in the sociology of youth, is about the extent to which young people are free to choose and act as autonomous individuals and the extent to which they are constrained by societal power structures and institutions. This develops into the *rationality versus culture* explanations of human actions. Here the debate is centred on whether young people's actions reflect the rational choice of autonomous adult individuals, or collective cultural beliefs, including culturally derived forms of rationality or defensive and largely unconscious collective responses to hegemonic power. Theories of reflexivity help to reconcile these 'alternatives'.

6 *Structure versus process* provokes debate about whether young people should be considered in a cross-sectional way as an age generation or smaller age group (perhaps because this facilitates policy development), or whether they can be best understood in relation to the processes of their transitions to adulthood. The recent 'Beings and Becomings' debate in childhood studies (Lee, 2001) warned that a focus on the *process* of childhood meant that children themselves could be lost from view. A challenge for researchers and policy-makers alike is how to reconcile the two.

7 *Contributors or dependants* debate – still largely to be aired – is over how the current complex and extended transition to adulthood is to be understood in terms of dependence. The dichotomizing of individuals into dependants or contributors does not reflect the complexity of young people's transitions. The shame associated with dependence feeds into young people's perceptions of their own guilt and public constructions of blame. This may prove to be the central problem of youth and is discussed in chapter 6.

Some of these themes are raised in the remainder of this chapter, while others are given more attention elsewhere in this book.

Nature or culture

The story of the concept of youth in social science begins in earnest with the Enlightenment, an intellectual movement in the eighteenth century which marked the beginning of the modern age, paving the way for scientific and technological advances. It represented the triumph of rationality over the fatalism associated with myth and tradition. In the case of young people, rationality was to be developed through education. According to Albert Einstein,[3] 'common sense is nothing more than a deposit of prejudices laid down in the mind before you reach eighteen'. Rousseau showed in *Emile, or On Education* (1762) how education could free children from tradition.

There is some ambivalence over whether young people are to be seen as in need of release from corruption by others or as untamed and untrained, 'savages' even, in their own right. Auguste Comte (1855), seen as the father of sociology, believed that the rationality of positivism provided the means of achieving social consensus. He suggested that an evolutionary process from myth to reason in society was mirrored in individual development, whereby knowledge passes from the theological or fictitious (associated with childhood), through the metaphysical or abstract (associated with youth), to the scientific or positive (associated with adulthood) (Jenks, 1996).

The first social scientist to comment specifically on adolescents was the American psychologist G. Stanley Hall, who described adolescence as both 'a marvellous new birth' and also as the age 'when most vicious careers are begun' (Hall, 1904: 325). He saw it as a perilous age, 'suggestive of some ancient period of storm and stress when old moorings were broken and a higher level attained' (Hall, 1904: xviii). Adolescence was on an unstable threshold between childhood and the rationality of adulthood.[4] It thus represented not only hope for society but also a threat to social stability. Like Comte and others,[5] Hall paralleled individual transitions from childlike pre-rationality to adult rationality with the evolutionary development of societies (to the detriment of each, according to Cohen, 1997). Referring to the United States, Hall (1904: xviii) wrote: 'In vigour, enthusiasm, and courage we are still young, and our faults are those of youth.' Cohen (1997) argues that Hall's conception of adolescents, as pulled by the contradictory forces of the primitive and the enlightened, set up the framework for future moral panics.

Psychological studies of adolescence proliferated. For many psychoanalysts, adolescence was a time when instability and disruption were to be expected. The 'storm and stress' observed during this period in life was seen to derive from the sexual and aggressive drives which followed puberty. Anna Freud (1937: 149–50) graphically described adolescents as oscillating between childhood and adulthood:

> Adolescents are excessively egotistic, regarding themselves as the centre of the universe and the sole object of interest, and yet at no time in later life are they capable of so much self-sacrifice and devotion. They form the most passionate love relations, only to break them off as abruptly as they began them. On the one hand, they throw themselves enthusiastically into the life of the community, and on the other, they have an overpowering longing for solitude. They oscillate between blind submission to some self-chosen leader and deviant rebellion against any and every authority. They are selfish and materially minded and at the same time full of lofty idealism.

Opinions in the world of psychoanalysis varied between those who blamed the individual psychopathology and those such as Bandura (1959) who blamed the external world, believing that reports of storm and stress were exaggerated. Both Bowlby and Winnicott refuted the idea that emotional disturbance was natural to adolescents. Shifting the emphasis from nature to nurture, they indicated instead the long-lasting impact of childhood experience, especially of parenting. From observations with evacuated children during the Second World War, Bowlby (1953) developed a theory of attachment and loss which suggested that delinquency in adolescence could be an outcome of early maternal deprivation. In a similar vein, Winnicott (1964: 228) indicated that a child needed a stable family life ('a circle of love and strength') from which to take risks and progress. For Winnicott, control was as important as care: thus, antisocial behaviour may not be the result of the child's psychopathology but an unconscious attempt to re-establish external control. Recognizing the significance of family relationships is an important step in moving beyond individual biology or psychopathology towards incorporating the social.

Rites of passage

With adolescence seen as a problem in western industrialized societies, anthropologists such as Margaret Mead (1943) and Evans-Pritchard (1951) studied transitions to adulthood in traditional societies – in their cases among Samoan girls and Nuer boys respectively. Their work had widespread influence on psychologists and sociologists of the time. They found that young people in the societies they studied, far from experiencing adolescent 'storm and stress', could make a smooth transition to adulthood through 'rites of passage'. These created clearly defined ritual structures (based on biological development) through which young men and women were accepted into adult status. Adult roles were known, desirable and achievable. There was consensus about them based on tradition handed down by elders – the 'guardians of tradition' (Giddens, 1994). This functionalist approach suggested an unproblematic fit between generations, and smooth transitions to adulthood which were unlikely to be interrupted or remain incomplete (the problems which in western societies were believed to lead to delinquency).

Reuter (1937) defined the basis of 'adolescent disorder' as cultural rather than biological, and identified the need for sociological research on adolescence. He suggested (1937: 419–21) that it was *only* in industrial societies, where there was neither appropriate training for adulthood nor a sure place in the social world, that young people faced an adjustment problem and could find themselves temporarily in a 'marginal world'. Jahoda and Warren (1965: 138) argued that in traditional societies, where physiological maturity and social maturity occur simultaneously, there are no problems with youth, and suggested that 'the level of civilisation seems related to the number of years which a society accords to youth.' They suggest that there is a vicious cycle: 'civilization' = extended youth = problematic youth = threat to civilization. Basically, the problems experienced by young people in industrial societies were created by the wider society and were not intrinsic to youth itself (or 'natural'). In a similar vein, Erikson (1965: 14) suggested: 'It is human to have a long childhood; it is civilized to have an even longer childhood.'

Developmental stages

The notion of life stages which dominated in the Middle Ages as a way of coping with biological fate became a tool of science. Sigmund Freud identified stages in the development of the individual psyche from infancy to youth (discussed in chapter 3). Youth came to be seen as a stage in ego-identity development, involving the shift of the individual from the family of origin to the external social world. The German psychologist Charlotte Bühler (1933) adopted a bio-social approach to human development. Identifying five life phases, she saw youth as the period between the acquisition of physiological maturity (puberty) and that of social maturity (defined by the social, sexual, economic and legal rights and duties of adults). Youth, for Bühler, provided a period for experimentation with ways to be adult.

Erikson's theory of ego development (1965: 254, and see also chapter 3) saw the adolescent mind as a 'mind of the *moratorium*, a psycho-social stage between the morality learned by the child and the ethics to be developed by the adult', and youth as a period of 'structured irresponsibility', during which young people should be allowed to experiment and achieve their own (non-ideological and non-traditional) ethics. He identified eight life stages associated with the development of ego identity, each associated with conflicts to be resolved: basic trust versus mistrust, autonomy/shame versus doubt, initiative versus guilt, and industry versus inferiority all formed part of pre-pubertal development; during puberty and adolescence, the tasks moved on to identity versus role-confusion, and among young adults to intimacy versus isolation. Erikson presents a model in which each task, though problematic, must be 'mastered' for the achievement of ego identity, but this, once achieved, is fixed. Erikson was a student of Margaret Mead and much influenced by her work, recognizing the importance of understanding the social context of ego development. His work has been criticized for failing to recognize that personal development can continue through the life course. The main problem with theories of life-stage development, however, is that they conflate difference and present a unified picture which is then adopted as the norm, any deviation from which can then be pathologized.

This is particularly the case with Jean Piaget's (1972) theory of learning, which fitted with the Enlightenment view but was an exception to a general trend towards the psycho-social. He argued that children acquire cognitive competences according to a universal sequence and can be assessed in relation to this normative sequencing. He identified stages of intellectual growth – pre-conceptual, intuitive, concrete, and reaching formal operations (capable of rationality) by early adolescence. The model represents steps in the expansion of the rational competence of the individual. Piaget's theory has been criticized for its claims of universality and lack of social and historical context (Jenks, 1996). The implication is that individuals should have achieved rationality by the time they become adolescent but may have failed to do so.

Age or generation

The move towards a sociological approach to youth began with explorations of how young people fit into social structures. Instead of simply seeing youth as a stage in the life course characterized by psychological instability, the challenge was to understand the nature of the connection between youth and society in terms of age and intergenerational relations.

This involved a shift in terminology from adolescence to youth. The former is still used, mainly among psychologists, to denote the period between the onset of puberty and adulthood and, being related to the teenage years, is relatively inflexible. Youth, on the other hand, is associated with the period between leaving school and becoming adult in socio-economic terms and thus currently covers the period, in most countries, between around 15 years and the mid-twenties, though both these age 'boundaries' are constantly rising, as this book will show. Youth and adolescence are therefore not interchangeable expressions.

Mannheim's theory of generations

Historical events such as wars, economic crises, natural disasters and mass cultural movements highlight the differences between those who experience them and those who do not, setting up a generational divide on the basis of age cohort. While the world stage was increasingly dominated by the opposing ideologies of communism and fascism, Karl Mannheim, who had been the victim of both, was developing a theory of knowledge which did not involve ideology. There was student unrest in Germany and a search for new solutions to the problem of explaining social change. Gradualist explanations were therefore likely to receive some support, and Mannheim proposed the idea of the free-floating intelligentsia as drivers of change: 'These intellectual elements then become the explosive material for bursting the limits of the existing order, leaving it free to develop in the direction of the next order of existence' (Mannheim, 1952 [1927]: 304).

An essential argument in Karl Mannheim's (1927) *The Problem of Generations* was that members of age generations, though located in the same historical time, were divided by their geographical and social location into 'differentiated antagonistic generation-units' (Mannheim, 1952[1927]: 306). He was referring to age generations (or age cohorts) rather than kin generations. Effectively setting the scene for the later development of the concept of 'peer group', Mannheim indicated that historical events were experienced differently by people in different social and spatial locations. 'The generation unit represents a much more concrete bond than the actual generation as such. Youth experiencing the same concrete historical problems may be said to be part of the same actual generation; while those groups within the same actual generation, which work up the material of their common experience in different specific ways, constitute separate generation units' (Mannheim, 1952: 304).

While the Spanish philosopher Ortega y Gasset (1998 [1931]: 15) saw the generation as 'the pivot responsible for the movement of historical evolution', Mannheim was much more cautious in his basic premise that structures of knowledge were context-specific. Indeed, his work was criticized by members of the neo-Marxist Frankfurt School of Social Research who considered it too relativist, though he thought of himself as 'relationist'. From his own Marxist standpoint, from which class conflict was the main driver of change, Cohen (1997) has more recently criticized Mannheim for producing a historical law of generational conflict, and questions why young people should be the privileged bearers of the *zeitgeist* (spirit of the age). However, Mannheim's insistence that age generations are divided into units seems to refute charges of either periodicity or 'age fallacy'. He was not arguing for chronological homogeneity.

Mannheim's theories have had an impact on theories of social movements. Wallace and Kovatcheva (1998: 41) describe the theory of 'juventization' in 1960s' Soviet society which proposed a similarly gradualist view of social change. Edmunds and Turner (2002) have recently applied Mannheim's theories, though differentiating between 'active' and 'passive' intellectual generations, with varying capacity for social change.

Functionalist theories of socialization

Talcott Parsons's focus was on continuity rather than change. According to Parsons and Bales (1956: 17), 'the central focus of the process of socialization lies in the internalization of the culture of the society into which the child is born.' Socialization theory is closely associated with developmental psychology. Parsons argued that, in a process of primary socialization during childhood, parents taught their children to conform to social norms and learn culturally prescribed future social and familial roles as workers in the labour market or in the home. He emphasized the importance of families as the 'factories' which produce human personalities (Parsons and Bales, 1956: 16).

In an industrial society where home and work had become separated, allowing scope for differing values and more varied biographies, primary socialization within the family could not prepare young people adequately for their future social roles (Reuter, 1937; Eisenstadt, 1973 [1956]). It was therefore necessary to supplement primary socialization within the family with secondary socialization in institutions set up by the state, such as schools. This 'professionalization of parenting' had the potential for further undermining the role of the family in primary socialization. Cohen (1997) suggested that socialization theory located youth at the point of tension between the competing value systems of the family and those of modern society, and it is thus not surprising that young people were confused about what was expected of them when they became adults. Parsons (1973) suggested that in such circumstances anomie can result. Erikson (1968) described how young people could be bewildered by their own feeling of incapacity to assume the role which society was forcing upon them. But there is a further problem. Because socialization theory was developed in relation to the normative values of male middle-class white Americans, attempts to apply it to other social groups 'inevitably led to a pathological view of their cultures' (Cohen, 1997: 187).

Culture or subculture

Their age peer group provided young people with one means of coping with the conflicting stresses. A debate ensued over whether peer cultures represented defiance, as suggested by functionalists, or were primarily a defensive response to oppression, as suggested by neo-Marxists. The period of national rebuilding following the Second World War had seen the development of the welfare state in Britain, along with the gradual relaxation of rationing, developments in communication technologies and expansion of consumer markets. The extension of education in the post-war period (in the UK, the Education Act 1944 raised the school-leaving age to 15, following many earlier extensions of compulsory education) meant that young people were increasingly segregated from the 'adult world', for which they were supposedly being prepared, in age-specific (youth) institutions. These developments increasingly opened up the experience of youth to working-class young people, who had previously been denied it. There was more scope for expression in language, style and music and, by the end of the 1950s, distinctive youth culture and styles were developing, influenced by access to US popular culture, from Elvis Presley to the outsiders portrayed in films such as *On the Waterfront* with Marlon Brando or *Rebel Without a Cause* with James Dean. It was the era when working-class culture came to the fore in Britain, too, with the 'angry young men' in theatre and film. It is hard to imagine now the shock impact of Elvis Presley on older age generations in the 1950s, but there was a feeling (yet again) that normative moral values were collapsing. In practice, what was happening was that the working-class popular or 'low' culture was gaining ground while middle-class 'high' culture was losing it.

Youth as culture

In the US, James Coleman (1961: 3) suggested that the school system created circumstances in which adolescents were 'forced inwards' towards their own age group, and developed a society among themselves, with its own culture, norms and status system, barely connected with adult society. For Parsons (1961) and Eisenstadt (1973 [1956]), the adolescent peer group formed its own separate social structure through which young people could transcend the status ascribed through the socio-economic status of their family, and achieve independent status within their own status system and according to their own specific goals and values. Musgrove (1969: 50) believed that young people were becoming a new form of age class 'relatively independent of the stratification system of adults'. Coleman (1961) considered age-based peer groups to be taking on a role of secondary socialization in competition with the school and diverting the energies of the young from its academic goals. Musgrove (1964) suggested that the segregation of young people led to their infantilization, young people behaving irresponsibly because they had no social responsibilities. Long before, Parsons (1942) had also referred to youth culture as a culture of irresponsibility. Charles Reich, in *The Greening of America,* declared that: 'Always before, young people felt themselves tied more to their immediate situations than to a "generation". But now, an entire culture, including music, clothes and drugs, began to distinguish youth. As it did, the message of consciousness went with it' (Reich, 1972: 253).

In the twists and turns of the career of the concept of youth, the paths now divided between those who stressed youth culture as a counter-culture in conflict with adult 'established' society, and those who saw it as subcultural and reflecting class continuity. In this debate, one of the big questions was whether young people were becoming marginalized by society or whether they were marginalizing themselves.

Conflict or conformity

Opinions differed over whether young people were corrupted by society (and needed to be freed) or were a corrupting influence upon society (and needing to be controlled). Young people have long been portrayed as disrespectful of their elders, as indicated by the earlier quotations from Socrates and Shakespeare. In the period following the Great Depression, there was an increased interest in the 'moral threat' posed by adolescent behaviour in the US. The Chicago School developed socio-ecological studies of young people. Robert Park (Park, Burgess, and McKenzie, 1925) began to study urban social groups as a means of understanding conflict and social change, finding that subcultural groups developed out of normal conditions of urban social life rather than individual or group psychopathology (Downes and Rock, 1982). Whyte's classic study, *Street Corner Society* (1943), proposed that deviant acts were a function of the relationship between the neighbourhood, the family and the young – in other words, they arose out of cultural conditions.

Even so, the increasing visibility of youth cultural styles set up the conditions for adult paranoia about a 'generation war'. With the appearance of Teds in the 1950s, mods and rockers in the 1960s, and hippies in the 1960s–70s, the apprehension of the 'older generation' increased – to paranoia at times (see S. Cohen, 1973; Pearson, 1983). The 1960s – described by Galbraith as 'The Affluent Society' (the Prime Minister Harold Macmillan had told Britain, 'you've never had it so good') – provided a seemingly class-free climate in which theories of generational conflict could easily take root. Studies of youth culture, such as that of Riesman (1950), suggested the relative omnipotence of the adolescent peer group. Suddenly it seemed that young people were becoming significant consumers (Abrams, 1961) and developing styles which were outwardly very different from those of their parents.

There were other reasons for trying to understand what was happening. Alongside the development of popular culture (music and style), there was a new political awakening among young people who were more openly critical of the performance of their governments than their parents may have been in their own youth during the war, when national loyalty was expected. During the 1960s, when the US and USSR came perilously close to starting a new world conflict during the 1962 Cuban Missile Crisis, and as a response to the Vietnam War, anti-war, anti-colonial and anti-nuclear movements led to demonstrations and marches in many countries. These events coincided with the spurt in development of sociology as an academic discipline during the 1960s and had an immediate impact on the formative years of many now established or retired academics, many of whom were, as students, involved in them. The student movement of the time seemed to represent a form of counter-culture. Commentators such as Wilson (1970), Musgrove (1964, 1974), Friedenberg (1973) and Rex (1972) suggested that the generation struggle was eclipsing the class struggle in the 1960s, especially when social class barriers appeared to be breaking down.

In the UK, the early 1970s saw the start of the decline of the trade union movement with conflict between the miners and the government. Having rejected a class analysis, functionalist commentators were drawn back into a crudely Mannheimian explanation of generational change. The concept of 'counter-culture' effectively meant intergenerational conflict. The question was whether the impetus was offensive or defensive. Musgrove (1974: 19) described the counter-culture as a 'revolt of the unoppressed', suggesting that it was not a revolutionary ideology but part of an 'exploratory curriculum' (of the type Bühler had proposed in 1933) and 'the pervasive spirit of a new generation'. Commentators such as Bensman (1973) and Mills (1973) considered that groups such as hippies were proposing an alternative society.

John Rex (1972) claimed that the extension of education was resulting in new challenges to the British ruling class as a new generation of highly educated young men and women emerged, outside the power class and bearing its own counter-culture and values.

Others saw the counter-culture as a response of the oppressed. Friedenberg (1963: 4) thought of adolescents as 'among the last social groups in the world to be given the full colonial treatment'. He wrote later (1973: 116) that generational conflict was inevitable, since 'adolescence is conflict – protracted conflict – between the individual and society,' though he also questioned whether this was really making a comment on adolescents, or a more fundamental statement about society. As Sheila Allen (1973: 53) indicated: 'It is not the relations between ages which explain change or stability in societies, but changes in societies which explain relations between different ages.'

Fears of a generational breakdown – 'generation war' – eventually faded, because of an increasing awareness of the continued significance of social class. Feuer (1969: 33) pointed out that generational consciousness, though important, was 'not strong enough to bind students and workers of the same age' (though this point is debatable since the May 1968 riots in Paris involved students and workers). There were indications that 'generational' conflict could take different forms in different social classes and was therefore not 'generational' in this sense at all. In all, there was still evidence to support Mannheim's concept of differentiated generation units.

Realization dawned that the student cultures of the 1960s, though expressed in the peer group, were often based on normative values also held by adults (Berger, 1963), indicating that young people were basically conformist rather than in opposition to adult society (Friedenberg, 1973; Zweig, 1963). This was put down to changing circumstances rather than an earlier misdiagnosis. In 'The Vanishing Adolescent', Friedenberg (1973) suggested that the 'stormy decade' of identity-seeking adolescence was disappearing because of the school socializing agenda to produce conformists. Whatever the youth culture, the norms remained those of the adult world, and the adults remained in control. Parsons conceded that: 'The general orientation appears to be, not a basic alienation, but an eagerness to learn, to accept higher orders of responsibility, and to 'fit', not in the sense of passive conformity, but in the sense of their readiness to work within the system, rather than in basic opposition to it' (Parsons, 1973: 50).

In other words, Coleman's (1961) analysis had failed to understand that youth culture is 'rooted in the parent soil' because he had taken an uncritical view of adult society and neglected the relation of adolescents to it (Berger, 1963: 399). Jahoda and Warren (1965: 138) argued for the adoption of a more rigorous analysis, saying that: 'It pays to be pedantic about a definition of this age group and to link it to the usual concepts in the social sciences.' By the 1980s, functionalist theories became discredited in much of the European research. However, some elements returned in the 'underclass' debate which entered the UK from the US in the 1990s (see chapter 4). It still continues in some elements of youth policy and, in particular, in the notion of normative transitions to adulthood and of individual responsibility for 'successful' and 'failed' (both normatively constructed) transitions.

Subcultural studies

Mike Brake's (1980) review of subcultural studies defines the relationship between subculture and culture. The term 'culture' refers to socially acquired or learned forms of beliefs and behaviours, often distinctive to particular social or ethnic groups. Cultures may represent a source of identity, belonging, legitimacy and social control. Within a post-traditional complex society there are different cultures, some associated with different social classes. Class subcultures are subsets of these 'parent' class cultures, containing some shared elements and some distinct ones, thus representing either an extension of the parent class culture or opposition to it. They exist where there is an organized and recognized constellation of values, behaviour and action perceived as different from prevailing norms – of the dominant class culture (Brake, 1980).

Following this approach, the middle-class student movements might have been seen as middle-class subcultures rather than as evidence of a youth counter-culture. Explanations of deviancy shifted away from seeing it in terms of individual psychopathology. In the UK, Albert K. Cohen (1955) argued that delinquency represented a subcultural solution to the exclusion from the opportunity structure experienced by working-class young people. In other words, youth behaviour was to be seen as collective action but at a subcultural rather than a generational level. Mays's study of young people in Liverpool concluded that delinquency was 'not so much a problem of maladjustment as adjustment to a subculture which was in conflict with the culture of the city as a whole' (Mays, 1954: 147).

Until now, the focus had been on middle-class youth, but it was now time to turn to what was happening among young people who were not students, and specifically the working class. Interest in working-class culture became widespread in the 1970s through the work of E. P. Thompson and Richard Hoggart (the first Director of the Centre for Contemporary Cultural Studies (CCCS) at the University of Birmingham). During the 1960s and 1970s, the social class basis of youth in the UK was examined through work at CCCS on the meaning of youth subcultures, and at Leicester University on subcultural processes (Brake, 1980). Subcultural studies came to dominate theoretical development in the sociology of youth in the 1960s and 1970s.

The theories appear in many ways to integrate many functionalist ideas within a structural perspective ('structural-functionalism'). Clarke et al. (1976: 21), like Coleman, suggested that secondary schools 'created the pre-conditions for the emergence of a specifically "adolescent society" '. Peer cultures were seen to have grown up in response to education policies and institutions, rather than spontaneously. In *Learning to Labour* (1977), Paul Willis described how the peer group contributed to the reproduction of manual labour through reinforcement of anti-school culture. This has some resonance with the functionalist concept of secondary socialization, but the emphasis was now on how and why working-class culture led young people to exclude themselves from the middle-class opportunity structure, drawing on Gramsci's

(1971) concept of 'cultural hegemony'. The overall finding (e.g. Clarke et al., 1976; Murdock and McCron, 1976) was that there was no such thing as a 'youth culture', standing in direct relation to the dominant culture of society; instead, youth *sub*cultures were articulated to the dominant culture via their own parent-class culture:

> The major cultural configurations will be, in a fundamental though often mediated way, 'class cultures', and so youth subcultures co-exist within the more inclusive culture of the class from which they spring. . . . The young inherit a cultural orientation from their parents towards a 'problematic' common to the class as a whole, which is likely to weight, shape and signify the meanings they then attach to different areas of their social life. (Clarke et al., 1976: 13)

These studies proposed a different construction from the studies of youth cultures of the 1960s. The move had been away from seeing youth as a homogeneous counter-culture, or age class ('a class in itself'), to seeing young people's values and actions as rooted in their social class positions.

Age or class

There followed a debate on the relative emphasis to be placed on social class and age, a debate which is still current. Eisenstadt (1973 [1956]) had asserted that age and age differences were crucial determinants of human destiny. Hall and his CCCS colleagues argued against what they saw as the functionalist 'obsession' with age. They criticized the life-stage approach of Havighurst and Dreyer's (1975) depiction of youth, arguing that there could be 'no sociology of youth, since differences of class, race and sex mean that young people experience very different types of youth in their trajectory to adulthood (and very different types of adulthood at that)' (Hall et al., 1976: 17). They insisted that, once pluralism is introduced, the concept of 'youth' is broken down, and that: 'Youth as a concept is unthinkable. Even youth as a social category does not make much empirical sense' (Hall et al., 1976: 19).

Marsland and Hunter (1976) defended their fellow-functionalists, pointing out that the emphasis on class in subcultural studies had led to a false denial of the significance of age, and arguing that it was necessary to conceive of youth as a period of transition in order to understand its essential nature. The assertions of Hall and his colleagues, they say, 'seem to us to represent an account of youth which is constrained to deny falsely the significance of one set of forces in social life – the psycho-social forces organized in the age system, out of fear that their recognition may challenge the determinative pre-eminence of another set of such forces – those of class' (Marsland and Hunter, 1976: 10). Murdock and McCron acknowledged that age was an important factor in structuring the social situation of young people, since some experiences are youth-specific: 'It is not therefore a question of simply substituting class for age at the centre of analysis, but of examining the relations between class and age, and more particularly the way age acts as a mediator of class' (Murdock and McCron, 1976: 10).

In a similar vein, though from a different perspective, Smith (1981) also criticized the 'New Wave' for confusing age and generation, and for failing to explain the difference in response of the young and of adults to what they described as a *class* problematic. The CCCS explanation for this was the 'specifically generational experience of the young' (Clarke et al., 1976: 49). This is where they confuse generation and age. The problem is that generational experience is concerned with age *relations* rather than age transitions – so here Marsland and Hunter really have a point. But there were other limitations too. CCCS still produced a very partial analysis of youth and did not indicate why some young people adopt particular youth styles and 'modes of negotiation and resolution', yet in similar situations others do not, as Murdock and McCron (1976) conceded.

The emphasis was on white male working-class peer subcultures. Perhaps it was important to the development of cultural theory at the time that this relative homogeneity be maintained. Later writers (Jenkins, 1983; Brown, 1987) partially redressed the balance by researching conventional working-class young men. However, young women and the middle class were still largely overlooked, as were young people's domestic lives.

Gender and pluralism

By the late 1970s, feminist sociologists were challenging the male dominance of subcultural theories. Most researchers were male, and concerned with subcultures which were acted out by males in the public arena (McRobbie and Garber, 1976). Subcultural styles, as identified according to street styles, confirmed female stereotypes, subordinating women to the role of followers and pillion passengers, there to satisfy the sexual and status needs of males (see McRobbie and Garner, 1976). Willis (1981: 67) later acknowledged that he 'did not specify clearly enough the oppression of girls in the male counter school culture'.

Female sociologists such as Angela McRobbie and Chris Griffin shifted the balance of subcultural studies to girls, identifying the 'culture of the bedroom' as the main setting for female friendships and the culture of femininity. Research on young women showed that for working-class girls, a dominant gendered ideology of romantic love led to commitment to marriage as necessity rather than choice (Leonard, 1980; Pollert, 1981). But there were criticisms that the feminist perspective on the sociology of youth had shifted the balance too far, and in focusing on seeing women as the victims of patriarchy, failed to recognize that they were victims of the whole capitalist economic system. Anne Campbell (1981), in her study *Girl Delinquents*, argued that, 'dizzy with monomania', women had become obsessed with their total uniqueness. As a result, it becomes difficult to understand female subcultures (as McRobbie (1980) also acknowledged). Should they be seen as a response to the same structural class constraints as those facing males or as the product of patriarchy? Nevertheless, Stuart Hall (1980: 39) acknowledged that the work of feminist sociologists 'sent certainties and orthodoxies back to the drawing board', since a 'theory of culture which cannot account for patriarchal structures of dominance and oppression is, in the wake of feminism, a non-starter.'

Other power structures, including heterosexism (Rich, 1981) and racism (Solomos, 1988), were perceived as also cross-cutting the class structures of industrial capitalism. However, there were dangers with this new recognition of heterogeneity. The pluralist and relativist approach can lose sight of the commonalities among young people and perhaps particularly the *dynamic* inherent both in youth and in the social structures which give it context. Increasing pluralism fragments the concept of youth to the point where any essential character risks being lost (as Hall and his colleagues indicated). But there is also the dynamic of social change, and battles over the meaning of youth are both continuous and historically specific. The world is changing and the concept of youth changes with it. The subcultural studies programme of the 1960s and 1970s represents, however, a high-water mark of youth studies in the modern age, and had theoretical strengths which have been less apparent since.

Youth in late modernity

The study of youth has gone through many stages reflecting shifts in societal concerns and structures. Commentaries on youth even a decade ago bear little relevance to the concept now. The following chapters will take up the story of developments in youth studies over the last twenty or so years but first a brief historical perspective is again needed.

Broadly speaking, grand narratives such as those of functionalism and structuralism associated with the height of modernity are becoming less relevant and we appear to be reaching the end of the modern age. Social class is now recognized as only one of several dimensions of social stratification and its cultural aspects are now considered to be as significant as its structural ones. The development of mass consumerism in most societies means that as much can be learned about social groups from their consumption behaviours as from their relationships to the modes of production. Globalization has led to massive socio-economic change, including greater migration shifts which in turn threaten intergenerational social cohesion. The political ideologies which framed much of twentieth-century history have nearly collapsed, to be replaced with religious fundamentalisms, and 1960s fears of impending nuclear war have been replaced with more immediate fears of suicide terrorism. These shifts have lent themselves to interpretations which move right away from those associated with modernity. Some commentators argue that we are now in a postmodern age; others that what we are experiencing is late modernity.

The two main streams in youth studies in the UK are split between these two perspectives. On the one hand, youth research has shifted to the holistic study of young people's transitions to adulthood, developing the theories of reflexivity of Giddens, Beck or Bourdieu and seeing the social world as one reflecting late modernity – with all its pluralities and relativities – and with its reframing of the concept of individual agency. This is an approach which has lent itself to use and abuse by researchers, policy-makers and practitioners. On the other hand, cultural studies have developed away from the neo-Marxist approaches of the 1960s and 1970s to apply postmodernist[6] or poststructuralist approaches to youth, focusing on surface and style rather than hegemonic resistance, in the wake of theories of the 'fragmented self' (Bauman, 1995), or adopting the nihilism of Baudrillard in an increasingly esoteric way.

This chapter has considered competing ideas about the location of young people in the wider social structure on the basis of generation, social class and gender. Many commentators, including Giddens, Beck and Bourdieu, have argued that these 'structuring' variables have lost their potency. What does this mean for youth studies? Basically it strips the concept of youth of much of the meaning accumulated since the Enlightenment. We are left with biological age and location in time – in other words, we are back to the conceptualization of youth before social science began. The increasing relativity in debates over how to locate youth in the overall social structure ended up almost annihilating it. As Griffin (1997) says, youth has become invisible. All we seem to have left are individualized young people, loose collectivities of 'tribes' and caricatures.

Does this mean that we are left with untheorized 'young people' now? Having begun to understand the complexity of youth, we now have to go back to the drawing board. Theories of reflexivity offer one way forward, potentially helping with the process of evaluating and, if appropriate, reconstructing the concept of youth. Pierre Bourdieu's development of the concepts of *habitus* and cultural capital has proved valuable to youth studies. Ulrich Beck's (1992) reflexive modernization thesis has been frequently applied to the study of youth. He suggests that social change resulting from scientific and technological developments has led to a new modernity associated with the 'risk society'. Fragmentation of the established structures of reproduction in society and a breakdown of traditional institutions mean that individual social roles are no longer clear. Individuals, free of these structures, are thus forcibly emancipated (or individualized) and must reflexively construct their own biographies; but emancipation brings risks. Anthony Giddens (1991) suggests that in late modernity an infinite range of potential courses of action (and attendant risks) is open to individuals and collectivities. His argument is that life is not so much a biographical project as a 'reflexive' one. Life transitions demand the exploration and construction of the altered self as part of a reflexive process of connecting personal and social change (Giddens, 1991: 33). This is very much the theme of this book, linking the individual with the social and trying to understand the source and impact of social change.

These theories have had an enormous impact on youth studies over the last decade but it seems that theories of youth have failed to progress. Although sociologists have often used youth as a laboratory for the development of social theory, youth studies have failed to reciprocate and draw adequately on these wider theories. Cohen (1997) complains of the atheoretical empiricism of youth transition studies, pointing out that policy-makers, politicians and professionals still widely believe in a 'bio-political model of youth'. Lash (2007) criticizes poststructural cultural studies for failing to engage with the problems of power and class. Roberts (2003) argues that youth researchers have been insufficiently proactive in defining and prioritizing youth questions, instead merely responding to policy concerns. Griffin (1997) argues that youth studies literature should have been more reflective and, in particular, should have been asking why there was so much interest in youth. What, actually, is 'The Youth Question' (Cohen, 1997) and why is it asked?

The organization of this book

This book is concerned with approaches to the study of youth, and as such it does not aim to review empirical research on young people. In the following chapters, I examine approaches to the concept of youth within broad conceptual themes – action, identity, transition, inequality and dependence. By electing to take this route rather than follow the more conventional route of organizing according to substantive areas of life, I am maintaining the focus on youth as a concept with reference to developments in wider social theories within these themes. The aim is to evaluate whether these theories can help inform current constructions of the concept of youth or prompt a process of reconstruction.

Youth studies have taken off in recent years in many areas of the globe and it would be impossible to do justice to all the research that has been undertaken. Youth policies show a similar proliferation, with countries which previously lacked any specific national youth policy now looking for international models from which to develop their own. Though the theoretical frameworks discussed in this book emanate from many different countries, mainly in Europe and North America, most of the substantive research programmes and almost all the policy initiatives discussed are UK-based. This has allowed me to evaluate the ability of a wide range of theories to illuminate the circumstances of youth in Britain but does not lead easily to direct generalization from the British case since, for a range of historical and other reasons, youth in the UK cannot be seen as typical of that in other countries.

The next three chapters evaluate changing theoretical perspectives in the main fields of youth research. Chapter 2 identifies a culture of blame which has developed around young people. It examines whether changing theories of action can explain what young people do, developing the debate over structure and agency, and considering the extent to which young people really can claim (or be attributed with) ownership of their actions. Thus, though the main focus is on the competing explanations of rationality versus culture as drivers of action, these have to be set in the context of theories of individual cognitive and social development. The chapter considers explanations of youth subcultures, old and new social movements, and the question of suicide terrorism – the latter probably the ultimate test of theories of action – before concluding with some policy considerations. Chapter 3 considers the theme of identity development in youth. It opens with a critique of recent attempts in social science to apply labels to age generations, before moving on to consider the shift over time from a modernist psychoanalytic preoccupation with the self, through the incorporation of a neo-Marxist sociological perspective, to concerns about identity in late modernity, and even nihilism in postmodern accounts. The chapter reconsiders youth subcultures in the light of poststructural theories of youth styles. It then considers the concept of reflexive self-identity, applying this to the idea of identity capital and learning identities in youth. Chapter 4 starts by considering how the idea of life stages has persisted and resulted in a further labelling of age generations in which they are often blamed for the phenomenon of extended dependence. It moves on to consider how the agenda of researching youth transitions developed in social science. The chapter considers whether the idea that there has been a shift from standardized to 'choice' biographies has any relevance, when young people's transitions are so structured by the institutions of the state. Then, drawing on individualization theories and the notion of reflexive biographies, it applies ideas on the nature of action, decision-making and strategy to the problem of how and whether young people 'manage' risk and opportunity during their biographies of transition to adulthood. It concludes with a discussion of how youth policies might be revised to create a structure of support for transition.

By chapter 5, it is time for a fuller consideration of the reasons for variation in youth transitions and thus to take on board the problem of heterogeneity in youth, so here we retreat from postmodernism (which seems to deny both structure and agency) to reassess the importance of the structural constraints associated with social class, gender and ethnicity in the lives of young people. The main emphasis of the chapter is social class. The chapter reviews the problems of applying social class analysis to young people because of their transitional status. It shows how political constructions of youth have shied away from social class explanations of inequality to focus on agency and individualized them through the concepts of underclass and social exclusion. It argues that inequalities in youth have their roots in structural disadvantage which may be acted out in cultural ways. Chapter 6 develops the problem of dependence which is at the core of transitions to adulthood and which makes it so difficult to apply theories designed around adults to young people. It argues that young people should be seen as social agents, socially connected through ties of obligation and reciprocity, but that social policies have created a situation which threatens this social bond by applying a model of dependence which breaks cultural norms and induces shame. It therefore considers the family as a context in which young people's actions and decisions are shaped. It is argued that the transition between private dependence and public independence is a key feature of the concept of youth which has received far too little attention, but which represents a way forward for youth studies.

The final chapter summarizes the book before drawing conclusions, partly in relation to the debates identified at the start of this chapter and partly in relation to new ones. It considers the precarious relativity of the concept of youth, whether a pluralist approach to youth can have integrity, and how the concept of youth can be developed within the broader study of age and generation relations in changing societies. The chapter considers how the concept of youth might be developed cross-nationally and its relevance to societies which may fit less comfortably within the model of late modernity. The emphasis on prescriptions for young people (reflecting political agendas) rather than descriptions of them is reassessed and implications for policy reviewed.

2
Youth as Action

Whatever young people do, they get blamed for. Even when they are just 'hanging about' and doing very little, the rest of 'society' seems to come down on them like a ton of bricks. Even as I am writing this, a new device called a 'mosquito' has been installed in some places in the UK: emitting a high frequency signal audible only to under-25s, it is being used to deter them from hanging around malls. Whether its use will continue may be in doubt, as it has been criticized for infringing human rights. The point, though, is that as a society we seem to allow very little 'public' space for young people; it seems that we would really rather they did not exist. It seems we live in a culture of blame.

It is clear that understanding the concept of youth means understanding the relationship between young people and society. Young people do not act in a vacuum but in a social context which helps to shape even the most apparently autonomous of actions. Nevertheless, there is still a societal tendency to blame young people for what they do, rather than the system which creates the ideology or structures the choices. In *Folk Devils and Moral Panics*, a study of mods and rockers, Stan Cohen (1973) showed how 'folk devils' were created out of youth subcultures through media discourse and how 'moral panics' could ensue. Cohen's work identified the importance of societal reaction in turning an event into a phenomenon, and he saw the development of moral panics as an ongoing

problem for young people: 'More moral panics will be generated and other, as yet nameless, folk devils will be created.
This is not because such developments have an inexorable
inner logic, but because our society as presently structured
will continue to generate problems for some of its members
– like working class adolescents – and then condemn whatever solution these groups find' (S. Cohen, 1973: 204).

Adult paranoia about young people ranges from concerns
that they will upset the boat by challenging the consensus to
blaming them for the current widespread fear of crime. Moral
panics, based on worries that normative values and practices
are under threat, develop too easily into a culture of blame,
centred on young people, while the responsibility of older age
groups for moral decline or criminal activity is barely acknowledged. The notion of social cohesion rarely seems to extend
to encouraging older people to recognize that much of what
young people do, including hanging around, is *faute de mieux*,
for want of something better. Bertolt Brecht had a point
when he wrote: 'Youth is when you blame your troubles on
your parents; maturity is when you learn that everything is
the fault of the younger generation' (quoted in Younge,
2006).

It is time to move beyond this culture of blame (which
seems in any case to be based on the idea that young people
are autonomous and homogeneous) to consider whether
images of 'youth', either negative or positive, really can be
constructed from the actions of young people? This chapter
is about the sources of actions attributed to young people and
conversely the ways in which young people may falsely claim
actions for themselves – thus, on occasion, feeding into the
common perception and building up the myth. It is therefore
about perceptions of responsibility for action – whether
young people have the autonomy and power to act freely and
can reasonably be judged according to their actions, or
whether they act within such constraints or such limited possibilities for *alternative* action that the responsibility should
be placed elsewhere, or at the very least shared. To put it
simply: are young people a problem for society or is it the
other way around?

The agency versus structure debate is at the heart of this
chapter. The two extremes are represented in the question:

did they jump or were they pushed? Do young people's actions represent conscious rational collective strategies by an age generation, or defensive responses to the oppression of disadvantaged cultural groups? There is a current emphasis in research, policy and practice on young people's agency but, rather than get carried away with this political agenda, we must understand agency in youth within a wider context of power relations, including age-generational power structures. Youth as a concept exists because adulthood exists – adults determine the 'consensus', create youth institutions and organizations (schools, leisure institutions), propagate moral panics and enforce social control.

The chapter starts with an examination of theories of action, and considers their applicability to young people. It then considers youth-as-action with a focus on apparently collective action in the form of youth culture and subcultures, youth organizations and new social movements and suicide terrorism. It concerns therefore some of the more public behaviour which feeds into (and from) public perceptions of 'youth', at local and global levels. However, rather than view youth as a static concept, it also begins to explore how and why 'individual' agency may increase as young people become adult, gain cognitive and communication skills, and gain the social and economic status which might enable them to engage more reflexively with the structures that controlled (and may have condemned) their actions when they were younger.

Theories of action

In social science, theories of action vary according to the weight given to precedent or tradition, emotion, rationality and agency, depending on when and where the theory developed, and whether the explanation derives from psychoanalysis, or economics, or structural or functionalist sociology. We can see emotional and traditional action as more typical of traditional societies; rational and cultural explanations as modernist; and poststructural and reflexivity theories as relating to late (or post-) modernity.

1 *Emotional or affectual action.* Anna Freud's description of the vacillations in adolescence, between narcissism and altruism, and rationality and emotion (see chapter 1), suggests that young people in particular may act according to emotional responses or unconscious motivations rather than consciously, and that these emotional responses may cut across other forms of action. Emotionally driven action has not yet received much attention in sociology. Theories of ego development suggest that the ego gradually takes control over the unconscious in the course of adolescence. The problems of the repressed unconscious self are discussed in the next chapter, but some of the ways in which actions are affected by the unconscious mind are considered below.

2 *Traditional or habitual action* occurs where unconscious, even mechanical, repetition substitutes for active and conscious choice, and is seen to relate to traditional societies. In a post-traditional society, adult individuals are supposedly becoming freed from these influences (Giddens, 1994). Myth and tradition, which are counter to the idea of rationality, are handed down via folk knowledge by the guardians of tradition, including parents. Young people who are dependent on their parents are thus particularly subject, through processes of socialization, to the influence of family myth and traditional practices.

3 *Rational action* covers a range of forms of action designed for economic or non-economic gain. The concept of rational action is key to the Enlightenment understanding of social consensus and self-restraint, as well as the role of education in freeing the individual from myth – hence the more educated are seen as more capable of rational and epistemological thought. The theory is at the basis of the concept of autonomous agency. The problems of understanding youth actions in this light stem partly from their lack of resources, including, if we are to follow Piaget's theories, whether they have 'achieved' the stage of rational thought.

4 *Hegemonic resistance* is a concept developed from structural-functionalist descriptions of working-class youth subcultures as representing symbolic resistance to hegemonic power, based on Gramsci's theories. The theory forms part of a general shift in sociology towards recognizing the significance of cultural explanations but also represents a shift from

seeing young people as agents to depicting them as 'cultural dupes'. It is based on the idea that ideologies infiltrate the unconscious and are acted out through a form of false consciousness or hegemonic resistance which in practice maintains the status quo. The question is whether this explanation still has currency in times of late modernity when power structures and therefore scope for resistance have been transformed.

5 *Postmodernist* explanations seem to portray young people as signifiers of signs, or conduits of ideologies, culminating in Baudrillard's portrayal of a nihilism where no agency exists and actions are merely responses to external stimuli. These ideas, discussed in chapter 3, may have explanatory power when it comes to current youth cultures which stress surface and style rather than the conscious or unconscious resistance associated with subcultures. They may also help to explain why those in power have on occasion seen young people as empty vessels waiting to be filled with ideologies.

6 *Reflexivity* theories tend to be more synthesizing. They relate to late modernity, where it is argued that the individual is obliged to have more autonomy. The theories are more difficult to apply to dependent young people than they are to adults, but are popular in youth research. In chapter 4, the reflexivity theories of Giddens and Beck are considered in relation to youth transitions. Bourdieu's theory of action is of particular value in examining youth subcultures and is considered below.

These theories reflect the changing historical context in Western Europe in which, as a result of the Enlightenment and industrial revolution, folk knowledge associated with traditional societies was replaced by expert knowledge, owned first by bureaucrats and later (in late modernity) by technicians (Giddens, 1994). Explanations of young people's actions and practices need to be sensitive to this changing social environment as well as to young people's individual development. No single theory of action is likely to work, even among adults, and there have been attempts to synthesize some of these explanations so that they no longer compete. Sayer (2005), for example, suggests that we move beyond seeing reason and emotion as opposed, to acknowledge that emotions are often perceptive and reasonable judgements about situations and processes. However, it is difficult to apply these theories of action to young people, as the following discussion of rational action and cultural explanations of action will reveal in relation first to youth subcultures and, secondly, to political action and new social movements.

Rationality as the basis of action

Rational action theories have their principal roots in the Enlightenment, when the model of *homo economicus* (economic man) was developed. Thomas Hobbes's *Leviathan* (1651) and Adam Smith's *The Wealth of Nations* (1776) both saw adult individuals as rational beings, motivated by self-interest and competing for wealth or power. Since the latter are limited resources, the problem of competition for them must be resolved through mutual cooperation and self-restraint (in Hobbes's term a 'social contract'). For Hobbes, and for functionalists later, mutuality and consensus must prevail for the social good. For Rousseau (*Emile, or On Education*, 1762), on the other hand, individuals must cooperate for their own protection against the potentially corrupt demands of social consensus. A problematic relationship between the individual and society is thus set up.

Can individuals really restrain their self-interest for the sake of social cohesion or can societies only function where there are external (legal or religious perhaps) controls on individual behaviour? Emile Durkheim argued in *Suicide* (1951 [1897]) that in stable societies a 'collective conscience' leads to individual altruism for the common good but, when a society becomes unstable, people no longer know where to look for the reference groups which would help them in their self-restraint, and they become prone to exaggerated hopes and fears; this is when anomie (a concept often applied to young people) occurs. Developing this idea, Talcott Parsons (1973) later argued that anomie could result when no consensus existed and the individual was thus subject to conflicting social pressures. The concept of the rational and goal-oriented individual, capable of translating goals into actions and modifying self-interest in the common interest, is thus both a modernist idea and a functionalist one. The theory is somewhat shaken when the 'consensus' represents the interests of the power elite who then seek to impose it in their own interests. In contrast to functionalist accounts, Robert Merton saw anomie as a product of social exclusion, occurring when their own experience leads people to question the normative consensus and they 'become estranged from a society that promises them, in principle, what they are denied in reality' (Merton, 1964: 218).

Actions are not only motivated by a quest for wealth and power. Max Weber (1978 [1922]) proposed the ideas of instrumental rationality to describe mainly economic motivations, and 'value-rationality' to describe seemingly altruistic motivations based on non-economic value such as religious belief or honour (where benefits may include social approval or intrinsic satisfaction). Value rationality facilitates the understanding of actions in the name of religious or political beliefs or, in the case of young people, perhaps the values of the peer group.

Rational Choice Theory (RCT) developed from these ideas. While popular in the field of economics, RCT has been criticized for stressing the economic over the social. Writers such as Lacan, Foucault, Bourdieu and Baudrillard have criticized it as ethnocentric and for its emphasis on the individual. Others argue that it fails to take account of collective actions and social relations (involving cooperation and interdependence between individuals), the problems of social norms (involving altruism and obligation), and wider social structures (Scott, 2000; Elliott, 2001). Also questionable is the concept of 'lines of action' from aspiration, through disposition to (conscious) action, which provides an essentially linear framework for the concept of strategy (examined elsewhere in this book) often inappropriately applied to the actions of young people.

John Goldthorpe's (1996, 1998) Rational Action Theory (RAT) was an attempt to bring rational choice into the realm of structuralist sociology. His objective was to explain why there are still social class differences in educational attainment even after controlling for academic ability. He argued against simple linearity, showing firstly that young people in the same social class locations may see different ways of 'bettering themselves', for example through education or through work, and thus have different goals and, secondly, that even people with similar goals may take different steps towards achieving them because their actions, far from representing free choice, are conditioned by the distribution of resources, opportunities and constraints produced by the social class structure as a whole.

There have been many critiques of this approach, too. Lash (1994) argues that RAT still implies a disembedded, cost-minimizing and benefit-maximizing, preference-scheduled actor. Devine (1998) doubts that individuals have goals and can make conscious choices on the basis of an informed cost–benefit analysis, and Bourdieu highlights the difficulty in identifying goals. One problem is that, in the late modern world of expert knowledge, many people have inadequate personal knowledge – the resource of cultural capital – with which to weigh up potential benefits, costs and risks. We shall see elsewhere in this book how ill-equipped many young people and parents are to make education decisions because of cultural as well as structural constraints. RAT has indeed been criticized for neglecting the significance of cultural and social resources in the reproduction of advantage (Savage, 2000). All these forms of resources may be hard for young people to access. If one accepts Robert Merton's (1964) formulation of anomie, there would be no point in disadvantaged young people aspiring to normative goals according to the rational choice model.

When, if ever, do young people become rational actors, capable of a degree of rationality which frees them from tradition and indoctrination or purely emotive action? This is not only a question of external resources. According to Piaget (1972), rationality develops during the course of childhood and should be achieved by the adolescent stage. This may still place young people in a problematic position with regard to theories of rational action. Nevertheless, ideas such as instrumentality and strategy and lines of action have all been applied in studies of transitions in youth, albeit in a more moderate form (see chapter 4).

Cultural explanations of action

Cultural explanations of action have dominated research on youth for some time because of the emphasis on collective behaviours associated with young people's leisure lives. The shift towards an interest in class cultures came at a time when youth cultural styles and peer groups were becoming more visible and engendering more concern among the older population. The theories of Habermas and Bourdieu provided the basis for understanding the social and cultural elements in young people's action.

Communicative action

The first step was taken in mainstream sociology when Jürgen Habermas began to examine the cultural basis of rational action. He was concerned with understanding how rational consensus developed in societies when it was no longer fixed by established traditional beliefs and codes. Through his *Theory of Communicative Action* (1984), Habermas distinguished between rationality at individual level and what he called 'communicative rationality', associated with embedded social practices. He argued that rationality relates to the way in which knowledge is used, rather than knowledge per se (an idea which sets him apart from commentators on late modernity who highlight the significance of expert systems). Thus, a rational action is one which an individual can criticize or defend (or justify) through a process of argumentation. Communicative interaction can lead to 'discursively redeemable validity claims' which challenge the consensus (Lash, 1994: 149). Habermas thus sees individuals as social rather than autonomous agents.

His theory can with caution be applied to young people. The idea that young people might individually or as peer groups seek validation of their actions or even challenge the consensus through argumentation is difficult to apply to those who lack cognitive and social skills (though this is where education potentially helps). However, their immediate peer subcultures and their families, which have their own language and values, may provide a setting and structure for the validation of individual action. The theory may thus help us understand how values may be negotiated among young people and form part of the development of peer-group culture, or among family members as a means of modifying beliefs about family obligations. Examples of the latter are discussed in chapter 6, where young people are seen to be obliged to validate their actions in their claims for parental (and state) support – though some young people need advocates to put their case for them.

Habermas was criticized for proposing a utopia of ideal speech (Savage, 2000) and ignoring heterogeneity. Later, Melucci (1989) similarly criticized Habermas's treatment of social movements as unified entities and his failure to differentiate the variety of actors and orientations within them. However, Habermas showed that the belief in autonomy which underlies theories of economic rationality was ill-founded, and paved the way for the recognition of the cultural and the study of collective action.

Bourdieu's theory of social practice

Pierre Bourdieu went further in developing the idea of the social agent and has been influential in developing understandings of decision-making in youth. He celebrates 'the return of the subject' (Bourdieu and Wacquant, 1992: 178), reclaiming the ground from French existentialism and the structuralism of Lévi-Strauss where the subject was denied (Jenkins, 1992; cf. Lash, 1994). Nothing is clear-cut in Bourdieu's work, though. He rejects the taken-for-granted dualities of modernity (agency and structure, freedom and constraint, conscious and unconscious) and focuses instead on reflexivity in social practice between the structural conditions of possibility (opportunity and constraint) and actors' use of these possibilities – a '*dialectic of the internalization of externality and the externalization of internality*' (Bourdieu, 1977: 72, original emphasis).

The concepts of *habitus* and *field* represent the thinking tools for his theoretical constructs and both designate bundles of relations (Wacquant, 1992). *Habitus* can be interpreted as the predispositions or orientations foundational for conduct (Bourdieu, 1977), both structured and structuring in a reflexive relationship. Fields are spaces of conflict or competition, representing external structural conditions of possibility. Bourdieu emphasizes that the field is a space of play requiring social agents, not autonomous and disembedded individuals. Each field has its own values and rules, thus requiring both acceptance of its values and mastery of its rules (Bourdieu and Wacquant, 1992). According to this analysis, the working class or minority ethnic groups may not share the values or possess the mastery of the rules required, for example, in the field of education.

Habitus engenders lines of action but, instead of displaying the regularity implied by RAT, these follow a 'practical logic', through improvised confrontation with endlessly renewed situations (Wacquant, 1992: 22). Thus, 'the logic of practice is logical up to the point where to be logical would cease to be practical' (Bourdieu, 1987: 96). Mastery of the logic of practice is acquired through practice (experience of the game). This suggests a reflexive process whereby individuals continually have to weigh rationality against practicality, but it also implies perhaps that young people, who are typically entering situations of which they have no previous experience, will inevitably lack mastery until they can gain it through practice and experimentation. According to Bourdieu (1987), actions may be rationalized retrospectively, according to their outcomes, rather than represent the product of a genuine strategic intention. (Thus Blackman (2005) claims that rave culture should be recognized as a form of resistance because it was treated as such by the police.) The question of whether such actions are conscious or unconscious becomes 'nonsensical' (Bourdieu and Wacquant, 1992: 129n) once it is recognized that it is the encounter of *habitus* with the peculiar conjuncture of the field that drives them.

> The lines of action suggested by habitus may very well be accompanied by a strategic calculation of costs and benefits which tends to carry out at a conscious level the operations which habitus carries out in its own way ... Times of crisis, in which the routine adjustment of subjective and objective structures is brutally disrupted, constitute a class of circum-

stances when indeed 'rational choice' often appears to take over. But, and this is a crucial proviso, it is habitus itself that commands this option. (Bourdieu in conversation with Wacquant, 1989: 45)

His work has been influential among those undertaking youth research, as the discussion in chapter 3 of identity capital will show, though it seems that his scepticism about the value of the concept of strategy is still neglected. His relevance to subcultural studies is discussed below.

Symbolic Interactionism

Subcultural studies in Britain came to the fore in a general trend towards recognizing the cultural explanations of deviancy. The forerunners were the Chicago School in the United States. Symbolic Interactionism (SI), as portrayed in the work of Goffman or Becker (and discussed further in chapter 3), introduces behaviour as socially rather than individually achieved, through the interaction of self and others. All action is thus situational. The individual does not simply absorb normative values and act in accordance with them for the social good, or alternatively resist them in acts of deviance. Instead, there is an iterative relationship between individual action and social reaction which defines the action. This perspective formed a key influence on later theories of reflexivity. Much of the focus of the Chicago School was on deviant behaviour and this has tended to dominate US research on young people ever since. Writing about marijuana users, Howard Becker argued that, whatever the social origins of deviant behaviour, it was through societal reaction that the deviancy was consolidated. It was therefore important to understand how consensus and deviancy were constructed through the relationship between action and reaction, rather than simply fall back on identifying 'social factors' leading to deviancy: 'From this point of view, deviance is *not* a quality of the act the person commits, but rather a consequence of the application by others of rules and sanctions to an "offender". The deviant is one to whom the label has been successfully applied; deviant behaviour is behaviour that people so label' (Becker, 1963: 9).[1]

Thus, it becomes important to identify reference groups and understand their cultures (McCall and Simmons, 1971). A young offender may be acting for status within the peer group (and according to its value system) rather than with any concern about the risk of social disapproval outside the group, though this does not mean that subcultural actions are only internally referential. There are current concerns that the tagging of young offenders is counter-productive because the tags become prestigious. Stan Cohen (1973) showed how media misrepresentations could feed 'moral panics' in the wider society and lead to the construction of young people as 'folk devils', in a manner similar to the witch-hunts of the past.

Hegemonic power and resistance

Following earlier work on anomie and deviance by the Chicago School, and particularly Albert K. Cohen (1955), studies in the UK by David Downes (1966) and others began to argue that, though the conditions for anomie existed, working-class youth subcultures (and not only deviant ones) were not merely defensive expressions but should be seen as active problem-solving. A new formulation of theory was needed and subcultural studies thus began to combine elements of the SI approach with a Marxist perspective deriving largely from the Frankfurt School in Germany.

The French philosopher Louis Althusser[2] provided a structuralist framework. His approach was determinist – he asserted that 'there are no subjects except by and for their subjection' (Althusser, 1971: 182). He saw social consensus as a tool of the power classes, and ideology as a 'real' and unconscious force *seducing* people via hidden determinations (Cohen, 1997: 48), with the result that through everyday rituals and practices (referred to by some as the 'life-world'), people are made to misrepresent themselves as autonomous agents. The Italian communist Antonio Gramsci (1971) spelled out the method of 'seduction'. He argued (in contrast to Symbolic Interactionists) that capitalism imposed a 'consensus' of values or hegemonic culture, as a result of which the working class identified common interest with the bourgeoisie and the survival of the capitalist system was ensured.

Subcultural studies in Britain

The concept of 'hegemony' came to crystallize UK cultural studies as a discipline, being understood largely in terms of resistance to symbolic power (Lash, 2007). The studies developed the idea that hegemonic power worked through ideology and discourse on the unconscious mind. Young people might therefore feel responsible for actions which are the product of their disadvantaged situations, thus displaying false agency.

Stuart Hall led a body of CCCS[3] work in the 1970s and 1980s which proposed that young working-class peer groups were operating in ways which unconsciously reinforced rather than challenged existing power relations (see Brake, 1980, for an overview). Hall and Jefferson (1976) thought of cultural style as text which was created as a collective symbolic response to real experience of subordination, and which resolved in an imaginary way problems which in reality remained unresolved (Clarke et al., 1976). The emphasis of one stream of work was on anti-school male working-class subcultures. Paul Willis's work, *Learning to Labour* (1977), in particular has become a classic text. He suggested that the real question for those seeking an explanation for social reproduction was not why middle-class young men get middle-class jobs, but why working-class 'lads' let them. Thus, the critical question was why working-class young men appeared to lack aspiration to better themselves (why they were not acting according to the model of *homo economicus*). Willis showed how the working-class young men in his study unconsciously colluded in their own domination (based on Gramsci's theory of hegemony): 'It is their own culture which most effectively prepares some working-class lads for the manual giving of their labour power' (Willis, 1977: 3). Their peer group was thus acting as a form of social control, a curb on aspirations which might otherwise have led them to compete with middle-class students. Willis's argument was that anti-school working-class male subcultures valorized manual labour (and rendered it attractive), so that the imagined 'goal' became an outcome for which they were destined in any case. The internal restraint was thus a cultural response to external constraints. Their resistance to the power of the dominant culture, expressed symbolically through ideology, was thus also symbolic, 'imaginary' rather than real.

Feminist writers Angela McRobbie and Chris Griffin identified the female equivalent. McRobbie and Garber (1976) refer to the 'the culture of the bedroom' (involving best friend relationships between girls) which emphasized 'feminine concerns', including a patriarchal 'ideology of romance'. This led young women to 'feminize' and aspire to the reality of their future gendered lives as wives and mothers, in a way similar to Willis's lads' valorization of their futures in manual labour (Pollert, 1981; Griffin, 1985). McRobbie (1978) pointed out that it was through processes acting through their own culture that working-class girls too ended up doing exactly what was required of them.

In both cases the subcultural resistance was symbolic, though real structural disadvantage was present. Both Paul Corrigan and Richard Jenkins thought that Willis had understressed the real power of the dominant class. Corrigan's own analysis found an 'instrumental working-class attitude to work, or alternatively the expectation of alienated labour'. In his more conventionally Marxist account, the actions of young people constitute a reaction to the use of *real* power by teachers and the state, rather than a rejection of normative values (Corrigan, 1979: 80). Jenkins (1983) criticized Willis for overestimating the degree to which the working class colluded in their own domination. For Jenkins, like Corrigan, social class identity was reproduced as much through labelling decisions in institutions of education, labour market and social control, as within the working class itself, but he emphasized a reflexivity between modes of power and modes of resistance and stressed the need to understand both sides, since 'power may be mobilised and legitimated simultaneously in consensus and legitimation, on the one hand, and resistance, coercion and grudging accommodation on the other' (Jenkins, 1983: 7). It can be argued that it was the structures of education and training systems which channelled some young people into manual work (see, for example, Bates and Riseborough, 1993).

It has been suggested that Willis's *Learning to Labour* was an ethnographic illustration of the interpenetration of *habitus* and action in Bourdieu's theory (Lash, 2007). Indeed, Bourdieu saw CCCS's work (particularly that of Willis) as the laboratory for some of his ideas, though he had a different interpretation, seeing anti-school masculine subcultures (as well as the 'black is beautiful' paradigm of emancipatory politics) as representing an 'irresolvable contradiction' rather than forms of resistance (Wacquant, 1992: 23). He proposed instead (Bourdieu and Wacquant, 1992: 193) that the subversive intentions of adolescents were often immature, imagined, utopian and unrealistic and that supposedly subversive practices were often in effect 'strategies of displacement' rather than transformative strategies. In contrast to Baudrillard (chapter 3) though, Bourdieu does not see action as the product of anarchy:

> The effects engendered within fields are neither the purely additive sum of anarchical actions, nor the integrated outcome of a concerted plan . . . It is the *structure* of the game, and not a simple effect of mechanical *aggregation*, which is at the basis of the transcendence, revealed by cases of inversion of intentions, of the objective and collective effect of cumulated actions. (Bourdieu, 1987, cited in Wacquant, 1992: 17)

Bourdieu's comments suggest then that Willis's lads' actions occur within the structure of the hegemonic game. 'Resistance can be alienating and submission can be liberating. Such is the paradox of the dominated and there is no way out of it' (Bourdieu, 1987: 184, cited in Wacquant, 1992: 24).

Style as resistance

The question of whether style and discourse can be considered forms of resistance is a thorny one. In its early days, CCCS had distinguished youth subculture, credited with symbolic social class authenticity (or at least working-class authenticity), from 'pop culture', which was a product of markets of consumption (Hall and Jefferson, 1976; Frith, 1978; McRobbie, 1994). Dick Hebdige's (1979) *Subculture: The Meaning of Style* marked a turning point in CCCS work. He saw the subcultural challenge to be at the level of *signs* of resistance, actually doing little to alter the social structure. The mods, Teds and punks in his study drew on the available cultural resources – music, dress and leisure activities which are the productions of consumer markets – and gave them new meanings, through *bricolage*, as strategies and responses to their specific social situations (Slater, 1997). Thus, according to Hebdige: 'The mod was determined to compensate for his relatively low position in the daytime status-stakes over which he had no control, by exercising complete dominion over his private estate – his appearance and choice of leisure pursuits' (Hebdige, 1976: 91). For Leong (1992), the notion of 'appropriation as resistance', reflected in the work of Hebdige, still represented a challenge to hegemony, albeit at the level of signs.

The structural anthropologist Claude Lévi-Strauss[4] (1966 [1992]) had coined the word *bricolage* for the process by which symbolic – or mythical – elements were combined into a new cultural form. The concept helps subcultural analyses by indicating how dominant ideologies such as consumer capitalism can permeate youth cultures while simultaneously allowing the culture to claim authenticity – such as through transformation of the original elements (though Bourdieu would question whether this really was transformation rather than mere displacement). Phil Cohen (1997) studied the processes of *bricolage* through which social contradictions were 'magically resolved' in different cultural codes and styles. Brake (1980) argues that elements from the consumer culture of popular music and artefacts were relocated and transformed into youth culture through a process of *bricolage*.

Subcultural studies in the UK focused on groups which cohered around particular activities, focal concerns and territorial spaces (Clarke et al., 1976), but they had plenty of candidates. Most were mainly concerned with what were seen at the time as ephemeral styles. Thus, the CCCS researched Teds (Jefferson, 1976), hippies (Willis, 1978), skinheads (Clarke et al., 1976), mods, Teds and punks (Hebdige, 1979), as well as producing Stan Cohen's (1973) study of mods and rockers.

The gradual proliferation of youth cultures gradually resulted in a shift towards research aimed at decoding the meanings of different styles. There were critiques that researchers such as Hebdige were ignoring the whole basis of subcultures as *shared* meanings and beginning to collude with the market against the interests of young people. Far from being emancipated through this approach, young people were being reduced to 'signifiers' and their subcultures reduced to 'signifieds' (Lash, 1994, 2007; Cohen, 1997). Under the influence of the French sociologists Jean Baudrillard and Michel Maffesoli, the concept of subculture is being replaced by terms such as 'neo-tribe' and lifestyle. The emphasis has shifted so far away from subcultural resistance, whether symbolic or real, that these ideas will be discussed in the next chapter in the context of identity construction.

From the 1980s, however, wider social changes made it increasingly difficult to see the styles and activities of young people in terms of hegemonic resistance. Scott Lash (2007: 55) points out that the concept of hegemony, which formed the underlying basis of British cultural studies from the 1970s, had 'truth value for a particular epoch', and that power is now post-hegemonic. His argument is that both power and resistance have shifted from the symbolic to the real: both domination and resistance should now be seen as working ontologically and as 'unutterable', working from within rather than through discourse. Thus power – for example the global power of the US – operates through real force and there is no longer a need for either hegemonic discourse or ideology. This presents a problem for understanding current anti-school cultures but helps our understanding of political action.

Political activism

Youth organizations

Over the last century in particular, young people have been formed into collectives which transcend their immediate peer groups. The original 'youth organizations' were not, however, grass-roots constructions but seem to have been based on the idea that young people's minds were empty vessels open to the influence of ideologies, and sometimes extreme ones, because their primary socialization and cognitive development were as yet incomplete.

Youth organizations arose in Britain and Germany in the late nineteenth and early twentieth centuries with the development of ideologies associated with nationalism and dominant religions. In Britain these included the Boys' Brigade (founded in 1883), the Scout Movement (1908) and the Woodcraft Folk (1925), while the German equivalent, the *Wandervogel*, also founded in the nineteenth century, was similarly associated with outdoor pursuits. Gillis (1981) has suggested that these organizations were founded on upper-class concepts of adolescence and boyishness, and in that light it may be significant that J. M. Barrie's play *Peter Pan* was published in 1904. It similarly reflected an adult construction of ideal youth and the shaping of young people to fit this image.

The more extreme youth organizations, in Germany, the USSR, China and Japan were all constructed around using young people to fulfil the aims of totalitarian regimes. In order to do this, young people needed to be separated from the socializing influence of their parents (Wallace and Kovatcheva, 1998). The Hitler Youth organization was founded in the 1920s, while Young Pioneers and the Komsomol were developed in Soviet Europe (Riordan, 1989; Pilkington, 1994). Events in post-war USSR suggested that young people could not be so easily moulded. At a time when overt criticism of the state was not permitted, the idea of 'juventization', developed in the 1960s by Mahler in Rumania and Mitev in Bulgaria, proposed that young people could also change society (Wallace and Kovatcheva, 1998) – in effect a Mannheimian proposition. When the Soviet system was coming to an end, it became apparent that young people were resisting manipulation by the state and that if they were going to change society it would be on their own terms and according to their own values; and indeed the political activity of young people played a part in the 'gentle revolutions' which toppled the communist regimes of Central and Eastern Europe (Wallace and Kovatcheva, 1998).

Counter-culture and new social movements

Mannheim's image had been of new generations changing society, rather than the socializing (or 'seducing') of young people to accept and live according to normative societal values. Theories of the 'counter-culture' in the 1960s interpreted the actions of young people as representing real resistance.

In the West, student movements of the 1960s were identified as counter-cultures, with the implication that there was a generational divide in values and aspirations across society. There was a fear that the normative consensus was being threatened by the alternative values of young people, mainly middle-class students protesting against the Vietnam war, or hippies seen as promoting an alternative lifestyle and thus challenging the foundations of society. Cohen (1997) argues that this was not the outcome of apathy but represented active cultural revolution. At the time, however, Musgrove (1974: 19) saw the counter-culture as an 'exploratory curriculum' rather than a revolutionary ideology, fitting it neatly with Bühler's perception of youth as a period of experimentation. The Marxist-Freudian Herbert Marcuse (1987 [1955]) argued that the cultural values of consumption, including the pleasure principle, provided alternative goals to the economic values of capitalism and introduced the notion of 'repressive desublimation' to explain how rationality had been reconciled with the pleasure principle with such apparent ease, giving the hippy movement as an example (Cohen, 1997; Elliott, 2001). So-called 'youth movements' were in many cases based on role models, gurus and folk heroes who were older. Reich's (1970 [1933]) sexual politics movement (offering, according to Cohen (1997) an 'erotic utopia') was originally presented as a less destructive alternative to fascism but, when it resurfaced in the 1960s, was seen as promoting a 'sexual revolution'. Wilhelm Reich and Herbert Marcuse were popular during the 1960s' student movements and sexual politics of the late 1960s (just as the poet Allen Ginsberg and Timothy Leary were icons for experimentation with drugs, and Che Guevara for revolution).

During the 1960s, there was an emphasis on what Giddens refers to as 'emancipatory politics' mainly evidenced through the women's movement and the Black Power movement, out of which emerged wider concerns for social justice. There appears, however, to have been no equivalent emancipatory youth movement, since young people aligned themselves with other causes. Student movements were not only left-wing – there were right-wing ones in the US, as Edmunds and Turner (2002) point out. Nor were they necessarily egalitarian. Habermas, who had been involved in the student movement in the late 1960s, later accused sections of it of 'left fascism' (Giddens, 1996: 173). Melucci (1989) criticized the student movement of 1960s' Italy for its integralist ambition and rejection of pluralism.

Why do individuals join social movements? From a Marxist-Freudian perspective, Reich (1970 [1933]) had suggested that in Nazi Germany repressed sexuality had been re-channelled into hatred and violence. Olson (1965) applied RCT to argue that rational individuals act primarily from self-interest[5] and would not join social movements unless either the collective concerned were small enough to serve their self-interest, or they were forced to do so. Alberto Melucci (1989) has thrown more light on why people join 'new social movements' and how collective action is constructed. Melucci argues that in order to understand why individuals participate in collective action, three levels of explanation must be addressed: the structural, the rational and the personal; it is the latter which is of particular interest to him. He argues that collective action affects not only social change but also transformations of individual experience. By striving to individuate themselves through social action, people experience personal growth – though paradoxically this is facilitated by the colonization of the lifeworld that Habermas describes (Melucci claimed that social movements were the product of the colonization of the lifeworld by abstract and reified economic and political mechanisms – the late modern equivalent of infiltration by ideology). He suggests (1989: 208) that much of the activity of new social movements occurs within 'submerged networks' which act as the 'laboratories of experience' before public display but that these groups are not necessarily liberating – some are limited and marginalized by lack of resources. His interpretation differs therefore from that of Habermas. Melucci recognizes that 'new social movements' are pluralist, ambivalent and often contradictory but rejects the idea of collective action as a pathological response to anomie and disequilibrium, arguing that there is always a degree of rationality involved. It is not just that anarchic behaviour can be interpreted as rational, but also that rational behaviour can be seen as anarchic.

> Even in less structured forms of collective behaviour, people do not act in a void. They are always enmeshed with other actors, and through this interaction they produce meanings, express their ideas and activate their relationships. Collective action is never a purely irrational phenomenon. It is always to a degree socially constructed and meaningful to its participants, even when it appears to be anomic or marginal behaviour. (Melucci, 1989: 191)

The investment of time and energy people make in such groups is therefore not purely defensive, and the various forms of collective action associated with identity politics are, according to Melucci, not the outcomes of structural social divisions. He argues that youth culture (his study included punks in Milan), the women's movement and ecological protest often take place outside political systems, rejecting representation in favour of direct action. In a post-hegemonic information society, action to change discourse is more powerful than action based on force, according to Melucci, and in this he differs markedly from Lash (2007) who stresses instead that both ideology and discourse are superfluous in a world where power is real. For Melucci, discourse can represent *real* resistance and is not just symbolic.

For Giddens, new social movements, including religious ones, mark an attempt at the re-appropriation of institutionally repressed areas of life (1991: 207). He distinguishes between the emancipatory politics of modernity and the life politics of late modernity (1991: 210ff). *Emancipatory politics* (such as the Black Power movement) are associated with the progressive liberation of the individual from constraints, but the emphasis is 'away from' rather than 'towards' an unspecified utopian vision. *Life politics* (such as the women's movement) on the other hand, is a politics of self-actualization in a reflexively mobilized order and represents the 'return of the repressed'. New social movements have now brought life-politics issues, which do not fit existing frameworks of politics (as Melucci also indicates), to public attention. This explains the shift away from more traditional political activity. It still involves emancipation from tradition and hierarchical domination but is less concerned with the processes of liberation than with choice itself. 'While emancipatory politics is a politics of life chances, life politics is a politics of lifestyle' (Giddens, 1991: 214). Giddens gives the student movement of the 1960s as a halfway example between emancipatory and life politics.

Youth activism now

With increased globalization of communications and political concerns (such as the environment and poverty), politics have become more globalized and issue-based: anti-poverty, anti-capitalist, Greens, CND variants. They have also become more pluralist – at the 2005 G8 protests in Edinburgh, for example, people of all ages were involved. Involvement in issue politics appears to be increasing while interest in and engagement with political parties and 'traditional politics' has decreased, though there is a danger of constructing a mythical golden age – usually 1968 – of conventional political engagement. Beck and Beck-Gernsheim (2002: 157) suggest that young people operate 'a highly political disavowal of politics' by rejecting political parties; and that their political engagement in issue politics, with organizations like Greenpeace, can also accommodate their desire to have fun (following Marcuse's pleasure principle?). Young people, especially working-class young people, have always had low participation in voting in general elections (White et al., 2000). An exception, at a time when mainstream politics appear bland, has been recruitment to the more extreme groups, from racist groups, such as the BNP in Britain and neo-Nazi groups in Germany, to religious fundamentalist organizations and global networks. The question as always is whether these movements and counter-movements are defensive or aggressive.

Some resistance is at local or national level. In 1981 and 1985, 'riots' involving young people occurred in some English cities. In 1990, widespread anger at the introduction of the 'poll tax' (a community charge which would particularly penalize young people) culminated in violent protest in central London. For Phil Cohen (1997), the riots occurred because young people lacked any other form of collective bargaining.

In recent years there has been plenty of evidence that, far from sinking into apathy, many young people in many countries worldwide have been actively involved in demonstrating against national policies seen as discriminatory. Do these represent emancipatory politics or life politics? Chinese students are said to have rioted in protest against increasingly profit-oriented educational authorities who had misled them about the value of their diplomas (*The Guardian*, 26 October 2006); left-wing protests in Mexico started as a demonstration against teachers' low pay (*The Guardian*, 31 October 2006). Since 2005, France has seen a succession of disturbances. Students and workers have protested against government youth employment and pension policies. Some student–worker demonstrations were sparked by an 'easy hire–easy fire' policy mooted as a means of reducing high youth unemployment levels. The government intention was that the lifting of employment protection would encourage employers to take on young workers but, paradoxically, the policy meant that they could be disposed of after two years without explanation. 'Hooded youths' fought running battles with police in the *banlieue* (the run-down suburbs in which most of the minority ethnic population live) of Paris in November 2005. There were further violent protests in 2006 against policy action which was seen as racist, and against a government clampdown on youth offending which included a ban on 15–18-year-olds going out in groups of more than three, and an order that under-16s should be accompanied by an adult – both orders later overturned as infringements on civil liberties (*The Guardian*, 31 May 2006; *The Guardian*, 30 October 2006). A newspaper article by Gary Younge (2006) quotes Daniel Cohn-Bendit, one of the leaders of the

1968 Paris uprising, as suggesting that, whereas the latter was a positive movement with a positive vision, the current disturbances are defensive, based on fear of insecurity and change. Younge points out, however, that the current protests have in many cases led to positive changes in government policy (as did the poll tax demonstrations in Britain in the early 1990s), in contrast to the 1968 protests which led to the reinforcement of right-wing policies, including those repressing young people, so that it was the generation of 1968 which unconsciously helped to create the circumstances against which young people are now rebelling. This interpretation sounds reminiscent of theories of hegemonic resistance, only working over a longer term. But the power to change may be effective only at local or national level. From a post-modern perspective, Baudrillard (2002) described the 9/11 al-Qaeda attacks of 2001 in the US as 'a form of action which plays the game' of the dominant power, rather than disrupting it, while Žižek (2007) argues that 'resistance is surrender' since it plays into the hands of the authorities in a symbiotic relationship of mutual parasitism, a division of labour in which anarchic agents do the ethical thinking and the state does the work of running and regulating society. His thesis may have more relevance to 1968 than to now.

Defensive reactions or resistance?

Ethnic differences in deprived multicultural urban areas have given rise to riots in Britain, too, but these have generally been regarded as defensive responses rather than forms of positive action. Those in the summer of 2001 have been seen as an expression of 'ethnic solidarity in the face of the threat of the far right', a defensive response to media hype about crime by South Asians against whites, and BNP activity in the 2001 local and general elections (Hussain and Bagguley, 2005: 417). Brake (1985: 142) similarly commented on Bengali defensive reactions to white racism. As Goodey (2001) points out, there has also been violence between South Asian groups, and 'blame' cannot therefore be easily apportioned. A recent report (Mirza et al., 2007) suggests that many young Muslims feel that media reports of

Islamophobia are exaggerated and have led to a feeling of victimization. There appears to be a growing minority of young British Muslims who are more politicized Islamist than their parents, suggesting that their actions are not purely defensive, but in the research this concept is widely defined and includes wearing the *hijab* as an act of identity politics. What we see is perhaps the result of interaction between two different groups, rather than cause and effect, or lines of action.

Terrorism

In the face of recent terrorist attacks, there has been increasing concern about the recruitment of some young people to terrorist organizations. Though terrorism has been around for some time, in some recent manifestations it has become global. Tosini (2007) identifies a typology of objectives associated with different terrorist organizations: nationalism (including the IRA in Northern Ireland, Tamil Tigers in Sri Lanka, ETA in Spain, PKK in Turkey, Hezbollah in Lebanon), revolution (Red Army Faction in Germany, Red Brigades in Italy, Islamic Jihad in Egypt), vigilantism (UVF in Northern Ireland, Ku Klux Klan in the US), symbolic (Aum Shinrikyo in Japan) and single issues (the anti-abortion Army of God in US, or the Animal Liberation Front). Why do people, often – but not only – young ones, join terrorist organizations or in extreme cases become suicide bombers? Tosini argues (in contrast to Olson, 1965) that there is no simple line of action from belief to action in the case of suicide terrorism. In order to understand the phenomenon, we have to go beyond individual explanations and understand motivations at three different levels: the terrorist organization, which determines the strategy and organizes it, the community, which provides the resources, and the individual bomber who carries it out. Tosini draws on Weberian theories of rational action and suggests that the organization uses instrumental rationality in developing suicide terrorism as a resource-efficient and effective strategy. This is especially the case where new recruits, rather than long-standing and trained members, of an organization are concerned (Pedazhur, 2005). The community achieves some consensus about the method through instrumental rationality (on the basis of previous success), through material and symbolic rewards, and through 'axiological rationality' (Habermas's communicative rationality), where the values of a culture of martyrdom form part of the ideology of the organization and come to be adopted by the community. The individual bomber may be motivated by revenge or in response to a status crisis, or through egoistic interest (the prestige of martyrdom) or, perversely, altruistic interest (helping their family and community, because the organization will support them), or through axiological rationality (Pedazhur, 2005; Tosini, 2007). Both Tosini and Pedazhur link the latter with Durkheim's (1951 [1897]) concept of 'altruistic suicide' on behalf of others or, in some more isolated cases, 'fatalistic suicide' as a response to personal oppression. In all, it seems that, far from abandoning rational action theory, we have continued to incorporate cultural and other elements into it. This allows us to consider the societal side, including recruitment into social movements, youth groups, jobs, and so on, and those who have the power to force, allow or reject memberships. In all, these findings challenge the conceptual division between individual and collective action.

Policy implications

Most of the research and theories reviewed in this chapter suggest that decisions are not made in isolation and, at the very least, young people should be regarded as social actors, and constrained ones at that. Emotional or habitual action may interfere with rationality; some action represents a defensive response; some actions appear to be collective rather than individual. Nevertheless, in several areas of social policy in Britain (as in the US), there is an assumption that young people can behave as autonomous and rational individuals.[6] Over the last twenty years or so, there has been an increasing tendency for policy-makers to develop financial incentives or disincentives intended to influence individual young people's behaviour. The trend towards this form of individualization started in the neo-liberal 1980s but has continued to the present day. The underlying assumption, seen in policies discouraging young people from leaving home or encouraging them to stay on in education or desist from offending, is based on economic theories of 'rational choice', seeing young people as rational, instrumental and calculative, motivated by money, and with access to the knowledge and intellectual capacity to undertake a cost–benefit assessment before deciding what to do. In practice, in applying this very limited model of individual agency, it denies them agency because it denies their social connectedness. Indeed, research has shown that one of the main reasons why young people begin to desist from crime is because they have formed social relationships and new responsibilities (Graham and Bowling, 1995).

The question must be asked therefore whether policymakers take notice of social research, even when a government is keen to stress that policies are evidence-based. It seems that theories deriving from economics and social psychology carry more weight than those deriving from sociology. The consequence is a denial of the social. Yet this denial is ironic when there is also considerable concern, shown in many countries worldwide, that young people are becoming less altruistic and less willing to take on responsibility for the growing numbers of older people. I will show in chapter 6 that, far from being characterized by irresponsibility as described by Parsons, youth is inextricable from social bonds of obligation. These are often private and family-based and so, although they do not receive public and policy attention, or indeed the attention of those youth researchers who are focused on peer activities, they still frame young people's perceptions of what can and cannot be done – their dispositions, in other words. The next chapter will pick up the idea of dispositions in the context of identity capital and consider whether this can be seen as a resource.

3
Youth as Identity

Youth is a vital period of identity construction during which young people separate from their families of origin and develop a sense of their selves through their interactions with others in new social relationships. Identity development is seen to be critical for social relations. This chapter is about the difficulties associated with this process and the problems which occur when young people lack a sense of their own identities. It also considers how identities are socially developed and how these processes may therefore have changed in the societal shift from modernity to late modernity.

The chapter will consider changing theories of self and identity in relation to youth and young people. These will also throw light on adulthood. First, I will consider some aspects of ascribed and achieved identities in late modernity. There will follow a summary of the main theories of self deriving from Freudian psychoanalytic theory and the concepts of the repressed unconscious and the distorted and superficial self-image developed through Marxist and later postmodern sociological theories. The chapter will then consider lifestyles and music styles in the light of these theories, and whether the concept of subculture still has relevance in the allegedly post-hegemonic age of late modernity. Finally, the concept of reflexive identities is discussed and applied to the concept of identity capital.

Labelling age generations

Images of youth prevalent in the media are often stereotypical and are both fed by and feed into moral panics. In their quest for target groups, market researchers reduce young people to marketing groups or ciphers which subsequently provide the sound bites for the media. In the consumer society, 'youth' is increasingly branded and commodified and marketed – such as in the preoccupation with youth as beauty and fitness, and the selling of youth as a lifelong attribute accessible through cosmetic surgery and chemical enhancement. Does this ideology of youth have anything to do with young people or is it simply the response of older people to the daunting prospect of their own greater longevity – and their need for reassurance that they will be cared for by the younger generation in years to come?

It appears to be hard to find appropriate terminology for describing young people in an extended period of transition between childhood and adulthood. They are variously described as youths, young people, young adults, youngsters, kids, adolescents, teenagers, or through neologisms such as 'kidults' or 'post-adolescents'. There are also age-generational labels. People born during the post-war baby boom have been labelled 'Baby Boomers'. Those born in the late 1960s–1970s, the children of the Baby Boomers, have been called Generation X and described as a 'lost generation', defined by the phase of transition from colonialism to globalization which culminated in the end of the Cold War (Howe and Strauss, 2000). One theme of these age-generational labels reflects concern about whether successive generations are more or less altruistic than the preceding one – and thus whether they are more or less likely to fulfil their social responsibilities. Twenge (2006) describes the cohort born in the US in the 1970s, 1980s and 1990s as egotistical (*Generation Me*) because of the discrepancies between their raised expectations and the crushing realities and suggests that they find fulfilment in helping others only as long as this does not conflict with their other roles. Howe and Strauss (2000) suggest that those born after 1982 ('Millennials') will show a return to civic responsibility and teamwork (thus splitting Twenge's cohort). These generation labels are all examples of period-icity and can be seen as associated with the persistence of functionalism in the US in particular. Shanahan and Longest (2007) suggest that images of adolescence have moved from the unhygienic, through the rebellious and the anomic, to the current image of the narcissistic individual incapable of achieving adulthood. I like to think of them as examples of 'yoofism'.

There are many problems associated with labelling age cohorts in this way. The use of such terms reflects the unease – if not paranoia – with which 'adult society' views social phenomena involving young people. The labels perpetuate homogeneous images of young people in which age is the paramount variable, dividing young people from 'the rest of society'. From their date of birth we can assign individuals an age and locate them in history but to learn more we need at the very least to know their social and geographical loca-tions (following Mannheim, 1952 [1927]). Bourdieu (1978) – like Bühler (1933) – distinguished between biological and social age, indicating that while age is a biological given, it is socially manipulated and manipulable. The act of ascribing common interest and social unity to a biologically defined age group can be seen as an example of such manipulation and therefore as a social phenomenon in itself.

Multiple identities

Young people may indeed have a sense of their 'age-generational identity' but contain and manage this alongside an age identity, a kin-generation identity, an immediate peer-group identity, a national identity, an ethnic identity, a gender identity, and so on. Whether, in the middle of juggling these various identities, they still have a sense of a 'youth identity' is open to question, though it is possible. Hussain and Bag-guley (2005), for example, found that young British Muslims stressed the multiplicity of their identities, Islam offering them a mode of being *within* the context of their identities as British citizens. It is time therefore to begin to get beyond misleading images and understand how complex identities are constructed. How much freedom do young people have to define their self-identities and act according to them? This links back to the theme of the relationship between agency and structure, and also that of the relationship between the real and the imagined or symbolic, which formed part of the discussion in the previous chapter.

In order to understand youth in terms of identity, one has to explore the relationship between self and society. Identity in youth is partly self-achieved and partly ascribed from social background. Peer groups can have a significant role in the formation of individual identity and separation from social background since they allow young people to explore through a collective identity and, 'within the parameters of their immediate class situation, certain elements of achieved versus ascribed identity' (Brake, 1980: 25), though they do not offer the promise of autonomy. The struggle to break free from ascribed identity and achieve self-identity is, according to some commentators, an agenda associated with the modern age and less relevant in late modernity (Bauman, 1995). Giddens (1991) argues that there has been a shift from preoccupation with social identity and personality to self-development as reflexively organized and self-referential in a lifelong process.

There are two questions we need to be asking here. The first is the relevance of ascribed identity in late modernity – is there still as much influence of social background, is there as much of a need for peer identity as a kind of intermediate stage, or is identity more freely and individually achieved? The second question is whether, in the case of young people whose independence from parents has been deferred, individual identity is now harder to achieve reflexively and more likely to continue to be ascribed by social background or restricted to the peer group. These two questions clearly conflict. In order to answer them we need to enter modernist accounts of the self and the more recent accounts of identity.

Self and society

The concept of the self is associated with modernity. Theories of the self have their roots in the Enlightenment construction of the individual as a rational being. Descartes's 'I think therefore I am' (*cogito ergo sum*) represented the rational self, seen as the basic requirement for altruism and self-restraint in the interests of social cohesion. According to Bauman (1995: 157), this has now mutated in late modernity into 'I am noticed, therefore I exist' or even 'I shout, therefore I exist'. The history of thought on self and identity shows how this mutation has occurred, from Freudian theories of ego development and the problem of the repressed unconscious self to the incorporation of a neo-Marxist perspective (as sociology began to infiltrate psychoanalytic theory) which examined the relationship between external and internal repression, to existentialist theory and later Symbolic Interactionism which saw the self as purely situational, and thence to the nihilism of postmodernist theories pronouncing the end of both the subject (the self) and society in a world dominated by signs. One way to encapsulate this story is to describe it, as Bauman has done, as the shift from a modernist pilgrimage of the self to an avoidance of being fixed. However, there is also a message of hope in theories of reflexivity which for the moment conclude the story and which offer some potential for the fulfilment of self-identity.

The repressed self

The distinction between conscious and unconscious behaviour was a sub-theme of the last chapter. Sigmund Freud developed the theory of the repressed self, which has had a major influence on social theorists since. Freud (1953–74) describes the self as split between rational and conscious thought (the ego presented to the outside world), and unconscious and therefore irrational desires and motivations, particularly with regard to sexuality, which are hidden within our private selves. The superego acts as an internal social control, operating through mechanisms such as guilt (or shame). Freud thus recognized a tension between individual repressed desires and societal needs for cultural order and social control (Elliott, 2001). This is contrary to the idea that altruistic consensus is reached, and also to the notion that individual behaviour is fundamentally rational.

Freud proposed that the individual psyche developed from *infancy*, when the psyche is closed in on itself and the infant is wholly dependent on others, through the *pre-Oedipal* stage, when there is no distinction between self and other, then the *Oedipal* stage, when the father is seen as intervening between the baby and the mother, and eventually to a stage when the mind opens out to consciousness of the self, distinguishing it from others and the outside world (see Elliott, 2001). It is crucial for the development of the adult self that the Oedipal stage be achieved because it involves a shift from the narcissism of the young child to recognition of culture and language and social relations (which are in effect the accoutrements of social and cultural capital).

Erik Erikson (1965) developed further the idea of ego development as consisting of stages, each involving tasks to be mastered by the individual in order, with adulthood, to control the unconscious and achieve rationality. He distinguishes between ego identity (the self, or 'I'), personal identity (individual characteristics) and social and cultural identities in which ego identity is anchored. According to his theory of ego development, adolescence (though post-Oedipal) is particularly problematic because 'role confusion' can occur when individuals have doubts about their sexual or occupational identities. Erikson suggests that this is why adolescents may temporarily over-identify with role models (an argument which might help 'explain' the present-day cult of celebrity). Successful completion of this stage is critical for adult social relations: young adults who have resolved the problem of their own identity are more outward-looking and ready for intimacy and commitment. Those without confidence in their own identities isolate themselves or try to damage the identities of others, and failure to complete this stage may lead, in Erikson's view, to delinquency. John Coleman (1974) drew on Erikson's work to argue that conflict resolution was needed for adult identity, and that conflicts were centred on awareness of sexuality in early adolescence, then on acceptance or rejection by the peer group, and later, on autonomy and independence from parents (cited in Banks et al., 1992).

While Erikson's ideas held sway among functionalist sociologists, a number of social scientists – some of them

Marxists from the Frankfurt School – developed Freud's ideas on sexual repression, including Reich, Marcuse, Lasch, Lacan, Foucault and more recently Žižek. Christopher Lasch's (1980) theory of a culture of narcissism follows Freud in stressing the significance of the Oedipal stage for the development of positive social relations. He saw the father figure as essential for resolution of the Oedipal stage, and was concerned about the effect of family breakdown. Lasch argued that consumer culture dehumanized the self: lacking any sense of social control over consumer capitalism (or indeed sense of historical connectedness through kin generations because of the demise of the family), individuals retreated to narcissism, becoming preoccupied with self-image, unable to form caring relationships, but at the same time longing for psychic security and well-being. In this situation, individual survival becomes paramount (Giddens, 1991).

According to Foucault and Lacan, the self could be crushed in the structured world of social interaction. Michel Foucault's work, rejecting both the Freudian theory of sexual repression and the calls for sexual liberation expressed by Marcuse and Reich, involved further consideration of whether individual behaviour involves self-restraint or is externally controlled. Foucault was politically active in the French student movement of the 1960s and his work started (1995 [1977]) from a Marxist stance, studying techniques of domination in a world where there was so much emphasis on surveillance. Foucault (1988) later recognized the part played by 'techniques of the self' and turned back to the study of sexuality to examine how individuals can actively engage with issues and rules of sexuality. He suggested that these had become incorporated into discourse, especially expert bureaucratic discourse, and that individuals act on their awareness about matters of sexuality to regulate their own behaviour. Operating in this way, power thus served not only to regulate sexual taboos but also to produce sexual pleasure. Furthermore, some forms of resistance were still feasible:

> Their existence depends on a multiplicity of points of resistance: these play the role of adversary, target, support, or handle in power relations. . . . There is a plurality of resistances, each of them a special case: resistances that are

possible, necessary, improbable; others that are spontaneous, savage, solitary, concerted, rampant or violent; others still that are quick to compromise, interested, or sacrificial; by definition, they can only exist in the strategic field of power relations. (Foucault, 1978: 95–6)

Jacques Lacan shifted the focus to the way the unconscious mind is structured and tied to language. He emphasized processes and mechanisms, seeing individuals as supports of language and symbolic identity (rather than the other way around) and the self as an *effect* of discourse. Ideology is thus reproduced by individuals through everyday repetitions of language rather than through history (Elliott, 2001) – an idea followed up by Foucault and Žižek. His key concept was the 'mirror stage', referring to the way identification with an external image leads individuals to a misrecognized sense of unified selfhood, and an emphasis on surface rather than depth (Lacan, 2002 [1949]). This 'self' is thus a delusion, and the ego a distorting trap, a narcissistic mirage which hides the fragmented mind. These ideas have been taken to evoke characteristics associated with the postmodern condition (Elliott, 2001).

Slavoj Žižek, the contemporary Slovenian philosopher, draws mainly on Lacan and Hegel in his analysis. He argues (Žižek, 1989) that ideologies work to fill the feeling of insufficiency within the self (following Lacan) but are only half successful. However much individuals try out different identities and lifestyles, their identities are always incomplete, because of the disruptive effect of the unconscious. Self-definition must always fail, and communication with others is only possible because we project conflicting passions and ambiguities onto them. In an analysis deriving from Lacan's 'mirror image', he argues that fantasy screens over the void because the self always fails to live up to some imagined version of identity – which can include negative projections associated with intolerance of difference, including racism (Elliott, 2001: 76). Thus, popular culture, deriving from the ideology of consumer capitalism and reproduced through individual lifestyles, can do no more than paper over the void. This analysis suggests that youth cultures in late modernity would lack both authenticity and transformative power. For

Žižek, unlike Foucault or even Baudrillard, there is no chance of resistance: 'Far from containing any kind of subversive potentials, the dispersed, plural, constructed subject hailed by post-modern theory (the subject prone to particular, inconsistent modes of employment, etc.) simply designates the form of subjectivity that corresponds to late capitalism' (Žižek, 1989: 216). In Elliott's (2001) view, Žižek excels at the sabotage of the self.

The death of the self

Existentialism

For Marxist existentialist philosophers, identity was not an innate (essential) characteristic of humans but developed as a result of action and commitment. As one of the characters in Sartre's 1944 play *Huis Clos* says: 'You are no more than the sum of your acts'. *Huis Clos* is about characters searching for their identities in the eyes of others and constantly brought back to their own (inadequate) self-identity. The act itself has no history or causality (no rationality therefore) but has only present and therefore ephemeral significance, as interpreted by the agent and others. Camus similarly presented this as *l'acte gratuite* (the gratuitous act) in his 1942 novel, *L'Étranger*. Elements of these ideas have resonance in Symbolic Interactionism and have had an influence on later French sociological theories. In practice, like Baudrillard later, they denied the 'subject', to the extent that Sartre felt the need to defend his philosophy from this charge, asserting that existentialism was a form of humanism (*L'existentialisme est un humanisme*).

The self and postmodernity

For some commentators, there has been a shift from the modernist self to postmodern identity, and the end of modernity marks the death of the subject (Elliot, 2001: 144). Lemert (1997) suggests that in a destabilizing world it is no surprise that the emphasis has turned from established social systems to the question of identity because identity has become just as unstable. For Richard Sennett (1998), changes in the labour market and industrial structure, and the increase in risk and uncertainty, mean that durable selfhood is replaced by super-market identity. This creates a problem for understanding 'adult identity' as a goal.

In his early work, Jean Baudrillard was influenced by the neo-Marxist critiques of consumer capitalism emanating from the Frankfurt School, while later he drew on theories of consumption as symbolic exchange (developing the work of Simmel, Douglas and Barthes).[1] He distinguished between traditional societies based on symbolic exchange, modernist societies based on production and postmodern societies driven by representation through *simulacra* (signifiers). In *The Consumer Society* (1998 [1970]), he explored how individuals were dominated through the symbols and signs associated with objects of consumption. Objects are bought as much for their sign-value (denoting wealth, power, etc.) as their use-value, and individuals thus gain status and identity through conspicuous consumption. He saw this, however, as the problem of 'simulation'. Baudrillard suggested that the transitory nature of symbolic meaning has become so universal that transitoriness itself has become culturally dominant. There are no 'lines of action' because there is no linearity and there is therefore no rationality: 'Everywhere, in every domain, a single form predominates: reversibility, cyclical reversal and annulment put an end to the linearity of time, language, economic exchange, accumulation and power' (Baudrillard, 1993: 2). Thus, fashion (other fields of interest to him being sport and the media) becomes a display of accelerated change and the alienation of meaning 'to the point of enchanting us – the enchantment and vertigo of the loss of every system of reference' (Baudrillard, 1993: 87). With the proliferation of signs and sign-value in the consumer society, the social content of meanings has become lost and signs and symbols have no logic. The outward is all there is and we are seduced by it.

Baudrillard developed the concept of 'hyperreality' to describe a world in which reality 'has incorporated the hyper-realist dimension of simulation so that we are now living entirely within the "aesthetic" hallucination of reality' (Baudrillard, 1993: 74). This approach is again related to the

Lacanian 'mirror stage'. Thus, Baudrillard argues, the 'superficial' defines the core of social experience, and the self is crushed and powerless (Elliott, 2001: 140). In his later work, Baudrillard came to see the domination of signs as marking the fragmentation of subjectivity and 'the end of the individual'. In *Fatal Strategies*, the subject recognizes the supremacy of the object, sides with it and surrenders to it (1990 [1983]). Because there is no structure, causal mechanisms cannot be identified and there is no external reality to try to understand and control. Further, the 'object world' which dominates the subject is out of control. It is also 'the end of the social'.

Not surprisingly, Baudrillard struggles to identify forms of rebellion. Nevertheless, fashion, he argues, has a subversive potential, precisely because 'it is this immorality in relation to all criteria, the frivolity which at times gives fashion its subversive force' (Baudrillard, 1993: 94). As Chaney (1996: 55) explains, the lack of order creates an anarchy of signs – a 'subversive meaninglessness' – which some have seen as a new form of revolutionary politics. Perhaps punk falls into this category. More recently Baudrillard (2002) has suggested that the world is without meaning and that acceptance of this would be liberating because it would allow individuals to play with forms, appearances and impulses without worrying about their ultimate destination (he thus posits an approach which is neither emancipatory nor associated with lifestyle choice).

Baudrillard's work obviously has resonance in the later work of CCCS, especially with the move away from understanding styles as forming through *bricolage* a subculture capable of hegemonic resistance, and towards the emphasis on decoding styles as signs. According to his interpretation, there is no need to hold a debate on whether power and resistance are real or symbolic.

Collective identity and postmodernity

If the individual self is dead, have collective selves survived? The French postmodernist Michel Maffesoli's work on identity and consumption has recently been influential, since his approach has been adopted as a way forward following the apparent demise of both subcultures and the self. In *The Time of the Tribes* (1996), he proposes that, although social class has lost significance, there are new 'tribal' determinants, collective associations in an increasingly consumer-oriented society – but shifting ones, as people switch from one group to another. Maffesoli suggests that 'neo-tribes' have emerged as a new social dynamic characterized by 'fluidity, occasional gatherings and dispersal'. He questions both the dominance of the idea of individualism, and the notion that collective ideals have been lost in late modernity. In fact, he argues that people are becoming more collective and tribal, neo-tribes having their own values and providing social support. The sexual, political and professional identities associated with modernity are being replaced by processes of identification with groups, with sentiments and with fashions; and contemporary identities are composed of experiences, representations and everyday emotions (Maffesoli, 1996).

The question is whether neo-tribes really provide the means for identity-building in the way that peer groups did in the past. Urry (1995: 221) describes as 'new sociations' non-traditional institutions such as youth cults or 'tribes', arguing that, although people may join or leave with rapidity, they can provide safe social spaces for identity-testing as well as providing a context for learning new skills; they also involve mutual aid reinforced by 'norms of reciprocity'. In contrast, Melucci (1992) argues that despite allowing individuals a multiplicity of memberships, achieved through a range of symbolic possibilities, they do not provide the necessary conditions for identity-building.

Zygmunt Bauman (1995) believes collective identity to be as problematic as individual identity. He describes collective identity as more contrived, postulated rather than even imagined, located in the future, and brought into the present, only ephemerally, 'through the combined force of individual loyalty acts' (1995: 187), suggesting at the same time that values are localized and person-specific. He suggests that, because of inbuilt uncertainty, such a community lives in constant anxiety, and he proposes that the neo-tribes described by Maffesoli are of this type. Concepts associated with 'culture' are still useful because they relate to the self-images within these neo-tribes whose attempts to appear less arbitrary, and internally more cohesive and consensual, lead to aggression and intolerance of others. At the same time, however, Bauman argues that 'humanity' enjoys no status advantages over neo-tribes, being equally postulated and equally constructed through affection and dedication. His analysis raises the question of whether the values and structures associated with neo-tribes represent an authenticity of self-image or a mirror distortion.

For Bauman, it is not a simple matter of substituting identity for self in a postmodern analysis. He does, however, distinguish between two strategic models of identity. Life in modern society was (and for some still is) a 'pilgrimage' in which identity-building was a key project, involving long-term objectives and planning, through which the pilgrim and his world gave meaning to one another. Within this model the desire for self-mastery – the guiding impulse of the modern self – takes the self into the work of rationality. Emancipation thus involves the assertion of an independent identity, and this is indeed the model which underlies theories of developmental psychology. For Bauman this search for self-mastery is illusory and self-defeating because it *leads people to believe* that life can be ordered, causing them to become dissatisfied with the present, alienated from social relations and constrained in their self-expression (Elliott, 2001) – not therefore because of a failure to master goals as Erikson had suggested but because the goals themselves are illusory, a false promise. In contrast, in the postmodern age, emancipation, the realizing of genuine (that is, not illusory) human potential, requires that the bounds of communities be broken and individuals set free from the circumstances of their birth. The project has therefore shifted from self-mastery and the logic of rationality associated with the 'pilgrim' to become the avoidance of being fixed – to an identity, to a relationship, or to a place.

Bauman (1995: 15) suggests that identity has become the surrogate of community, and (quoting Jock Young) says, 'Just as community collapses, identity is invented.' He proposes that 'in the same way as the pilgrim was the most fitting allegory of modern life strategy preoccupied with the daunting task of identity-building – the stroller, the vagabond, the tourist and the player offer jointly the metaphor for the postmodern strategy moved by the horror of being bound and

fixed' (Bauman, 1995: 91). The stroller (*flâneur*) is disconnected, unattached (Bauman draws on Dick Hebdige's analysis for examples). The vagabond's movements are unpredictable
and she or he has no set destination, so 'cherishing one's
"out-of-placeness" is sensible strategy' (Bauman, 1995: 94–
5). The tourist, on the other hand, though also on the move
and afraid of home-boundedness, maintains the notion of
having a home to return to, as part of a safety package (the
idea is similar to that of 'ontological security' discussed in
Giddens, 1991). The player plays a game, with conventions
(including a beginning and an end) involving anticipation,
risk, intuition and precaution-taking, but without conscience
or morality. For Bauman (1995: 99, original emphasis), '*The
mark of postmodern adulthood is the willingness to embrace
the game whole-heartedly, as children do.*'

Reflexivity and the self

Theories of reflexivity offer an alternative track to that of
postmodernism, which ultimately proves to be a blind
conceptual alley. They have their origins in Symbolic
Interactionism.

Symbolic Interactionism

Freud's theories and those of his followers conflict with the
interactionist theories of G. H. Mead and Symbolic Interactionists where the self is constructed through social interaction rather than being crushed by it. In contrast to Freud's
view, according to the interactionist perspective there would
be no tension between individual desires and societal needs
as the latter would be subsumed within the construction of
the self (Elliott, 2001).

The forerunner of Symbolic Interactionism was George
Herbert Mead. In *Mind, Self and Society* (1934 [1974]), he
describes how the 'social self' (the 'me') is created through
engagement with significant others and thus peopled with
the attitudes of others. Self-awareness means distinguishing

between 'I' and 'me'. Jenkins (1996) points to an affinity here with Freud's distinction between ego and superego. Erving Goffman's *The Presentation of Self in Everyday Life* (1956) was concerned with techniques for the social representation of self and developed the concept of the self as purely situationally defined, distinguishing therefore between self and mind. Elliott (2001) quotes Alvin Gouldner's criticisms that Goffman was creating an amoral universe where everything was situational and the ideology of the market was thus able to penetrate personal identity and the self (suggesting that the 'me' was not acting as moral censor). Goffman's ideas provide a means of understanding the way alternative identities (roles) can be brought into play in different social settings, through cognitive or expressive processes or actions.

Reflexive self-identity

Elliott (2001) suggests that these early sociologies of the self failed to take account of emotion. This omission is partially resolved in Anthony Giddens's works on self-identity (1991) and intimacy (1992) which incorporate many psychoanalytic ideas. He (1991) argues that the self has undergone massive change. He compares traditional societies, where there was continuity from generation to generation on the level of the collectivity, and changed individual identity was clearly defined through rites of passage, with modernity, a 'post-traditional order', in which the self becomes a reflexive project to be explored and constructed as part of a reflexive process connecting personal and wider social change. He refers to self-identity as 'the self as reflexively understood by the individual in terms of his or her biography', in a narrative of the self (1991: 244) through which individuals define both their identities and their life courses (discussed in the next chapter). This moves away from the distinction between 'I' and 'me'.

According to Giddens, the relationship between self and society is dynamic and fluid, involving negotiation, change and development. This contrasts with the idea of a linear pilgrimage. He argues that as tradition loses its hold, and myth is replaced with expert knowledge, individuals are *forced* to negotiate 'lifestyle choices' (1991: 5) which have become increasingly important in the constitution of self-identity and daily activity despite the standardizing influence of commodification in the consumer society. This is still a far cry from Lasch's (1980) perception of a consumer society which dehumanizes the self. For Giddens, like Bauman, emancipation is illusory; he describes a tension in modernity between the promise of emancipation and the reality of 'mechanisms of suppression, rather than actualization, of self' (1991: 6). Stressing that the conditions of modernity affect all sectors of society, he points out that lifestyle decisions can be constrained. Elsewhere (1994) he distinguishes between choice, which has become obligatory, and decision-making, which requires power.

Youth culture and style

A picture seems to be building of young people as chameleon-like, lacking selfhood and capable of changing to fit their changing contexts and circumstances. This image may be perpetuated in the styles associated with present-day youth cultures. There is an emphasis on the ephemeral as well as the pluralist quality of postmodern styles, and a question about whether they possess authenticity. In recent UK commentaries on youth cultures, there has been a debate about the relative merits of structural and 'poststructural' cultural analysis. On the one hand, Shane Blackman and Stephen Miles have continued to put forward the more structural view which acknowledges the power of global consumer capitalism. On the other hand, Andy Bennett and others have taken a poststructuralist stance.

Identity-building is difficult. In practice, individuals have a multiplicity of memberships, achieved through a range of symbolic possibilities, but these do *not* provide the conditions necessarily for identity construction (Melucci, 1992, in contrast to Maffesoli). There are simply too many possibilities to allow choice. Žižek's (1989) analysis suggests that membership would be merely 'papering over the void'. Ken Roberts (1997) argues that leisure lifestyles are prone to quick disintegration and cannot therefore assist in the task of identity construction. Miles (2000), however, argues that young people are no longer as dependent on peer subcultures for their identity construction but that their lifestyles, however fragmented or unstable, can provide a rational and modernist way of stabilizing their everyday lives. He does not problematize the concept of identity but draws on Žižek and Melucci to argue that the meanings underlying young people's lives as consumers represent the fundamental building blocks of their identities. 'Young people do not construct their identities directly through what they consume, but consumption plays an important role as a vehicle for the construction of young people's lifestyles and it is largely within this context that their identities are constructed' (Miles, 2000: 128). Though he declares himself less swayed by Baudrillard's analysis, his work does have strong associations with it. Miles and colleagues (1998) suggest that consumption allows young people to feel that they 'fit in', at the same time allowing them a semblance of individuality, and this combination potentially gives them a sense of stability not otherwise available in the risk society. Miles (2000) subscribes to Baudrillard's description of signifiers and sign-values in suggesting that purchasing a pair of trainers, for example, means buying comfort and a communal sense of well-being. But he also argues that the purchase in practice legitimizes consumer society and thus only *appears* to be emancipatory of the individual, drawing on Žižek to argue that there is an essential contradiction in late modernity between the loss of the subject in a consumer world and the apparent emphasis on the subject in an individualizing society (ideas which are incorporated into Giddens's and Beck's explanations of reflexive individualization). Furlong and Cartmel (1997) refer to this contradiction as an 'epistemological fallacy', but it might be more appropriate to conceive of it as a tension between the individual and society. Individualization does not imply agency. Miles finds more explanatory power in the work of Melucci (1992), who argues that a gulf has developed between traditional and contemporary identities and as a result people have fewer fixed reference points against which to plot their life courses; they are *obliged* to actualize themselves as consumers in isolation. Giddens (1994) similarly distinguishes between obligatory choice and constrained

decision-making, while Beck (1992) refers to 'forced emancipation'. Bourdieu (1984: 379) comments that working-class
culture and consumption are determined by 'the choice of the
necessary' rather than aesthetic choice, not from poverty, but
because the necessary is defined through *habitus*. These theories of reflexivity thus acknowledge the extent of external
constraint, especially if social class is seen as 'collective
habitus' (Lash, 1994).

Music styles offer a setting for considering collective identities and behaviours in contemporary societies – or at least
some of them. Poststructural approaches have been taken to
the study of rave culture (Redhead, 1993, 1995), 'straightedge' (Wood, 1999), club cultures (Thornton, 1995), black
musics (Briggs and Cobbley, 1999), gangsta rap (Riley, 2005),
and other music styles. Andy Bennett (1999: 599) argues that
in the postmodern age the concept of subculture fails to
account for the 'pluralistic and shifting sensibilities of style'
which have characterized post-war youth cultures. Bennett
refutes the authenticity of 1960s' and 1970s' subcultures as
artefacts of research (created by subcultural theorists) and
suggests that youth styles both then and now are instead
'free-floating' (referring to Redhead, 1993, 1995) and concerned with surface and self-authentication (referring to
Muggleton, 1997, 2000). He quotes Maffesoli (1996) as
arguing that the concept of tribe can illustrate the deregula-
tion of solidarity and identity based on class occupation,
locality and gender, and the resulting shifting nature of collective associations in an increasingly consumer-oriented
society – people switching from one group to another.

Bennett applies these notions to music styles, arguing, from
his study of the urban dance-music scene (bhangra, hip hop
and progressive rock) in Newcastle, that they should be seen
as having permeable boundaries. Indeed, the internet raises
the possibility of virtual global subcultures – even more
hyperreal and deterritorialized. From a study of 'virtual psy-
trancers' (people who visit psychedelic trance dance style
discussion forums on the internet), Greener and Hollands
(2006) are keener to represent youth styles as global rather
than local and class-based, but also reject claims that they are
lacking depth, transitory and internally fragmented. They
identified a cohesive and homogeneous global culture, loosely

articulated around a particular style (though one could argue that this too could be illusory, following Baudrillard).

Though seen as ephemeral, some music styles have proved to be long-lasting, although attached to particular age cohorts. Hesmondhalgh (2005) indeed argues that popular music should not be conceived as the privileged domain of young people. Bennett's (2006) study of ageing punk fans really raises the question whether the popular music styles commonly associated with youth should be regarded as youth-specific at all, if styles can both hold long-standing and now middle-aged fans, and attract newer younger recruits. This casts doubt on how age-specific some styles and activities associated with youth really are, as well as whether they really reveal the fluidity associated with neo-tribes. We are faced with the possibility that their ephemeral quality may be artefactual.

Bennett's comments on identity are in practice not dissimilar to those of Miles. Bennett too is concerned with the collective cultural meanings which may be inscribed in commodities, and insists that his aim is to locate consumption (broadly defined to include music styles) in the construction of social identities and social relations. He counters that his critics underestimate the agency of young people – which he suggests is exemplified in the emergence of hip-hop style. Bennett (1999) sees musical tastes and stylistic preferences of young people as examples of late-modern lifestyles in which notions of identity are constructed rather than given, and fluid rather than fixed. Individuals move between site-specific gatherings and build up a sense of self through multiple identifications – 'a self which can no longer be simplistically theorized as unified' (Shields, 1992: 16). This runs counter to Melucci's argument therefore.

Collective identity, according to Elliott (2001), gains its power through the establishment and recognition of common interests, built upon forms of solidarity involving battles over social exclusion, class, nation, etc. Bauman (1995) suggests that neo-tribes could think of themselves as cultures and attempt to appear cohesive through intolerance of others – thus creating less permeable boundaries than those suggested by Bennett. Some commentators have argued that styles can be divisive and associated with status maintenance within the group, functioning in a subcultural way. Croghan and colleagues (2006) examined the ways young people use style as a vehicle of status and self-expression within 'style groups', and consider the social costs of 'style failure' when the rules are broken. Riley and Cahill (2005) studied body art (piercing and tattoos) which, they argue, has become pathologized and found that, although for some young women body art represented authenticity (the outer appearance reflecting the inner person) and was part of identity construction, for others it represented adoption of a consumer-style practice. Those siding with authenticity operated as a 'mythical mainstream' to exclude the others by denying them meaning, and thus prevented cultural dilution. Thornton (1995: 163), in her study of club cultures, combines Bourdieu's concept of social capital with subcultural analysis and posits the concept of 'subcultural capital' as the criteria for acceptance or exclusion, and the means 'by which young people negotiate and accumulate status within their own worlds'.

Subcultures or styles?

There has been debate over whether youth styles present new forms of subcultural resistance. Hebdige (1979) described punk music and style as 'youth music', seeing it as a strategy of resistance among working-class young people but Bennett (2006) reminds us that punk had middle-class art college origins. Siegel (2005) sees Goth culture in terms of resistance to regimes of sexual normalcy. As Shane Blackman (2005) points out, the rave culture which existed during the 1990s was, whatever its origins, certainly treated by others as oppositional (with clampdowns by the police, negative reporting by the media) and thus should be recognized as a form of resistance; however, this links with Bourdieu's idea of strategy being claimed retrospectively, or Becker's description of deviancy as the outcome of societal reaction rather than the act itself. Raby (2005) suggests that Foucault's perception of the multiplicities of resistance offers a way of incorporating micro-resistance into postmodernist analysis.

Reluctance to present young people as cultural dupes leads to attempts to stress the emancipatory potential of music styles. Thus, according to Smith and Maughan (1998), new technologies mean that dance cultures are becoming more and more of an underground (rather than commercialized) scene, and young people who are acting as DJs or establishing labels are becoming the producers as well as consumers of this often informal economy. Blackman argues that although the idea of collective resistance is lost in postmodern interpretations, postmodern constructions of youth culture as creative and emancipatory still align them with subcultural analyses. According to him, the concept of subculture describes forms of solidarity, focusing on the existence of 'groups with different patterns of behaviour and alternatives values from the mainstream who pursue and act out their own cultural solutions' (Blackman, 2005: 2). He points out that Maffesoli himself suggests that tribes can challenge the logic of domination of the dominant classes. According to Blackman, postmodernist accounts still have elements of a structural analysis.

According to other critics, however, they do not go far enough. Shildrick and MacDonald (2006) argue that the focus on music, dance and style has been detrimental to understanding the experiences of the majority of young people because insufficient account has been taken of social divisions in youth and the ways youth cultural experiences intersect with their wider biographies. Their review of recent but sparse literature which does this suggests that cultural 'choice' is limited to the more privileged. Lash (2007) argues that 'post-hegemonic' cultural studies are the poorer for their neglect of social class at a time when inequality has worsened, especially on a global level, and he argues that the task of cultural studies is to be more political, and engage with the culture industries (rather than be part of them).

Working-class masculinity in late modernity

Currently there have been concerns about poor education achievement levels among young men in Britain, highlighted by the improved education levels among young women. Those most seen to be missing out on education, and ending up without qualifications and poorly placed to compete in a job market where qualifications increasingly matter, are white and African-Caribbean origin working-class young men. Research suggests that in these groups anti-school cultures are, outwardly at least, similar to those studied by Willis (1977). However, where he explained anti-school behaviour in terms of a subcultural resistance to the ideology of a hegemonic power, we must consider whether this explanation still holds. It is possible to apply a Gramscian explanation of anti-school culture if production capitalism is replaced in the analysis with consumer capitalism: the lads still end up doing what is expected of them, albeit in the consumer industry, and their own peer subculture still plays a part in this. However, Lash (2007) has argued that power is no longer hegemonic because it does not need to be – it does not have to work through ideology because it is real. Where does this place symbolic resistance, and does it challenge the authenticity of 'traditional' working-class cultures?

One explanation of anti-school cultures lies in the problem of identity. Several recent studies have shown that current male anti-school cultures are bound up with particular models of masculinity also described as hegemonic (Johnston et al., 2000; McDowell, 2001; MacDonald and Marsh, 2001, 2004). This leads them to affirm their male identities through aggression and intolerance, especially of women, gays and ethnic minorities (Mac an Ghaill, 1999). McDowell (2001), for example, found an 'assertive masculinity' among the white, working-class young men she studied, in which they were disparaging about girls and expected to become traditional breadwinners. It is not new to associate male subcultures with assertive masculinity: Brake (1980) described subcultures as explorations of masculinity. Where Willis's lads affirmed their masculinity through their future roles as manual workers, young men in the current, restructured and 'feminized' labour market were unlikely to be able to do so and faced a 'crisis of masculinity' in which their ideals of masculinity were not matched by their experience in service industry jobs. These studies bring back to mind the work of Lacan, Lasch and Žižek on the ways in which an imagined, incomplete and distorted sense of identity can lead to intolerance of others. Whatever the young men thought they wanted to be, they were quite likely to be working in McDonald's or other temporary, casual or part-time work. They had little awareness of the changing realities of the labour market, but clear beliefs about the kinds of jobs appropriate for men and no fears about finding one.

Young people in poor communities with goals set so low may well not see the relevance of education to their lives, and their beliefs can be reinforced by anti-school peer cultures (MacDonald and Marsh, 2004; West et al., 2002; Furlong and Cartmel, 2004). If they resist peer pressure, they risk being bullied and some withdraw from school. Being a 'swot' may not be compatible with maintaining an existing peer identity and membership of a peer network (Johnston et al., 2000), though the authenticity of these peer cultures is in question, and they may simply be papering over the void rather than offering an opportunity for identity construction. This also raises a further issue for analysis: whether the function and functioning of the peer group constitutes 'subcultural capital' (Thornton, 1995), but of a 'bonding' kind from which it is difficult to escape (see chapter 5), rather than offering a transitional (and bridging) social environment in which individuals can begin to achieve new identities and develop competences and control beliefs with which to assess and negotiate risks.

Identity capital in youth

James Côté (2000), a Canadian social psychologist, suggests that youth and adulthood have been individualized, so that adulthood is seen as individually rather than socially achieved. His work attempts to update Erikson's developmental theory by locating it within Beck's (1992) individualization theory. He argues (Côté, 2002: 119) that individualization takes two forms. On the one hand, following Beck's analysis, he sees *default individualization* as the passive acceptance of mass-marketed and mass-educational pre-packaged identities. Drawing on Erikson's developmental psychology, he suggests that this distracts young people from their main agenda of developing into responsible adults and can lead to 'arrested development' or deferred membership in an adult community. This idea links with the difficulties described by Melucci in developing identities through multiple memberships. In contrast, *developmental individualization* involves active, strategic approaches to personal growth and life projects. Côté argues that for developmental individualization, the resource of identity capital is needed.

Identity capital refers to the personal resources which people may be able to develop and draw on to construct their biographies – for example, in abilities, appearance and inter-action skills (Côté, 2002). This is clearly associated with Bourdieu's concept of *habitus* or dispositions (discussed in chapter 2). Some elements of identity capital are very indi-vidual: for example, Brown (1996) identifies individual 'cha-risma' as an increasingly important element of human capital, applied as a selection criterion by prospective employers, in the face of increasing credentialism among job applicants. But some qualities seen as individual may in practice be socially achieved. The question is whether identity capital is 'mas-tered' in the course of a developmental process, negotiated through interaction with others, or ascribed as a product of an individual's history. This takes us back to the question posed earlier about the relationship between ascribed and achieved identity. For Côté (2002), it is self-concept – the Me – which links to elements such as self-esteem, suggesting that identity capital is achieved through social interaction. Bynner (2005) similarly proposes that a fruitful way of understand-ing youth is in terms of 'capital accumulation', particularly in relation to social capital and identity capital. Emler (2001), on the other hand, found that self-esteem, an element in identity capital, is mainly derived from parents, and over time may become aligned with peer approval, but is also affected by previous experience of success and failure (and is therefore the product of personal history). This is a point also made by Bourdieu.

When faced with a choice, young people's dispositions are framed by their perceptions of what can be done. Flammer (1997) refers to the importance of control beliefs, comprising two components: *competence beliefs* (about capabilities to act in ways which will produce the desired outcomes) and *contingency beliefs* (about the probability that certain actions will affect outcomes in particular ways). Control beliefs, though held at an individual level, are socially and temporally embedded; thus, competence beliefs depend largely on experience of success or failure. The evidence is thus that poor motivation is as much a consequence of negative experience as a cause of it (Catan, 2004).

Young people construct 'learning identities' around their 'successes' and 'failures' within the education system and through this they develop dispositions with regard to questions of choice and risk, adjusting their aspirations accordingly (Jenkins, 1996; Cieslik and Simpson, 2005; Reay, 2005). They may be reluctant to take advantage of education and training opportunities, for example, to avoid risk of further failure. Though there may be a degree of reflexivity in the construction of learning identities, as Jenkins suggests, in practice young people may have little power to control the outcomes. The labelling in schools of young people as achievers or non-achievers can reflect an institutional bias against young people with disabilities, from minority ethnic groups, or in care (Berthoud, 1999; Bignall and Butt, 2000; Britton et al., 2002). Dispositions are not therefore individually achieved, as Bourdieu also pointed out. Lehmann (2004) suggests that young people form dispositions on the basis of a reflexive understanding of their place in the social structure and the degree of risk associated with this. Lawler (2000) suggests that labels of cleverness and intelligence can become metaphors for knowledge which is class-specific. Personal resources such as resilience and self-esteem have been proposed as reasons why some young people achieve 'against the odds' but Schoon and Bynner (2003) found that, although young people could make the most of their individual resources and enhance their competence by deploying a range of 'protective factors and processes', they do not overcome disadvantage; while Emler (2001) found little evidence that self-esteem could be viewed as an individual resource which can enable disadvantaged young adults to succeed against the odds. Reay (2005) speculatively develops the idea of a 'psychic economy of social class', comprising affective elements including feelings of ambivalence, inferiority and superiority (constituents of *habitus*), which influence 'the ways we are, feel and act' and which are the result of the internalization of social class.

Henderson et al. (2006) found, however, that young people's identities were not necessarily centred on their academic labels. They develop different identities in different areas of life, reflecting different degrees of competence in each – according to a combination of self-assessment and assessment by others as competent. Those who failed to gain competence through education tried to do so in other fields, such as employment, or leisure and consumption, or the domestic sphere of caring and parenthood. These constructions of competence were central to their 'imagined futures', constraining or shaping their life plans (Thomson et al., 2004). Like Côté, they indicate that investment is needed. Investments of time and energy made in relation to these different areas of competence depended, firstly, on whether young people had a feeling of efficacy (but this can change in response to the accumulation of experience) and, secondly, on whether they had access to material, emotional, social and cultural resources (which can reconfigure over time, making available different identities, tactics and strategies). Thus, young people's identities can change over time in a 'continuous project of self' (Thomson et al., 2004: 224), as proposed by Giddens and Beck, rather than being fixed by adulthood in the manner described by Erikson, or free-floating as proposed by Bauman.

Some of these ideas have found currency in youth policy and practice initiatives while others have been overlooked. Initiatives to enhance individual capital still fail to take account of the significance of structural inequalities. However much forms of identity capital such as self-esteem, resilience and employability are enhanced, other forms of capital such as social, cultural and economic capital are still needed for decision-making and, being held at family level or not at all, may not be accessible to those in need of them.

4

Youth as Transition

It is time to consider the central dynamic in youth: the transition to adulthood. Here it is hard to disagree with Marsland and Hunter's (1976) criticism of CCCS for failing to recognize that it was as a period of transition that youth gained its essential nature. Where the two previous chapters noted the impact of forms of repression on young people's ability to express themselves and their values, and develop a sense of their identity, this one is concerned with the impact of state institutional structures (the apparatus of bureaucratic knowledge) on young people's ability to define their own lives. In doing so it takes a more holistic view, beyond the more visible and public domains of consumption and politics, to 'the mundane worlds of family, school and work which most young people still inhabit' (Cohen, 1997: 198–9).

The chapter begins by charting the ways in which life transition has been conceptualized in social science, and consides the value of this approach to understanding youth as a concept. It presents an overall picture of recent trends in transitions to adulthood, to map the extent to which these trends are specific to youth or reflect wider social change. It thus reviews the ideas of standardized biographies and biographies of choice, through discussion of the idea of reflexive biographies. The theoretical work of Giddens and Beck provides a framework for considering whether young people's biographies represent pathways which are mapped and pre-packaged by institutions, or personal projects. There follows a review of how young people manage their lives, either pragmatically and defensively, or instrumentally and strategically, or even experimentally and more freely, and how over time their approaches may change, giving rise to hope that there really is scope for second chances or even third ones, and that the concept of 'failed' transition should therefore be abandoned in favour of support for ongoing biographical projects which are unrestricted by poorly conceived 'life stages'. The chapter concludes with some reflections on ways that government policies could be designed to enable transitions as well as to frame them.

Conceptualizing transition

Limbo and moratorium

In addition to the more generalized labelling identified in the last chapter, social science has followed the example of market research in applying labels to young people who are experiencing extended youth. These are founded on the idea of deviation from normative models of transition as linear, one-way, and relatively brief: thus 'Twixters', or 'Kidults', are apparently in limbo between childhood and adulthood. Apter (2001) refers to 'thresholders', while Holdsworth and Morgan (2005) draw on the related anthropological concept of 'liminality' to describe the situation of young people on the threshold between youth and adulthood, in a limbo between the social world of their family and that of the external world into which they have not yet integrated (following Turner, 1967). The idea that young people are on the margins of society is not new (e.g. Coffield et al., 1986), but the extension of the period of dependent youth brings the issue more sharply into focus. The terms 'freeters' (*furītā*) and 'parasite singles' (*parasaito shinguru*) have been used in Japan to describe young people who are not fully integrated into the labour market and are seen as dependent-by-choice, free-loaders and a threat to generational and social cohesion (Kosugi, 2002; Miyamoto, 2001). The terms 'Boomerang Generation' and 'Yo-yo Generation' have been used to refer to those returning home and to dependence on parents. Galland (1984, 1990, 2001) proposed there was now a new age in life, 'post-adolescence', and more recently suggested that the categories of youth and young people should be replaced by the concept of 'entry into adulthood'. In the US, Arnett (2004) similarly uses the term 'emerging adults' to describe young people who are relatively independent of age-normative tasks, experimenting with social roles, and lacking commitment to social and organizational relationships. His work has been influential in the US, but is also criticized for overstressing agency and neglecting institutional and structural factors and exclusion mechanisms (Bynner, 2005).

Part of the difficulty lies in the continued use, especially in the US, of the psychological term 'adolescent' to describe young people who, far from being teenagers, may be in their early twenties (European social policies are generally based on youth as the period from 15–16 to mid-twenties). Because most of these labels derive from developmental psychology, they are used to promote the idea of normative linear transitions towards the destination of adulthood, but they neglect social change and social variation and thus pathologize transitions which do not correspond to the norm. There is a whole terminology associated with such deviance, including the concepts of 'failed', 'stalled', 'broken' or 'blocked' transitions. The assumption is that young people who have not achieved their transitions to adulthood are somehow in limbo, trapped in their youth.

From life stage to life cycle to life course

The notion of life stages was developed as a means of making social sense of biology – especially birth and death (Ariès, 1962) – and now fits more comfortably as a descriptor of traditional societies where 'rites of passage' still structure and to some extent standardize individual lives. In developmental psychology, as we have seen, conceptions of life stages assume linearity and sequencing from childhood to adulthood, each stage to be achieved (or mastered) before moving on. Thus, for Bühler (1933), youth is the period of experimentation with aspects of adulthood between physiological maturity and social maturity – with the assumption of the social, sexual, economic and legal rights and duties of the adult. The question of how the transition from one stage to another is effected remained unanswered.

As the study shifted from theories of child psychological development to theories of change across the entire life course, new approaches were needed. At first, the concept of life cycle, deriving from biology, was applied to humans – somewhat unsuccessfully because the term 'life cycle' carries connotations of cyclical continuity more suited to the butterfly. During the 1970s, the life-course approach was developed in the US, still following a functionalist tradition. Modell and Hareven (1978), Marini (1984) and others studied transitions to adulthood in terms of life events such as age at leaving education, entry into the labour market, age at marriage, and (among women) age at which they gave birth to their first child, and sought to explain the determinants of these social timetables. The approach provided an opportunity to explore historical change through cohort comparison, and variation between social groups. But as Howard Becker (1963) indicated with regard to deviance, the identification of associated social factors is not sufficient to explain a phenomenon.

The life course is the social biography of the individual, and is structured not only by biological age, but also socially. Chris Harris criticizes approaches to transition which misuse and reify the space-time categories associated with life events and neglects the social content which gives the processes their meaning and diversity.

> Wilful ignorance of ascriptive variables results in the use of space-time as a mere analogy of social processes . . . so that the history of social life becomes a dance of social categories to the music of historical time, and we become concerned with the trajectories of social categories through social space, as if these categories themselves were capable of action, and did not have to be embodied in concrete actors whose distribution in material space-time did not necessarily condition the speed and duration of the movement of social categories. (Harris, 1987: 20)

Transitions through the life course have therefore to be understood as socially, rather than individually, constructed and achieved. Tamara Hareven (1982) describes the life-course approach as the meshing of individual careers with the family as it changes over time. Daniel Bertaux (1981) has argued that it is the context of social relations between individuals with differing life histories which brings biography into the realms of sociology.

But youth was changing. The life events which were seen to constitute developmental social tasks were losing much of their meaning in the shift to late modernity. There was an increasing problem about viewing 'adulthood' as a destination, when adulthood was itself becoming less stable in terms of jobs, marriage and parenthood. The normative linear timetable of events which informed earlier research (leaving school, starting work, marriage and parenthood) was becoming out of date, and may in any case have belonged to a mythical 'golden age'. Models and measurements of life stages may provide policy-makers and researchers with tools of convenience for their day-to-day work but, once these models become more than convenient tools and become crystallized, they begin to form an ideology of the life course which corresponds less and less to lived experience. For the people experiencing them, life events have relevance primarily in relation to the changing social relationships of dependence and obligation which surround them. This means understanding the relationship between young people, their families and the state. Simmel (1994 [1909]) pointed out that crossing a bridge or going through a door is always both an event and a process; somehow, both these elements need to be maintained in any explanations of youth. However, when research is dominated by a focus on life events, even if it includes the study of 'sequential' processes between events, it still does not consider the social context in which young people's lives are lived – the structures of the bridge or door.

Young people's biographies are structured to a very great extent by government policy and the institutions through which they pass. These draw on particular models of youth. The problem is that policy models do not reflect current reality. Guillemard (2000) describes a 'crisis of normativeness' in which people's lives have come adrift of policy structures. This does not just apply to young people. She suggests that the welfare state, based on age thresholds, effectively standardized the life course into three phases, of education (childhood), work (adulthood) and rest (old age), thus accentuating the differences between these states rather than the relationships between them. However, with the increase in longevity, and changes in patterns of responsibility and dependence across the life course, the life course has been de-standardized. Jones and Bell (2000) argue that 'youth' has never been successfully incorporated into UK policy thinking. Instead, various age-based frameworks have developed in different policy contexts and been crystallized in legislation over the last century, leading to a somewhat haphazard policy formulation of 'youth'. The upshot is that the study of life transitions which are in practice structured by government policies are probably going to tell us as much about the political agendas underlying institutions and structures as about young people as actors (Crow, 1989; Raffe, 2003).

Transition studies

The focus of transitions research shifted towards a more holistic and socio-biographical (rather than event-mapping) approach to young people's lives. The biographical approach requires that the lives of the young are seen as an integrated whole. The sociology of family life in the late 1960s and 1970s made a start in opening up the 'black box' of the family household, in terms of adult partnership relations (see Brannen and Wilson, 1987), but the changing relations between young people and their parents or carers were still neglected (though Leonard, 1980, was a notable exception). Subsequently, Wallace (1987), Hutson and Jenkins (1989) and Allatt and Yeandle (1992) all used qualitative methods to examine the family contexts of young people. In the late 1980s, a major ESRC research programme, the *16–19 Initiative*, studied young people's social and economic 'trajectories', though the age range was restricting (Banks et al., 1992). Research on young people's transitions took off in the UK in the 1990s with new research programmes (Catan, 2004, and Jones, 2002, provide overviews). Debates ensued about what transitions should be called – flux, itineraries, biographies, pathways, niches, navigations (see, for example, Passeron, 1990; Evans and Furlong, 1997) – but the broad agenda had been established. Transition studies have shown major changes in the ways in which young people in Britain become adult compared with the transitions experienced by their parents a generation before. These changes need to be seen in the broader context of a wider social shift from modern to late modern society.

The shift from normative timetables

The argument is that the normative timetables upheld in previous research and in policy structures may represent patterns associated with modernity, or even with the patterns of a generation ago, but not those now experienced. This is particularly curious since current patterns of extended transition are to a very great extent the result of policy changes. Though the period of dependent youth has been extended for a growing majority of young people, independence continues to occur earlier for others. This is not new but reflects long-standing social inequalities (Ariès, 1962; Bourdieu, 1978). Typically, middle-class transitions and parental support for them have been more protracted than working-class ones and male ones more than female ones (Leonard, 1980; Jones, 1988, 1995). There has been considerable change in the course of a generation. Parents interviewed in a recent study thought that, though their own transition to independence was more abrupt, the current pattern of transition is more difficult for young people to manage, mainly because 'the jobs aren't there' (Jones et al., 2004).

In the UK, there was a strong working-class pattern of early entry into employment at the minimum school-leaving age, and the wage was once seen as the key to adulthood (Willis, 1984). The youth labour market has now been marginalized and the structure of opportunity has changed. The 'feminization' of the labour market, resulting from industrial restructuring and an increase in service industry jobs and loss of manufacturing ones (Stafford et al., 1999: 3), has created new sets of problems for working-class young men who are underachieving educationally and who might have expected to get traditional working-class manual jobs. Many of the jobs once held by unqualified school leavers have disappeared. Traditional craft apprenticeships and manufacturing jobs have been replaced by jobs in the service industry, often low-paid, insecure and marginal. Instead of being able to work their way up from the factory shop floor through 'stepping stone jobs', young workers are now more likely to be trapped in low-grade jobs or experience early unemployment, which in turn can lead to later unemployment and lower earning power in a 'scarring' effect (Bynner et al., 2002; Furlong and Cartmel, 2004). John Bynner and colleagues conclude that this is why, despite economic growth and a decline in the numbers of young people available for work, a 'core' of youth unemployment persists. But there is a problem when policies focus too exclusively on the barrier between work and non-work and indeed it has been argued, especially in countries such as Spain and Portugal, that it is government employment policies which result in the preponderance of insecure and low-grade jobs (see Bradley and van Hoof, 2005). The real barrier, according to Furlong and Cartmel (2004), is between insecure and secure employment, and the real need is therefore for policies designed to help vulnerable young people gain the competitive edge which might help them get better jobs. Sennett (2004) makes a related point, arguing that welfare policies oriented towards putting people into work can have the negative effect of increasing a sense of inferiority and low self-esteem among those at the bottom of the occupational structure. Inability to integrate into the labour market is thus due not to individual deficiency but to labour-market characteristics (Furlong and Cartmel, 2004; MacDonald and Marsh, 2001, 2004).

Young people are being encouraged to stay longer in education and training and delay their entry into full-time employment and economic independence, so that they gain the qualifications and skills needed for the contemporary labour market. The current aim is to improve young people's life chances, prevent social exclusion and increase the national's economic competitiveness in global markets. In practice, the raising of the school-leaving age has been ongoing over the last century (Jones and Bell, 2000). The changes in patterns of school-to-work transition over the last thirty years have been immense. Since 1976, staying-on rates in education and training have increased and the proportion of young people entering higher education has risen (Dolton et al., 1999: Bynner et al., 2002). As a result, only 11 per cent of 16–17 year olds in the UK were in employment in 2000, compared with 33 per cent in 1984 (ONS, 2000). UK government policy is that by 2013 all under-18s will be in education or training, rather than the labour market. Access to the benefits of education is not evenly spread, as analysis by class, gender and ethnic grouping shows (see Berthoud, 1999, for example), and so the most vulnerable may not get the step up they need. The challenge for policy-makers is to persuade 'non-traditional students' – such as young men from working-class families or young women from some minority ethnic groups – to take up the education and training opportunities available and this means understanding economic and cultural barriers, including the implications for individuals and their families of deferred economic independence (Jones et al., 2004).

With the withdrawal of most of the state support for higher education, young people and their parents must foot the bill. However, as access to education widens and qualifications become more common, its benefit, put alongside its increasing cost, is eroding (Bynner et al., 2002). This is important because it seems that parents and young people are increasingly taking an instrumental and rational approach to education, needing evidence that it is worth the economic investment and feeling less swayed by its intrinsic value (Jones et al., 2004).

There have been changes in domestic transitions too, associated with household, partnership and family formation. A generation ago, though the timing and shaping of individual domestic biographies differed by social class and gender (Jones and Wallace, 1992), there were 'normative timetables' (Finch, 1989: 175), an expectation of 'proper' ages and sequencing for transition events. Parents had a responsibility for keeping children on the right track; thus, cohabitation and single parenthood were frowned upon, but normative timetables were also brought into play by young people themselves when, faced with economic uncertainties, they needed a sense of order in their domestic lives (Allatt and Yeandle, 1992). Transitions were gendered. Women have traditionally left home, entered partnerships and become parents earlier than men, tending to have partners older than themselves (Jones and Wallace, 1992; Jones, 1995). For many young men, commitment to relationships meant being tied down and bearing the responsibility of breadwinner (which required a solid economic base). In contrast, women, influenced by media representations of romantic love and faced with lack of opportunity in the labour market, saw marriage as the key to independence (Pollert, 1981; Wallace, 1987). Individual choice was thus compromised by gender and social-class constraints. Women in particular saw courtship as a mystery beyond their control (Leonard, 1980), leading to an 'unmapped plateau' of marriage (Allatt and Yeandle, 1992).

Over the last few decades there has been considerable change, reflecting characteristics of late modernity. Widespread cohabitation emerged as a new phenomenon in the 1970s (Kiernan, 1992). The new pattern of partnership is more likely to involve serial monogamy over the life course (Ferri and Smith, 2003). Giddens (1991, 1992) has argued that partnership formation now involves a greater element of choice. The gendered domestic roles associated with modernity and sustained by the ethos of romantic love have been transformed, so that partnerships have become more equal and mutually 'companionate'. It seems, however, that this is not across the board. Some working-class young men still expect to become breadwinners and see partnership as a constraint on their scope for personal growth, and some young women still feel that they lack control over partnership processes (Johnston et al., 2000; McDowell, 2001; Jamieson et al., 2003).

Patterns of leaving the parental home have changed considerably (Jones, 1995; Rugg, 1999). Until fairly recently, leaving home was not regarded as a separate phenomenon and not studied as a life event; instead the age at leaving home was imputed from the age at marriage and treated as a one-off event (Young, 1987; Jones, 1987). It is now far less common for young people to remain in the parental home until they marry, and far more likely that they will experience some form of relatively independent housing before they establish a partnership home of their own. This independent home is not always an owned or rented flat but may be student housing, a bed-sit or shared flat, or a hostel, so the degree of independence associated with it will vary (Rugg, 1999; Heath and Cleaver, 2003). Patterns of returning home have also changed: where returning was once unidentified in research or mainly associated with students who returned home when they had finished their studies, returning is now a wider phenomenon, and is no longer uncommon among working-class young people who would once have found it shameful and evidence of failure (as many working-class young people seem still to do) (Galland, 1995; Jones, 1995). Where Goldscheider and Goldscheider (1999), from a functionalist perspective, comment on 'insufficiently launched young adults' in the US, reinforcing the idea that returning constitutes failure to achieve a developmental task, it is now more analytically appropriate in Britain at least to think of the whole process of leaving home as a complex one which can involve several leavings. Returning home can be for a range of reasons, mainly the ending of the reason for leaving in the first place, but also can be symptomatic of the deficiencies in the housing market, which has never catered for young people and rarely offers the levels of affordability, security and basic standards that they need. As is the case with unemployment, when looking for a cause of changing transition it may be advisable to look first at the structures involved rather than individual psychopathology.

For the majority of young people there are intermediate stages (such as training, apprenticeship, post-16 education or intermediate households) between events such as leaving school and entry into the labour market, or leaving home and becoming a householder (Jones and Wallace, 1992). The significance of individual life events has therefore changed. Leaving home has become a significant life event in itself rather than in association with marriage (Harris, 1983; Jones, 1995). On the other hand, leaving school becomes less significant *as an event* when it is not followed by entry into the labour market (Jones and Bell, 2000). Where adulthood was once closely associated with marriage and parenthood, cohabitation and later parenthood are now common. The normative transition biography along linear pathways no longer exists, if it ever did (Jones, 1995; du Bois-Reymond, 1998). Transitions can involve false starts, returns to dependence and second or third attempts. Age has become less reliable as a marker of adult independence, though it is still adhered to as a means of targeting delivery of policies and thus of structuring experiences in youth. The legal age of majority (18 in the UK), for example, is not accompanied by recognizable adult status in terms of welfare rights and responsibilities, which are scattered across a wide age range. This unpacking of unitary transitions could be seen as the development of a new form of youth, reflecting late modernity, and characterized by more choice but less freedom.

Patterns of transition have also changed across Europe, though the UK is exceptional in several respects, having a low age at leaving education and leaving home, a high rate of teenage pregnancy, and a shorter period of parental support (Iacovou and Berthoud, 2001). These reflect working-class patterns. There has also been a trend within all European countries for family formation to be deferred by all but a minority. Where young people still typically leave home in order to marry, and the median age at marriage is rising, then the age of leaving home will also rise. But young people seem to be increasingly leaving home for other reasons, such as to study or take up a job, and in these circumstances the age of *first* leaving home may become lower. In northern European countries (UK, Denmark, Netherlands, Germany, Austria), young people tend to leave the parental home earlier. In southern European countries (Spain, Italy), young people may remain in the parental home until well into adulthood, only leaving in order to set up a marital home (Holdsworth and Morgan, 2005; Jones, 2005).

Extended and complex transitions

Rather than persist with the idea of unitary and linear transitions, it is now more helpful to conceive of the transition to adult independence as consisting of interconnecteds strands (from education to labour market, from child to partner/ parent, from living in parental home to forming households and starting housing careers). Young people can become 'adult' along one strand but not another. Thus, they can become economically independent from their parents through employment but still live in the parental home (including sometimes with a partner), or live as a single individual in an independent home, but still need parental support. They may return home but still be employed. This might make the problem about what adulthood *is* less significant. Everything is negotiable: there are many different ways of claiming adulthood and reducing loss of face, and young people unpack the concept of independence to suit their circumstances. Young people with disabilities may find difficulty accepting simplistic normative definitions of social and economic independence which they will probably never be able to achieve, and construct appropriate alternative definitions (Valentine et al., 2003; Pascall and Hendey, 2002). For Emily, a lone mother aged 21 (Jones, 2004), independence built up in stages:

> You know, you learn to do different things at different times, and you can still build up various areas of your independence while you still live with your parents. You know, financially. When I lived with my mum and I was working full time, I paid my mum money towards food and things anyway, so I was learning that you can't just get freebies everywhere. They made me do my own washing and stuff like that.

A generation ago, young people thought of adulthood in terms of work – the key to financial independence (Willis, 1984) – and marriage – the key to home and family (Leonard, 1980). A recent study of constructions of adulthood among 16–21-year-olds (Thomson et al., 2004) found perceptions of competence to be more significant than age or event markers, but that individualized constructions give way to relational ones, as young people 'settle down'. Young people initially think of independence in terms of autonomy, responsibility and maturity, but as they experience setting up home, becoming a parent, gaining an adult income, etc., they retrospectively begin to identify adulthood with these 'event markers' (Jones, 2004; Holdsworth and Morgan, 2005). It seems that most young people still chiefly associate adult independence with earning an income from work, which gives them greater control over their consumption and leisure lives (Jones, 2004). Age has become less significant to young people themselves.

While 'social adulthood' is withheld from some young people, others are catapulted into one form of independence at a young age. Children involved in caring responsibilities in their families of origin, such as looking after a chronically ill parent or sibling (Dearden and Becker, 2000), or who have to look after themselves because their parents have alcohol and drugs problems (Bancroft et al., 2004), or care leavers and those who have been evicted from the 'family' home, may well feel that they have had to take responsibility too soon. Roger, a care leaver who when interviewed (Jones, 2004) was unemployed and homeless, said he 'sort of got a bit old-headed' by the time he was eleven.

Despite the stereotyping of transitions as extended, recent UK research shows persisting inequalities in youth, reflected in increasing polarization in education, work, health, family formation, civic participation, and incomes (Jones and Martin, 1999; Schoon, 2002). Bynner and his colleagues (2002), on the basis of age-cohort comparison,[1] found increasing polarization in occupations (between career jobs and insecure ones), qualifications (between those with higher qualifications and those with no qualifications) and earnings (between the better-paid and the low-paid). While some young people are on extended transitions to adulthood, others are not (Bynner et al., 2002; Jones, 2002).

- *Slow-track* transitions typically involve staying on in post-compulsory education and delaying entry into full-time employment and family formation, in a pattern previously dominated by the middle class. With the extension of education, there are more young people from working-class backgrounds on this type of transition path, but they can have particular difficulties because working-class families would traditionally not expect to continue to provide financial support and may not be able to afford to do so (Jones et al., 2004). Policies aimed at reducing inequalities can therefore increase risk. 'Failed' slow-track transitions typically involve drop-out from courses.
- *Fast-track* transitions may involve leaving education at around the minimum age and entering a diminished

youth labour market, risking unemployment or insecure and badly paid work (Bynner et al., 2002). For some young people, these patterns represent a continuation of traditional working-class practices which, with the demise of the youth labour market, are no longer sustainable, though young people may have to experience this in order to understand it (Bourdieu's idea of the 'logic of practice' may be helpful here). Because of deficiencies in the labour market, housing market and welfare system (or at least lack of fit between current structures and young people's expectations), 'failed' fast-track transitions result in increased risks – young people ending up unemployed, homeless, teenage lone parents, or in some cases offending, or abusing drugs and alcohol. The group most likely to be referred to by policy-makers as socially excluded is mainly recruited through the fast track, though those who unsuccessfully attempt to enter slow-track transitions are also at risk (see chapter 5).

Reflexive biographies and 'lifespans'

Bauman (1995), as indicated in the previous chapter, believes that there has been a shift away from the idea of life as a 'pilgrimage', which was associated with life in modernity. According to Beck's individualization thesis, life is still a project, but it has become self-reflexive, because 'status-influenced, class cultural or familial biographical rhythms overlap with or are replaced by *institutional biographical patterns*' (Beck, 1992: 131; original emphasis). Apparently 'individualized' biographies are thus still subject to standardization by external controls, 'contrary to the image of individual control which establishes itself in consciousness', since the traditional commitments and support relationships associated with modernity are exchanged for the constraints of existence in the labour market and as a consumer. The private sphere has become 'the outside turned inside and made private' (echoing Bourdieu's terminology and Habermas's description of the colonization of the life world), of conditions and decisions made elsewhere with general disregard for their private, biographical consequences (Beck, 1992: 133). This leads to increasing susceptibility to risk. The standardized biographies defined by institutions are vestiges of the fading industrial period and are now representative of a diminishing minority. Beck (1992: 134) argues that 'the edifice of industrial society threatens to slip into normative legalism'.

One of his main points is that in late modernity risks are spatially and temporally limitless, but no one can be accountable for them because of the way institutions can adapt procedures and their presentation to maintain credibility (Lash and Wynne, 1992). Beck (1992) argues that there has been 'forcible emancipation'. Linking ideas from Kafka and Sartre, he suggests that the age of the self-determined life is produced by a dense fabric of institutions which 'condemn' everyone to freedom on pain of economic disadvantage (Beck and Beck-Gernsheim, 2002: 163). New forms of 'guilt ascription' come into being. Decisions must be made and, even where 'decisions' are not feasible, individuals will have to pay for the consequences of decisions not taken (p. 135). How one lives becomes a 'biographical solution of systemic contradictions', such as between education and employment or between legally presumed and actual biographies (for examples of such contradictions between youth policy and family policy in the UK, see Jones and Bell, 2000). Beck gives as an example the way in which access to apprenticeship training in Germany means the difference between entering society and dropping out of it. For Beck, individuals must recognize, however, that the institutional conditions which determine their lives are the products of the decisions they have made – but he is, implicitly at least, speaking of adults. Young people have no bargaining or political power to change them.

Giddens (1991: 146–8) suggests that the idea has developed of an internally referenced 'lifespan' – a trajectory which is enclosed and distinctive and, most importantly, 'distanced from the life cycle of the generations'. External givens or certainties associated with tradition and habit have been replaced with expert knowledge systems which represent contested knowledge. He suggests that the removal of prior supports ('the sequestration of experience') allows individuals to achieve greater mastery over social relations and social contexts, so that lifespans become 'internally referential open experience thresholds' rather than ritualized passages or rites of passage. There is also a problem, because trust, linked to achieving a sense of ontological security in early life, allows the leaps of faith which engagement demands but there has been a loss of ontological security – loss of sense of continuity, order and ritual, an 'evaporation of morality'. As a result, life transitions can become a series of identity crises (he appears to be referring to Erikson here) – which individuals need to recognize, anticipate and resolve. 'Fateful moments' are times when a particular configuration of events forces an individual to take stock, assess risk and make a life-changing decision.

Giddens sees strategic life-planning (organized in terms of the individual's projected lifespan and focused through the notion of risk) as an increasingly dominant temporal outlook involving colonization of the future and control of time. Thus, he describes the teenager who drifts around and has no thought for the future as opposing this outlook (Giddens, 1991). In contrast, Sennett (1998) argues that, in an uncertain world, making decisions does not necessarily create a sense of control over the future.

According to Giddens, living in the 'risk society' described by Beck 'means living with a calculative attitude to the open possibilities of action, positive and negative, with which, as individuals and globally, we are confronted in a continuous way in our contemporary social existence' (Giddens, 1991: 28). Rationality is therefore involved. Like Beck, he argues that decisions must be made, but also (1994) that it is important to distinguish between choice and decision-making. So many day-to-day activities involve choice that choice has become virtually obligatory. Decision-making, on the other hand, usually involves expert knowledge rather than individual rationality and is a medium of power: 'Analytically it is more accurate to say that all areas of social activity come to be governed by decisions – often, although not universally, enacted on the basis of claims to expert knowledge of one kind or another. *Who* takes those decisions, and *how*, is fundamentally a matter of power' (Giddens, 1994: 76). Bourdieu makes a related point in indicating that 'We can always say that individuals make choices, as long as we do not forget that they do not choose the principles of these choices' (Bourdieu in conversation with Wacquant, 1989: 45). Melucci (1992: 65) suggests that too many possibilities can result in a lack of choice. Although young people have more choice, this is often imposed and defined by others; nor are they equally positioned to capitalize upon it.

Reflexivity in youth

It is helpful to remember that individualization does not imply that individuals are free agents – neither Beck nor Giddens has implied this. Although young people's transitions have become *individualized*, this does not mean that they are able to determine their own biographies.

Reflexive biographies depend not only on a degree of rationality but also on access to a range of external and personal resources which will affect approaches to risk. Mary Douglas (1990)[2] indicates that approaches to risk assessment are determined by resources and social responsibilities, and Sennett (2004) argues that young people from privileged backgrounds have safety nets in the form of cultural capital which allow them to ignore risk. Skeggs (2005) ironically points out that, while risk-taking may enhance personal exchange-value and speed promotion for the middle class, it is more likely to lead to imprisonment for the working class. One problem is that young people constantly have to experiment with risk because they are constantly facing situations which they have never encountered before. Where young people are seen as indulging in risky behaviour, it is worth remembering that much of the risk occurs in very mundane situations simply because their ability to assess risk is affected by their ignorance of the rules of the game or their lack of power to change them. For example, the 'last in–first out' employment practice means that young workers are often the first to face redundancy during a recession, though they might also be first to be taken on again during economic recovery (Payne and Payne, 1994) in what Makeham (1980) refers to as a 'pendulum effect'. In the 'risk society', risk is gendered: among young men it may be associated with unemployment or marginal employment; among young women, risk may be associated with teenage pregnancy (McDowell, 2001; Johnston et al., 2000; Ferri, Bynner and Wadsworth, 2003; Bynner et al., 2004).

Choices at 16 years (whether to stay on at school or leave) have become more critical in recent years in terms of adult outcomes by the age of 23 years (Dolton et al., 1999) but 'decisions' may be the result of a perceived lack of alternatives (Biggart and Furlong, 1996). For some school leavers, the local job opportunity *now*, however menial, is still more attractive than the vague promise of a better job in an uncertain future. Youth research also suggests that increased choice can be problematic because it is bound up with individual responsibility. A study by Karen Evans and colleagues compared the impact on young people of the different structural frameworks in Germany (where youth transitions are more closely structured, for example through the apprenticeship system) and England (where the approach is more diverse and unregulated). They found that young people in England needed to be more proactive and to maintain a positive approach to opportunities, but also that they felt more responsible for their failure or success, in other words, more 'individualized'. Though unemployed young people in England felt forced onto schemes and not in control, they still felt responsible for their situation and experienced what the researchers refer to as a sense of 'frustrated agency'. Evans indicates that the least advantaged become the most exposed through processes of individualization, and reports that young people feel individually responsible for their own circumstances *even when they are not*, thus reconstructing fate as choice (Behrens and Evans, 2002; Evans, 2002; Evans et al., 2001).

Other research has shown that young people *feel* responsible for their own situations and actively decide between the options on offer (Allatt and Dixon, 2000; Anderson et al., 2005), whether or not this is the case. For some young people, ability to choose is an important element of independence. Graham, aged 21, stresses the importance of choice and recognizes the responsibilities involved (Jones, 2004); Patricia, in an earlier Scottish study (Jones, 1995), stresses her need to be able to make her own mistakes.

Graham: I mean for me, independence is having the freedom of choice to do what you want to do, to be able to understand the consequences of your actions, and being able to, you know, obviously be responsible for yourself and others.

Patricia: I wanted just a bit of freedom so that I could make my own choice. But my choices were getting made for me, so I wanted to say 'Right. OK, I'll make that decision.' And most of the time it was the wrong decision, and I learned from my mistakes, but if I could make that mistake myself that was fine. It was my mistake. I made it.

The concepts of 'bounded agency' (Evans, 2002) and coping strategies (Thomson et al., 2002) recognize the limitations on individual agency in youth. James Côté (2002) (see chapter 3) distinguishes between 'developmental individualization' – according to which young people are able to take strategic approaches to their personal life projects – and 'default individualization' – which involves passive acceptance of pre-packaged identities devised by policy-makers and into which young people are expected to fit (and indeed they are blamed if they do not). According to Côté, it is in the context of developmental individualization that reflexive biographies can develop, and young people with sufficient identity capital can negotiate 'individualized life-course passages' through 'the institutional holes and deficits of late modernity' (Côté, 2002: 119).

The young people quoted above clearly believed that they had freedom of choice. Are they duping themselves, and if so, why? How much unconstrained choice do they really have to create their own biographies, and to what extent are their pathways mapped out for them?

The management of personal biographic projects

The concept of 'strategy' – used by Giddens as well as Goldthorpe – views individuals as capable of exercising a degree of rational choice in facing opportunities and risks. Crow

(1989) warns that the term implies conscious and rational decisions and can thus overstate the degree of agency involved in decision-making. The concept is particularly problematic when applied to defensive behaviours such as 'survival strategies' or 'coping strategies'. De Certau (1988) distinguishes between the 'strategies' of those with power and the 'tactics' of the powerless. Crow (1989) suggests that the study of 'strategies' developed under conditions of extreme constraint (that is, tactics) can probably tell us more about structures than about individual actors. Thus, strategies to cope with a school system perceived as alienating might lead either to studies of anti-school subcultures, or more usefully to studies of the school system itself (as Jenkins, 1983, and Corrigan, 1979, pointed out). In sobering contrast to the notion of strategy, Reay (2004: 1019) reports that many children, experiencing schools differentiated by ethnicity and social class, 'confronted schooling as academic fate'.

A range of 'strategies' may be consciously or unconsciously employed by young people either to cope with (and make the best of) their situations, or more proactively to deploy whatever resources may be available and change their situations for the better. Some behaviour among young people may reflect tactics in the face of powerlessness – survival 'strategies' may take this form. Some strategies depend on some form of collective action within the family. Furlong and Cartmel (2004) stress the importance of the family in helping young people to develop strategies for coping with unemployment and financial hardship, while Gillies (2005) shows how poorer parents are actively involved in developing their children's survival skills (though these non-normative practices may then be blamed for causing disadvantage rather than representing an appropriate response to it). In many working-class families, however, the emphasis is on chance rather than planning (Evans, 2002). Few young people have made provision for risks such as unemployment (Hutton and Seavers, 2002). While some parents 'keep the door open' for a return to dependence, others continue to expect transitions to be one-way – that is, out (Jones, 1995).

The decisions young people make at 16 are likely to affect the rest of their lives since many are unable to get a second chance. Research suggests that many young people nevertheless take a short-term view, based on immediate benefits or pressures. This does not apply to all young people, however. Some young people can be identified as planners, more able to identify longer-term objectives and to work towards achieving these. Ford et al. (2002) studied young people's housing transitions and found them to be of four main types: chaotic, unplanned, constrained, or planned. Mansfield and Collard's (1988: 73) study of newly-weds distinguished between 'planners', 'venturers' and 'roamers', but found that partnerships were more usually conducted along a 'haphazard' trail, while more recently Jones et al. (2006) identified planners, searchers and escapers among those involved in partnership formation.

Brannen and Nilson's (2002) study of young adults in Norway and Britain found three models of individual control – deferment, adaptability and predictability. Younger students and trainees emphasized present options and concerns and deferred thinking about adulthood (a pattern also observed by du Bois-Reymond, 1998); older students thought they could shape their futures through short steps and adaptations; others were planners following clearly charted courses.

Short-term and survival strategies

Young people's aspirations are affected by their knowledge and understanding of local structures of opportunity, as experienced and reported to them by the people they know. The offer of a job and income here and now may be hard to turn down for the sake of an extension of education and training and the possibility of a better job later. Younger people with difficult family relationships and anxious to assert their independence from their parents may find this immediate 'solution' appealing.

Thomson and Taylor (2005) describe tactics as the tools of the powerless but exhibiting a kind of false agency. Tactics, or survival strategies, can be seen as ways of responding to and attempting to avoid perceived risk. Young people leaving home and facing inequalities of opportunity in the housing market find ways to improve their housing chances, young people who have nowhere to live find ways of surviving in the open, and young people without any money may beg. Often in such situations the strategy adopted is short-term, and is not the outcome of rational and conscious choice over which the young people concerned have control. Short-term strategies are most likely to be adopted by those with the least power to change their circumstances. Those most likely to take a shorter-term view have been found to have experienced family crises (Catan, 2004), to be in insecure circumstances and to have experienced failure (Anderson et al., 2005). Some are seeking immediate and urgent escape from untenable current circumstances, such as unhappy family lives (Jones, 1995). They therefore lack the economic, family and individual resources needed for strategic thinking. The result can be 'chaotic' housing careers (Ford et al., 2002), a drifting between jobs, and further experience of failure and rejection. Some young people find risky (and possibly short-term) escape routes: some young women may enter a risky and unequal or even abusive partnership as a means of leaving home (Jones et al., 2006), though partnership formation can also be seen as a strategy for finding housing, especially in some rural areas (Jones, 2001).

Pragmatism is recognized. This seems to reflect Bourdieu's idea of the weighing of rationality against practicality. Wyn and Dwyer (1999) find that many young people are making pragmatic choices which enable them to maintain their aspirations despite structural constraints, and the authors interpret this as proactivity in the face of risk. Hatcher (1988) finds that young people make educational choices on the basis of pragmatically rational decisions, opportunist and context-related, though both Hatcher (1988) and Boeck et al. (2005) point out that emotion may interfere with rational choice. Young adults try to formulate realistic plans, based on probability of success, rather than pipe dreams (Anderson et al., 2005). They might therefore lower their aspirations to reduce the risk of failure associated with disadvantage (Lehmann, 2004, in contrast to Wynn and Dwyer above). One construction of anti-school cultures is that they represent a defensive peer-survival strategy.

Short-termism does not necessarily lead to fast-track transitions, however. It has been observed that young people can avoid economic and housing risk by continuing to live with their parents (Hutton and Seavers, 2002). Their increased spending power and the scope for greater participation in leisure activities are unconsciously short-termist attractions, however, because by spending they are unable to save towards the costs of future independent living and become trapped in the parental home (Jones and Martin, 1999).

The longer-term strategic view

For the most part, longer-term planners are young people who have resources and who are able to deploy them in pursuit of their defined aims. They therefore tend to be middle class and from advantaged social backgrounds. Jones et al. (2004) found that the decision to defer entry into the labour market and obtain better qualifications requires not only the prospect of family support but also family encouragement to take a longer-term view. There appears to be developing instrumentality in approaches to education (MacDonald and Marsh, 2004; Jones et al., 2004; Brown, 1987), sometimes involving juggling with scarce resources in order to be able to capitalize on the choices available (Catan, 2004; Scott, 2000; Scott and Chaudhary, 2003; Schoon, 2002; Schoon and Parsons, 2003). Those who continue into higher education or plan to do so take an instrumental approach, seeing education as a means of getting better jobs, but in the process incurring considerable family and individual investment. In these circumstances, leaving home, and partnership-and-family formation, may have to take second place to academic ambitions – in other words, life plans in one sphere are likely to impact on those in another sphere of a young adult's life, such as when partnership formation interferes with existing education and training plans (Jones et al., 2006).

Evans et al. (2001) found that planning only occurs on a solid foundation of past success, in education or the labour market. Long-term strategies are the realm of the most privileged, including those with the highest levels of competence and control beliefs (dispositions), who may formulate strategies in the knowledge that they have the resources (various forms of capital) to put them into effect. Some planning may, however, simply involve replication of patterns set by parents or following the paths laid out by policy-makers (examples of traditional or habitual action, perhaps, where repetition substitutes for choice). Brannen and Nilson (2002) identified planners who followed established tracks set by their parents. A distinction between 'trail blazers and path followers' has been made in connection with rural out-migrants, with the latter group following a generational pattern of migration (Jones, 2000). Though habitual action is revealed in the actions of these groups, instrumentality may still have been involved since, by following a traditional path, young people may be more likely to make a successful case for parental support, including financial backing (Jones et al., 2004, 2006).

Changing perspectives

Static typologies based on long-term planners and short-termist non-planners – and various 'stages' in between – fail however to take account of the dynamic nature of young adulthood. Some young adults say that, when they were at the decision-making age, they had not been sufficiently mature to think ahead and had no clear idea of what they wanted to do, or why higher education would help them. Over time, the ability to make longer-term plans increases. After experience in employment, young people may develop longer-term plans which could include returns to education, and this has also been observed in relation to housing, partnership and other decision areas (Jones et al., 2004, 2006; Furlong and Cartmel, 2004; Ford et al., 2002).

Anderson et al. (2005) found a willingness to modify plans, especially among the short-termists. Anderson et al. (1994) found that young people's strategies could be reviewed and altered in the light of events and changing contexts. The majority of young adults in their study felt more in control of their lives by their early twenties but this was not merely the result of becoming older. Furlong and his colleagues (2003) researched young people's life-management strategies and found that, on leaving school, young people broadly divided into 'strategic planners' and 'drifters'. At this stage, the family played a critical role because young people lacked the knowledge needed for decision-making (though it is also hard for parents to stay up to date with education, training and labour-market knowledge). 'Drifters' were demotivated by the experience of failure and underachievement in secondary school. However, their motivation could change over time and with experience if they began to place more importance on work as an area of achievement or source of status. As a result, some began to take more strategic control of their lives. In Bourdieu's terms, perhaps they were learning the rules of the game and developing the dispositions (*habitus*) needed to play it. Furlong[3] suggests that external pressures (from family, partners or peers) could make young people realize that they were being left behind. MacDonald and Marsh (2004) similarly found that some young people moved from disaffection with education to instrumental engagement with it as they neared the end of their compulsory schooling. Young adults who had become unemployed or lone parents after leaving school were socially isolated,[4] but with hindsight began to see a link between education and labour-market success despite the deficiencies of the local labour market, and wished they had worked harder at school. Perhaps simply leaving the institution that had negatively labelled them also had an effect.

As we saw in the last chapter, competences can change. Some young people can thus become strategists on the basis of reappraisal of their competences, particularly if they have access to new resources. The significance of this is that young people should not be written off as failures but should always have the opportunity for 'second chances', or even third or fourth ones, in the spirit of the concept of 'lifelong learning'. This point was made by Carter (1975) in the early days of transitions research but is even more relevant now.

Policies for transition?

Many governments worldwide are beginning to develop youth policies where these have not previously existed. Japan is an example, and it is to be hoped that there, as elsewhere, youth policies can be evidence-based, drawing on youth research. Despite the relatively long histories of youth research and policy in the UK, however, it seems either that policy-makers are not listening, or that youth researchers are failing to send out clear messages, because there is still a mismatch between policy models of youth and the reality of young people's lives which cannot be explained entirely by the idea of a mutual time lag as each (reflexively but slowly) responds to the other. Chapter 2 has concluded (following Bynner et al., 2004) that policies need to take account of the cultural beliefs of young people and their families; we can add some more challenges here.

Policies are still based on normative standardized bio-graphies. The institutional structures through which young people pass in the course of their transitions to adulthood – structures of the education system, labour market, housing market, health provision and so on – assume a particular (out-dated) model of youth as linear. Although rites of passage may no longer have relevance to young people's lives, there remains a persisting belief that biographies comprise stages, each to be achieved before moving on, in a manner deriving from devel-opmental psychology. The policy model builds up a false con-struction of success and failure in youth, which valorizes success in education to the detriment of success in childrearing or even in early employment, and which can somewhat arbi-trarily construct leaving education or leaving home too early and having children too soon as social problems. In the next chapter I will show that this can add fuel to the culture of blame. Again, it seems that adults make the rules.

The linearity of policy models of youth also leads to a continuing dependence on age-structuring in policy legisla-tion. This ignores heterogeneity in youth and the wide varia-tions in living conditions and needs of young people of the same age but different social class, gender and ethnicity. Age is a very poor indicator of individual economic need (Jones and Bell, 2000), yet, despite the great disparities and com-plexities in the ways that young people now effect their transitions to adulthood, many policy provisions for young people are still structured according to age. This leads to welfare policies which assume dependence and independence at particular ages. As a result, age barriers are erected which affect young people's access to state provisions and government services at times when they could be most at risk, a critical threshold developing at eighteen or nineteen years, when young people enter a world where they may have a great need for support and protection but a diminished right to these. There are increasing calls for appropriate support arrangements to enable smoother transitions to adulthood for over-19s (Social Exclusion Unit, 2005; Bynner et al., 2004).

This chapter has highlighted some of the heterogeneity in youth and in particular the increasing polarization in experience between those on slow-track transitions experiencing extended dependence, and those on fast-track transitions attempting to support themselves. The next chapter will examine more closely the sources of inequality in youth with a particular focus on an element which policy-makers have tended to overlook in recent decades: social class. Policy approaches to social problems in youth will then be examined more closely.

5
Youth and Inequality

Youth is a luxury to which the poor have no access. By this, I mean that youth was, until recently, a mainly middle-class phenomenon, and also a male one. For the working class, childhood was until fairly recently succeeded by early adulthood, not youth (Ariès, 1962; Bourdieu, 1978). Despite the intended 'levelling effect' of UK policy frameworks for youth, there is still inequality in access to youth, evidenced by an increasing polarization in paths of transition to adulthood, between the majority who are on extended paths involving deferred economic independence, and those who in various ways become socially and economically adult on leaving school or before (Bynner et al., 2002; Jones, 2002). This polarization reflects either structural disadvantage or differences in individual choice – within the framework of 'biographies of choice' – depending on one's perspective. In considering the sources and outcomes of inequalities in youth, we need a dynamic model of inequality in youth which can reflect both societal and individual change. The foundations of this project are developed in this chapter and the next.

Chapter 1 reviewed theories about the social location of young people according to generation, age, class, gender or as individuals, and the social conditions which gave rise to these different theories. 1960s' researchers described middle-class students as an 'age class' outside the social class structure of adults. Subcultural analysis introduced a social class analysis, examining working-class subcultures as systems of social reproduction, but still took little account of social class relations or how an unequal power structure contributed to social stability. The CCCS work on subcultures was of its time (Lash, 2007), forming part of a trend in sociology towards exploring the cultural origins of action, celebrating the ability of the working class to survive through collective class cultures. Although these working-class cultures *appear* (to some) not to have survived, in reality it was the study of class cultures which died, not the cultures themselves. Studies of school-to-work transitions from the 1960s onwards (such as Halsey et al., 1980) had begun statistical explorations of the association between structural inequalities of class and gender and access to education and jobs, and causal analysis became more possible with the availability of longitudinal birth cohort data and new methods of analysis. However, this too has faded from view in current research on holistic transitions, where 'factors' have taken over from structural explanations, and in poststructural cultural studies, where the shift away from structural determinism is even more extreme. Recently, qualitative methods have been used to get at the underlying class cultural meanings and microprocesses, just as Willis (1977) did. Yet, structural inequalities in youth also persist, even though they too may be masked or overlooked in an 'individualized' society.

This chapter is first about the changing and different ways of understanding the *causes* of inequalities in youth. Inequalities in youth arise and change because of a wider (and changing) structure of unequal power relations across the wider society. Since it is unlikely that young people would choose to be homeless or poor, it is the role of social scientists to understand how they got to be that way, and inform the policy-makers who, with the political will to do so, might develop means of redressing structural disadvantage.

There seems to be more emphasis in current youth research and policy on achieving 'against the odds' than with any serious analysis of what the 'odds' are. To what extent do structures of inequality persist in late modernity, and how do they function? We need to think more about what constitutes the *structures* involved in 'structured individualization' (Roberts, 1997) and also move on to reconsider the role of the cultural in social reproduction, and its relationship with the structural, at a time when the structure has, undeniably, changed.

From modernity to late modernity

The main dimension of social stratification, the concept of social class, has held decreasing currency in late modernity in academic as well as policy circles. There has been a shift from determinist approaches to class as historical fate (as exemplified by Althusser for example), through more optimistic studies of social mobility, to ideas of culturally practised, reflexively organized or even 'individualized class' (Savage, 2000).

Social class is essentially about power relations as well as wealth distribution and social status, but this is sometimes overlooked. Skeggs (2004: 5) argues that classes are produced through conflict over power, and that 'Class (as a concept, classification and positioning) must always be a site of continual struggle and reconfiguring precisely because it represents the interests of particular groups.' The original concept of the welfare state in the UK was based on the knowledge that, although welfare citizenship could help raise a household's living standard closer to the prevailing level in society, it could not eradicate class inequalities (Marshall, 1952). There has been an overall increase in affluence since the Second World War but this has not been evenly spread and has led to a polarization (sometimes called the 'wealth divide') in terms of the accumulation of wealth, housing, property, jobs and so on. On average, young people in employment are 'better off' financially than their equivalent age cohort were 15 years ago, but the visibility of their immediate spending power can mask the inequalities between young people, and income disparities have grown, both relative to adult earnings and among young people (Abrams, 1961; Jones and Martin, 1999). The residual youth labour market for school leavers is dominated by low-grade and low-waged jobs. Both unemployment and second jobs run in families, so that while some families are work-intense, others are work-free (Pahl, 1984;

Payne, 1987). Similarly, some people have second homes while others are homeless. The belief that 'we are all middle class now', living middle-class lifestyles, ignores the 10 per cent or so at the lower end of the class structure, who may be described as an 'underclass' or 'socially excluded', and the unknown numbers just above them who are at risk of joining them or may recently have left them. This polarization is clustered geographically as well as in families. Pockets of visible disadvantage range from inner-city estates to rural communities, reflecting the limitations of local labour markets and housing provision, and the stresses on communities from population movements.

Structuralism and social class

Social class has a particular position in post-war British social theory. Savage (2000: x) comments that because the concept of class was 'historically defined in legislative ways', it acted as an intellectual bridge between policy and political debates and broader academic concerns. He argues that if the concept of class is lost, then 'one of the main intellectual spaces for critical social inquiry also disappears.' Debates on class were thus not purely theoretical but related to practice. However, with the breakdown of the relationship between social science and politics in the 1980s especially, the link was broken and academic work became 'more esoteric, specialized and self-referential' (Savage, 2000: 7). The focus of debate shifted from meaning and application to the difficulties associated with its measurement.[1] The heart of the problem lay in the changing division of labour, not only in the wider society but also at the level of the family household. Factors include changes in labour-market participation, the changing occupational structure, the changing household structure and associated models of the household economy.

Trends in industry and the global economy resulted in a changing occupational distribution, with an increase in non-manual service industry jobs and a loss of manual primary, agricultural and manufacturing industry jobs. The distribution of social class positions is affected by changes in the occupational distribution, so that much of the observed upward mobility was structural, not achieved. It was not that people had improved their relative social positions, only that different social positions had opened. To some extent, therefore, the 'embourgeoisement' of the working class in the 1960s was artefactual (Goldthorpe et al., 1969). In contrast to the Weberian model of socio-economic status applied in the US, which assumes the possibility of movement up and down the entire social structure, in the UK a more Marxist model of the class structure assumes that although there is movement within the middle class and working class, a boundary exists between the two which, though not impermeable, is hard to breach. It has been argued that social reproduction through intergenerational processes is likely to falter, allowing more scope for intergenerational mobility, in conditions of late modernity, but Marshall and colleagues (1997) found that the class boundary seems to be no more (or indeed less) permeable now than in previous decades, suggesting that social mobility has *not* become easier. The problem for social science is to distinguish between relative and absolute rates of social mobility therefore.

The second set of circumstances was associated with changing gender relations, particularly as a result of the rise of feminism. Increased participation of women in the labour market, particularly women who returned to work after childbirth, led to the decline of the notion of the male breadwinner and increasing numbers of dual-earner households. Though this contributed to greater household affluence in some households, some commentators argued that it also contributed to an increase in poverty because higher rates of marital breakdown led to an increase in the numbers of lone parents. Here, one problem for social science was to find ways to represent dual earners in analysis. Another more fundamental one concerned how and whether to incorporate women, including lone mothers, into class schemata which from the first had been based on male occupational structures. Reay (1998) argues that basing the social class of women on their labour-market position denies the complexity of the relationship between social class and gender. Feminist writers have tended to stress the importance of theorizing class in terms of everyday social processes and interactions –

how class is lived, as well as how class structurally affects life chances. For Reay (2005: 924), 'class is a powerful psychic force', embedded 'in struggles over identity, validity, self-worth and integrity'.

Social class in youth: ascribed or achieved?

Young people have never held a very clear place in structural social class analysis. Analysis tends to focus on their attachment to the labour market, their job status and education inequalities as outcomes rather than causes. Sometimes their class is based on their own occupational status and sometimes on that of their father (or mother in a lone-mother household).

There are particular difficulties in identifying, studying and redressing inequalities in youth. Inequalities *within* households (inequalities of gender and age) make it difficult to determine individual-level poverty, especially in relation to dependants. Youth poverty tends to become more visible when young people are no longer able to be dependent on their parents and may become jobless, homeless, or trapped in the poverty associated with teenage parenthood. There are therefore some problems for the analysis of inequality which are integral to youth, namely the transition from private to public worlds, during which young people's social status broadly changes from ascribed to achieved, at first through the medium of the family's and peer group's own status structures, and later through 'achieving' their adult social and economic status. How has this configuration changed in conditions of late modernity, when ascribed status has arguably become less significant and individual biographies more reflexive?

Social class in quantitative research is typically based on adults, usually male ones, and the social class of 'dependants' measured according to the occupation of the head of household, the male 'breadwinner' (in the language of the welfare state). The most common measure of social class for young people living in their parental homes draws on their 'ascribed class' as dependants (whether or not they are), according to their father's occupational class. The problems for researchers are thus similar to those of policy-makers trying to tackle youth poverty: some young people live independently of their families of origin, alone or with others, or are homeless. Even if they do live in the parental home, this does not mean that the standard of living is equally shared among household members, and the ascription of social class – or of poverty/ wealth – is thus likely to mislead.

The notion of basing social class on young people's own jobs is equally problematic when young people are subject to unemployment (as in the 1970s) or increasingly delaying their entry into the labour market (as currently). Increasingly, young people may be in training schemes (and other intermediate statuses) which are hard to differentiate from jobs, or in several part-time jobs, or in the informal economy, none of which is readily amenable to social-class analysis. Structural explanations based on current occupational class are problematic because jobs are insecure and changing (some of them may still constitute stepping-stone jobs to better occupational positions). Employment and unemployment histories were better predictors than current labour-market situation of outcomes in adulthood (Wallace, 1987) and it seems that this is still the case (Bynner et al., 2002).

There have been attempts to take account of intragenerational and intergenerational mobility and develop class schemata which might be more appropriate in relation to youth. The social 'class trajectories' (to use Eric Olin Wright's expression) defined in my own work represent a longitudinal social class schema[2] which combined ascribed and achieved social class and was applied to young people aged 16–25 years (Jones, 1987). This schema of class in youth, which aimed to encapsulate some of the dynamic of young people's class careers, proved of more value than using class of origin for studying class and gender variation in the timing and spacing of transition events such as leaving home and family formation (Jones, 1988), and also for studying voting behaviour among young people (Jones and Wallace, 1990). In both cases, the intragenerationally mobile were found to reflect class practices and beliefs which had shifted away from those of their class of origin, in contrast to those who had not changed their class positions.

Without the prospect of social mobility, class would be seen as 'fate' and young people's life chances in adulthood determined by the social class of their family backgrounds. Talcott Parsons (1940: 78–9) suggested that in maturing industrial societies ascribed status gave way to achieved status ('the valued results of the actions of individuals'). Marshall et al. (1997) refer to this as liberal theory. Young people are at an early stage in 'class careers' which may or may not take them into new achieved class positions through intra-generational mobility (Jones, 1987). Eric Olin Wright (1978) suggested that young people were in 'pre-class positions' and Goldthorpe (1980) considered that the working class did not reach 'occupational maturity' until their mid-thirties. However, the kind of occupational security and stability once associated with adult 'destinations' has now largely disappeared.

There is social inequality in access to paths to upward mobility from the lower social strata – the basis of achieved social class and escape from the class associated with one's family background. Traditional working-class pathways, such as from the proverbial 'shop floor', no longer provide a pool for recruitment to higher occupational levels. Indeed, as we saw from youth transitions research, work routes to upward mobility such as through traditional apprenticeships or 'stepping-stone' jobs have virtually disappeared, leaving the education route as almost the only prospect.

The trend in expansion and extension of education should in theory reduce the effect of class of origin on class of destination – but in practice it has limited ability to do so. State support for students has decreased and the costs for their parents have increased. Educational achievements become devalued as more people gain qualifications (Bynner et al., 2002). Access to education continues to be related to social class (Halsey et al., 1980; Marshall et al., 1997; Forsyth and Furlong, 2000). Educational expansion has had limited success in reaching the most disadvantaged and there are still many young people who are not in employment, education or training, or who are surviving precariously on the lowest rungs of the occupational ladder. It is important to understand what is keeping them there so that effective policy interventions can be designed.

Multidimensional structures

But structuralist explanations based solely on social class are not enough. Unemployment and homelessness, and other indicators of poverty in youth, emanate from a complex and multidimensional structure of stratification, the dimensions of which include social class, gender, ethnicity and indeed age, which severally or in combination structure disadvantage. Because it is not always clear how these dimensions of inequality relate to one another, there is a tendency to refer to them as 'factors', but this is to deny their potency.

Young people may experience disadvantage because of a disability or their sexual orientation (Pascall and Hendey, 2002; Valentine et al., 2003). Care leavers are particularly disadvantaged because they often lack the family resources which can allow others to escape structural disadvantage (see Stein and Carey, 1986; Social Exclusion Unit, 2003; Jackson et al., 2005). Current inequalities among young people have their origins in wider social structures even though these are mediated by their families and communities, or even individual-level factors classified as identity capital. Recent research in the UK has found a continuing social class effect (as measured by class of origin) on labour-market outcomes, though heightened by local labour-market structures and also other factors associated with family background (Dolton et al., 1999; Scott, 2000; Dolton, 2002; Harris et al., 2003). Through a process of reductionism, age – as a policy-driven construct – is becoming more significant just at a time when culturally it should be becoming less so. Young people are discriminated against through age thresholds in many policy areas, including employment, housing and welfare. The UK Age Discrimination Act 2006 has removed an under-18 age barrier for entitlement to redundancy payments, but young people still face age discrimination in terms of their access to basic rights (the UN Convention on the Rights of the Child only covers those up to 18 years). While some inequalities reduce with the achievement of adulthood, others continue into later life (suggesting a cohort effect), or into the next generation (suggesting more deep-seated structures of inequality). It is important to retain awareness of the underlying structures of inequality alongside mediating or time-limited factors because 'factors' lack explanatory power. This is a point made by Gillies (2005) when she identified a tendency among policy-makers to separate out parenting practice from socio-economic status and then use it to 'explain' the inequality in which it is grounded.

The effects of social class interact with those of gender. Gender was brought into the youth debate from the 1970s with the work of Pollert, Leonard, Wallace and others. McRobbie and Garber (1976) and Griffin (1985) both showed how hegemonic resistance could derive from feminine as well as masculine working-class subcultures. Gender inequalities have undergone transformation in recent decades. Young women are now outperforming young men educationally, for example, and Irwin (1995) found that the pay of young women had begun to converge with that of young men. Nevertheless, gender inequalities continue to affect young women's life chances (Women and Equality Unit, 2002) and surface in continued income inequality, in occupational segregation and in the domestic division of labour. While the position of women (particularly in education) has greatly improved, that of many working-class young men has deteriorated. In the UK, young women are less likely to be unemployed (though there are different patterns elsewhere in Europe, according to Bradley and van Hoof, 2005). Because some gender inequalities have been redressed, the problem of remaining ones may be ignored – or the balance shifted to improving the situation of young males.

Inequalities on the basis of race and ethnicity are equally complex. Young people in black and minority ethnic groups can be disadvantaged in many respects (Berthoud, 1999; Bignall and Butt, 2000; Britton et al., 2002). Unemployment rates are two to three times higher for young people aged 16–24 from ethnic minority backgrounds, regardless of educational attainment (Social Exclusion Unit, 2000). Simmons (1994, cited in Bradley, 1996: 173) indicates that nearly half of homeless young people in London are from minority ethnic groups. There is, however, considerable variation between ethnic groups in both participation in post-16 education and labour-market outcomes, and inequalities between ethnic groups are increasing (Berthoud, 1999). While some, such as those of Indian, Chinese and West African origin, do well in education, others of African-Caribbean, Pakistani or Bangladeshi origin tend to fare worse in the education system (Tomlinson, 2005; Savage, 2000). British Bangladeshis and Pakistanis have the highest poverty levels in the UK (Platt, 2007). The question which studies raise is the extent to which this inequality is the effect of ethnic discrimination or a structural class effect, masked by ethnicity. Platt's (2005) study of intergenerational social mobility among different ethnic groups (comparing Indians and Caribbeans with white non-migrants) found that the impact of class origin (based on father's post-migration occupation) varied with ethnicity among men, but concludes that women may be more constrained by their gender than by their ethnicity.

We now also have to consider the effect of global structures of social stratification. There is variation cross-nationally in social structures of inequality, and particularly in the emphasis placed in different countries on different dimensions of inequality. Migrants therefore reflect inequalities relating to their countries of origin as well as their countries of destination. The number of 'factors' proliferates. Wyn and Harris (2004) suggest that the subjective meanings of social divisions vary according to local conditions: in the case of Australia and New Zealand, their colonial histories, and relationships between colonizers, colonized peoples, and later immigrants, have led to more hybridized identities and belief in the effectiveness of personal agency among young people.

Individualization and social class

One of the problems of understanding late modernity is the apparent contradiction between the idea that the structures and institutions which have acted as determinants of life chances are crumbling and the idea that life chances and risks remain unequal. Giddens's (1984) theory of structuration described a duality of structure, whereby structures made actions possible but were also created through actions, and this formed the basis for his later development of the idea of reflexivity, which continues to recognize the effect of structural constraints on action. Beck (1992: 91) argues that as a result of shifts in the standard of living, 'subcultural class identities have dissipated, class distinctions based on "status" have lost their traditional support, and processes for the "diversification" and individualization of life styles and ways of life have been set in motion. As a result, the hierarchical model of social class and strata has increasingly been subverted. It no longer corresponds to the reality.' He stresses (1992) however that, though risk has been individualized, risks are not equally shared. Bourdieu (1977) suggests that the most 'individual' projects arose out of subjective expectations (*habitus*) which were largely structurally determined.

There have been critiques however that reflexivity theories fail to explain these continuing structural inequalities. Scott Lash (1994: 118) argues that 'reflexivity chances' are unequal, and there are still winners and losers, and asks how much freedom from the necessity of structure and structural poverty a single mother or an unemployed young man has to self-construct their own life narratives. He suggests that the structural conditions of reflexivity have changed so that life chances are now based on *non*-social information and communication structures (the mode of information, rather than the mode of production).

Savage (2000) argues that Giddens and Beck have failed to theorize adequately the relationship between the individual and society, reminding us that social class is based on exploitative relationships and involves inequalities of power as well as wealth and status. Class interests are therefore significant for both social science theory and social policy. 'If there is still a role for class analysis it is to continue to emphasise the brute realities of social inequality and the extent to which these are constantly effaced by a middle class, individualized culture that fails to register the social implications of its routine actions' (Savage, 2000: 159). This agenda entails understanding why the middle class hold onto their wealth (rather than Paul Willis's approach which would be why the working class let them). An example would be the self-interest of homeowners keen to see their own house prices rise, to the detriment of first-time buyers desperate to gain a foothold on the housing ladder. Savage accepts the view that social classes can no longer be seen as collective agents and suggests instead that the decline of class cultures should be understood in terms of a shift towards 'middle class modes of individualization' (Savage, 2000: xi). He concludes (2000: xiii) that class processes work biographically through the individual, and that 'we can understand social change in Britain as an example of the reforming of class cultures around individualized axes.' The paradox of class, he explains, is that although individuals do not recognize that life chances are still clearly differentiated by social class, and have no clear sense of their own *class location* as objectively ordered, they nevertheless have an individualized sense of their own *class identity*, defined through subjective comparisons. Indeed, according to the British Social Attitudes Surveys, though more people identify themselves as middle class, 57 per cent still call themselves working class (Park et al., 2007), partly, we might conjecture, because of the increasing perception that social class is associated with wealth rather than relative power (e.g. Savage, 2005). Like Lash, Savage criticizes the view that individual biographies can be constructed free of class identities, and stresses that it is therefore important to examine the relationship between cultural identity and power.

Class as culture

The concepts of social and cultural capital help us understand the relationship between structure and culture without abandoning power relations or class interests. Bourdieu saw social class as a form of collective *habitus*, and his unpacking of the concept of capital has proved useful to youth research. Apart from economic capital, there are other forms of capital which potentially have resource potential: social capital, cultural capital and symbolic capital. Individual or human capital was discussed in chapter 3. For Bourdieu, capital and power are closely related.

Social connectedness – being a *social* agent – is integral to the concept of social capital, which broadly refers to social networks and the norms of reciprocity and trustfulness that arise from them (Bourdieu, 1986; Putnam, 2000). Social capital creates a framework for the transfer of cultural and economic capital between individuals. In Bourdieu's construction, cultural capital is a rather vague concept, incorporating language use, manners and orientations/dispositions (Jenkins, 1992). In contrast to James Coleman (1988, 1990) who believes that social networks carry resource potential for conversion into other forms of capital, Bourdieu (1986) sees cultural capital as convertible only *under certain conditions* into economic capital, and therefore as part of a broader system of social reproduction. With the 'right kind' of cultural capital, young people are more likely to succeed academically, access to this being determined to a large extent by social class of origin. Cultural capital is defined as a means of transmission of *middle-class* advantage in the education system, largely as a result of socialization within the family (Bourdieu and Passeron, 1973), though Bourdieu does not otherwise specify the processes by which cultural capital is mobilized across the generations (Thompson, 1997; Devine, 1998). Thompson suggests that a family's cultural capital may be mobilized where an individual faces downward mobility or blocked upward mobility, but that family cultures may otherwise operate in conservative ways. Families can thus be involved in the intergenerational transmission of not only wealth, but also skills, social networks, aspirations and values, but not unproblematically (see Bertaux and Thompson, 1997).

While some parents may encourage their children to succeed academically, and create the conditions for them to do so, other parents encourage their children to succeed in the work place. These different stresses on education and work have their origins in wider social divisions. The work ethic is a strong and persisting tradition in working-class communities which see adult status as gained through employment, and progression through work experience rather than qualifications (Jones et al., 2004). The cultural beliefs of many parents do not therefore equate with those of policymakers who value education and training. In order to provide support for extended education, parents must believe either in the intrinsic value of education or its instrumental value for social mobility in leading to better jobs, drawing on their own cultural capital (Jones et al., 2004). Since only a very small proportion of (mainly middle-class) parents themselves continued into higher education on leaving school, many (mainly working-class) parents (or lone parents) may lack the social and cultural capital needed to support the belief that education has an intrinsic value. As Goldthorpe (1996) has argued, disadvantaged families need more convincing that the outcomes warrant the costs. These patterns thus place a limit on intergenerational social mobility.

It would be naive to imply that the working class lack access to cultural capital. Rose's (2002) study of the education tradition among some sectors of the working class is a move towards breaking down some of the class-education stereotypes, and suggests that cultural capital could also be held by the working class – or that education alone (without social capital) does not necessarily transform into cultural capital. Studies of anti-school cultures by Jenkins (1983) and Brown (1987) both differentiated working-class school students according to their levels of conformity to the norms of the school and their orientations towards the future. There are other forms of cultural capital among the working class, constructed according to the work ethic, and these can be powerful in different ways. A generation ago the transmission of cultural capital among the working class might have taken the form of helping with job introductions (including a father putting in a word with his own employer), or migration (Grieco, 1987). The processes through which sons tended to follow in their fathers' footsteps (and, to a lesser extent, daughters in their mothers' footsteps) are disrupted when manufacturing jobs have been lost and there is more emphasis on qualifications than on reputation and respectability. This is likely to be detrimental to class continuity rather than mobility. However, the ability of working-class parents to offer up-to-date guidance and information to their adult children, for example to provide education and training as well as non-traditional job information, has been restricted (Forsyth and Furlong, 2001; Jones et al., 2004). Parents have been deskilled, 'replaced' by professionals (in this case careers teachers and guidance staff) who continue the socialization process. This would suggest that parents are less able to transmit social and cultural capital – but does this mean more social mobility?

Sources of social and cultural capital

Families act as mediators of external structural factors, and transmitters of both advantage and disadvantage (Halsey et al., 1980). Halsey and his colleagues used parental academic achievement as an indicator of the amount and quality of cultural capital in the home. Coleman (1988) argues, however, that the breakdown of family networks as a result of divorce, separation and loss affects the accumulation of social capital. Both these comments appear to hold true. A stable family environment with parental commitment to education has been found to help override the effects of poverty and disadvantage (Schoon, 2002; Scott and Chaudhary, 2003; Schoon and Parsons, 2003). With increased educational achievement and labour-market participation among women, it is perhaps not surprising that a significant factor in labour-market achievement among unqualified young people is the educational level of the mother (Halsey et al., 1980; Reay, 1998; Stafford et al., 1999). Thomson et al. (2003) showed the type of support, advice and encouragement offered by mothers to be crucial.

Families are not the only sources of social and cultural capital, however. Dolton (2002) found that young people's decisions about education and training had little to do with the information formally available and more to do with the opinions of family and friends obtained by chance. As (most) young people grow up, their social networks widen and change: their relationships with their friends, partners (and in-laws), and neighbours become potential alternative sources of cultural capital. Seaman and Sweeting (2004) suggest that when family networks are restricted, young people can still actively develop community-level social capital through 'between-family links'. Entry into employment may enhance social and cultural capital and bring with it new forms of social support; thus, an employer who encourages and supports good quality education and training can be key to 'successful' adult outcomes among those at risk (Webster et al., 2004). Personal relationships provide access to a range of resources, and lead to new social bonds of responsibility and obligation. Emler and McNamara (1996) cast doubt on the scope of the peer group: they found that roles in their families, workplaces and education institutions provided young people with almost all the basis for their informal social lives, and lack of such roles was not compensated for in other ways but meant lack of informal social contacts.

Social capital can be bridging or bonding

The intergenerational transmission of social capital can both lead to social reproduction of the middle class and act as a barrier to social mobility among the working class. Putnam (2000) distinguished between social capital which is 'bridging' and that which is 'bonding'. A study of young offenders (Boeck et al., 2005) found that bridging social capital enabled young people to navigate risk, while bonding social capital, though providing protection and support, restricted young people's dispositions. The 'subcultural capital' of the peer group proposed by Thornton (1995) is likely to be of the bonding type.

Bridging social capital enables links to new social networks, labour markets and education opportunities. Young people with geographically scattered (and typically middle-class) families have a resource they may be able to draw on to escape disadvantage and move to more prosperous areas to study or work (Jones, 2001; Jamieson, 2000; Thomson and Taylor, 2005). Leonard (2004) points out that, as a result, bridging capital benefits individuals – and perhaps also their families – rather than communities.

Bonding social capital may be a characteristic of disadvantaged communities or groups, where tight bonds and solidarity create boundaries through which it becomes difficult to pass, thus acting as a barrier to other forms of capital rather than as a resource. Community solidarity (bonding social capital) confirms the distinction between the community and the world outside, and is protective, allowing the community to tolerate negative labelling by outsiders (Jones, 1999; Ghate and Hazel, 2004). There is a tendency for dissenters to leave a community and 'conformists' to remain, thus further strengthening the community ties among those remaining (Bulmer, 1978). These ties can be important sources of support, and Leonard (2004) argues that the transition from bonding to bridging capital (as advocated by Putnam) can lead to the reinforcement of existing inequality.

Paul Willis's (1977) study of anti-school young men indicated that they generated a working-class solidarity which supported social stability and maintained their social ties to their peers and community. Sennett (2004: 97) refers to this research as showing how a working-class fear of standing out from the crowd might lead to the suppression rather than nurturing of personal ability, while Savage (2000) similarly comments that ordinariness is a cultural force among the working class which militates against the social legitimacy of cultural capital.

Cultural values and beliefs such as these help explain the lag in behavioural change that follows new policy initiatives (Bynner et al., 2004). The cultural norms of a community can be supportive of beliefs and practices which policy-makers would like to change. An example is attitudes to teenage pregnancy, where local cultures may be at odds with policy targets. Turner (2004) found that young women from disadvantaged areas perceived fewer negative implications of becoming a mother and were more likely to continue with a pregnancy. Studies in the north-east of England (Johnston et al., 2000; Webster et al., 2004; MacDonald et al., 2005) found that informal social networks in the community helped many individuals manage their lives (whether as workers, unemployed, drug users or criminals) rather than challenge or change them. Several commentators have indicated that in order to get on, young people have to 'get out'. Those wanting to avoid postcode discrimination by prospective employers, or wanting to get off drugs, may need to leave their communities and form new social networks elsewhere. The loss of their earlier supportive networks may be difficult (Johnston et al., 2000; Pavis et al., 2000). A study of young people in north-east England found a very strong sense of identification with their locality which, though it had a negative side, sprang 'from a familiarity with the geography of the district, and a feeling of being a cherished part of a close network of relationships' (Coffield et al., 1986: 141–2): as a consequence of this 'localism', the quality of these young people's lives would have been lowered had they left the area. MacDonald and his colleagues (2005) however are anxious to stress that bonding social capital is a mediating factor in individual disadvantage rather than a causal one, and represents a resourceful way of negotiating local economic decline.

According to Giddens (1991) and Bauman (1995), the stayer with fixed identity is a product of traditional societies. Urry (1995) argues that in the postmodern world, cultural capital needs to be transferable for individuals to cope with detachment from the institutions (generations, place, kinship and rituals of passage) which formerly gave order to their lives. One of the expectations of present-day life is that people should be prepared to move to where the career opportunities are. Indeed, in restricted labour markets unwillingness to move away could result in downward mobility (Thompson, 1997). Geographical mobility has long been associated with social mobility, and thus with the middle class. The result is that middle-class families in particular have extended kinship networks (Jones, 2000; Finch, 1989; Bell, 1968). Grieco (1987) demonstrated that 'chain migration' could result in the re-establishment of kinship networks in the new location. Thus, some young people are socialized and supported into migration while others are not. Cultural capital thus provides migrants with both rationale for migrating and a means of doing so; lack of cultural capital would similarly inhibit migration or increase risk among those who migrate anyway.

Does the disparity between cross-national structural conditions, combined with the trend towards individualization in late modernity, make it impossible to explore the commonalities and differences between young people cross-nationally? It is becoming more important that commonalities are recognized, since we now need to be able to deal with inequalities at a global level. The polarization which is developing within nations also occurs across them, with countries becoming ultra-rich or ultra-poor. Globalization of inequality has led to increased migration, forced and unforced, political and economic, and once again, as at the time of urbanization following industrialization in the nineteenth century, young people appear to be at the forefront (UN, 2007).

Inequality and policy

Policy interventions in the UK have had a chequered history from their poor law origins, to the universalist welfare state, to individualist neo-liberalism, and more recently to the 'Third Way' approach to inequality with its emphasis on social exclusion. In recent decades, we have seen three different models of the relationship between research and welfare. First, there was a close relationship between class analysis and welfare capitalism. Next, individualization was seen in practice when neo-liberal policies (which included the dismantling of the increasingly costly welfare state) and an emphasis on individual responsibility gained ground in policy circles in the Thatcher era in Britain. It was from this context that the underclass debate took off in the early 1990s. Later, the 'Third Way', advocated by Giddens and applied by New Labour on taking office in 1997, continued the shift away from a social class perspective by focusing on multiple disadvantage and socially excluded groups, though it appears that concerns about the social class basis of social exclusion may now be resurfacing. In the next few pages these recent models will be explored in more detail.

The concept of 'underclass'

Approaches to the concept of 'underclass' have taken one of two forms, individualist or structuralist. According to the latter, the underclass are the victims of wider socio-economic trends (Gallie, 1994). Some saw the long-term unemployed as a seventh social class, below the occupational class structure but nevertheless working class in terms of their political beliefs – culturally affiliated to the working class rather than forming a separate culture (Gallie, 1994; Runciman, 1990). In contrast, the individualist concept of 'the underclass' was developed in the era of neo-liberal

monetarism in the 1980s and provides a case study in how
to ignore power relations and blame the individual. The
underclass thesis represents a response to what was becoming
seen as a cosy relationship between structural determinism
and the welfare state. Margaret Thatcher's (1987) comment,
that 'there is no such thing as society, there are only individual men and women, and there are families', was a political
example of a theme paralleled in sociological debate, as structuralist explanations of the social world were being challenged by postmodern ones (Baudrillard, for example,
claiming the end of the social). Sennett (2004: 105) refers to
this as the apotheosis of the denial of social connection.

The American Charles Murray brought an individualist
construction of the concept of underclass to Britain through
his 1990 essay, *The Emerging British Underclass*. He suggested that there was a 'type' of poverty which bred an
'underclass culture' of dependency among the poor. He identified three indicators: illegitimacy, violent crime and drop-
out from the labour force: 'If illegitimate births are the leading
indicator of an underclass and violent crime a proxy measure
of its development, the definite proof that an underclass has
arrived is that large numbers of young, healthy, low-income
males choose not to take jobs' (Murray, 1990: 17).

The emphasis here was on individual rational *choice*.
Murray saw the problem of unemployment in terms of the
absence of male role models for young men brought up in
the increasing number of lone-parent households. According
to his theory, the 'nanny' welfare state had led to a breakdown of family life and consequent failure of socialization.
There were calls to re-create the 'normative nuclear family'
in the interests of a return to 'traditional values'. Dennis and
Erdos (1992) argued for women's withdrawal from the labour
force and a return to normative gender roles. How did such
reactionary views take hold? As Giddens indicates (1994), in
the modern world, tradition defies logic, requires no defence,
discourages dialogue, and is invented for the purpose of
power. When the normative structures of modernity were
seen to be breaking down, the underclass thesis represented
an attempt to reconstruct them. This is the kind of thing Stan
Cohen (1973) meant when he suggested that deviancy is

defined and 'deviants' scapegoated in order to 'clarify normative contours'. In his commentary on Murray, Walker (1990)
suggested that the poor were seen as poor because they did
not conform to prevailing social values.

The underclass concept in its neo-liberal sense was adopted
by the New Right under Thatcher, fitting neatly within concerns about increased levels of unemployment, crime, family
breakdown and an increasingly unmanageable social security
bill. During the Thatcher era, and continuing under John
Major in his 'back to basics' campaign (which fostered the
idea of a golden age of family life based on Victorian values),
the concept of 'underclass' came to the fore as a means of
describing marginalization as self-inflicted. Prospects for collective resistance through class consciousness had receded in
the 1980s as trade unions were stripped of much of their
power. The government response to the 1984 miners' strike
in protest against pit closures and loss of jobs was arguably
the last straw in the crushing of working-class organized
resistance, leaving many individuals exposed. By 'blaming the
victim' (Walker, 1990), the UK government fed this individualized vulnerability and sought to justify its reluctance to
intervene with policies to reduce the widening gap between
rich and poor. Various government ministers condemned
teenage mothers 'who jump the housing queue' and jobless
'shirkers' who 'live off the state' at taxpayers' expense, while
the housing minister described 'the homeless' as 'the sort of
people one stepped over on the way out of the opera' (Jones,
1997). The 'folk devils' of the day were among the most
vulnerable groups in society.

Both Murray's (1990) underclass hypothesis and the policy
thinking deriving from it were based on a model of instrumental rationality. The entire responsibility was thus laid at
the feet of the individual. Murray encouraged policy-makers
to use the stick rather than the carrot and reduce benefits
which, he believed, acted as incentives for illegitimacy and
long-term unemployment (1990: 30). He argued that job
creation was not a solution, and that even if homeless people
in 'cardboard cities' were given work, the powerful dependency culture of the underclass would cause them to 'revert'
to unemployment and joblessness within two years. In other

words, it was the underclass culture itself which was holding people back, not structural inequality (unlike subcultural theorists, he did not see the culture as a defensive response to oppression). These were the arguments behind the Conservative government's welfare reforms in the late 1980s which removed welfare benefits from young people such as income support, housing benefit and Exceptional Needs payments, all identified without evidence as 'incentives' for them to leave their parental homes. The aim was thus to reduce youth homelessness by regulating housing demand rather than improving the supply of affordable housing, placing the responsibility for youth homelessness on young people themselves (Jones, 1995, 1997).

Murray's comments on generational transmission of the underclass culture contained, as Walker (1990) points out, elements of the eugenics movement, as well as Oscar Lewis's (1959) view of the 'culture of poverty' as perpetuating poverty. Keith Joseph, a leading monetarist Conservative, had similarly suggested in a 1972 speech that deprivation was transmitted culturally through an intergenerational 'cycle of deprivation', and was therefore resistant to interventionist welfare policies, an idea discredited by Rutter and Madge (1976) among others. In contrast to Murray, many commentators, including Morris and Irwin (1992), have stressed the heterogeneity of the long-term unemployed. Lydia Morris points out in her book *Dangerous Classes* (1994) that the 'underclass' concept relates back to the Poor Law, to late Victorian distinctions between the deserving and undeserving poor, and also to Marx's concept of the *lumpenproletariat* (see also Marshall et al., 1997). The contributors to MacDonald's (1997) volume on the underclass criticize Murray's view as too static and homogeneous. Research has shown that most unemployed young people want jobs (Furlong, 1992) as do homeless ones (Jones, 1995) – the question is more whether they feel they have the power (control beliefs) to change their situations. There seems to be little evidence that choosing to be unemployed is a feature of a 'culture of poverty' though, as this book shows, it is also possible that young unemployed people will blame themselves, thus offering themselves as cannon fodder for neo-liberal views.

Social exclusion

Despite the evidence of persisting inequality, social class was not re-adopted under New Labour in 1997 as a concept of policy value, though the underclass theory fell from view. Alternative explanations were sought.

New Labour made a pragmatic withdrawal from its traditional ideological position as defender of the welfare state and began to think of targeted benefits rather than universal ones, stressing the responsibility of individual citizens (or, in the case of young people, Their parents). There was a new approach – referred to as the Third Way and proposed by Giddens – between structure (welfare capitalism) and agency (neo-liberal monetarism). Education was seen as the key to escaping social exclusion and gaining upward mobility, but there was also an emphasis on reducing the numbers who were dependent on public welfare through policies aimed at getting more people, including those with disabilities and lone parents, into work. Young people were clearly in an ambiguous situation here, being not yet able to work and needing to be dependent either on public welfare or on their parents.

Although the European Commission in 1995[3] described social exclusion as the disintegration and fragmentation of social relationships and hence the loss of social cohesion, social exclusion is mainly seen in the UK in terms of individual life course and intergenerational processes (Bynner et al., 2004). Policies since 1997 have tried to address problems such as unemployment, poor skills, low incomes, poor housing, high-crime environments, bad health and family breakdown, all seen as linked within the concept of social exclusion (Social Exclusion Unit, 2001). Social exclusion is seen as an outcome of a range of structural, cultural and individual processes, relating to multiple disadvantage rather than poverty. This approach, both holistic and focusing on processes, represented progressive thinking after neo-liberalism. However, the policy theme 'tough on crime; tough on the causes of crime' which appeared near the start of the Blair government in 1997 disappeared after a short while and the concept of social exclusion appears to have been increasingly interpreted at an individual or community level rather than as an outcome of structural inequality.

The Social Exclusion Unit was set up in 1997, charged with developing evidence-based and joined-up policies (joined up between government departments) to combat social exclusion.[4] This gave added impetus to youth research which had advocated a holistic approach and was ready to provide evidence. The underlying agenda was to improve the economic competitiveness of the UK in a globalized economy. One of the main areas for development was youth policy. Social exclusion policies are especially relevant to children and young people not only because of the risks they currently face, but also because of a recognition that early interventions could prevent social exclusion in later life and in the next generation. A policy action team set up to examine the problems and needs of young people (Social Exclusion Unit, 2000) highlighted evidence of economic disadvantage in youth and produced reports on rough sleeping, teenage pregnancy, and other concerns. It also found relative disadvantage at national level: young people in the UK were more likely to be growing up in workless households than in any other OECD country; one in eleven 16–18-year-olds were not in education, training or employment, though this figure included teenage mothers; and one in sixteen young people left school without qualifications each year, with the result that the UK had one of the lowest levels in the European Union of education participation among 18-year-olds.

The focus has been on targeting vulnerable groups and disadvantaged neighbourhoods. In practice, many of the groups previously defined as an underclass are now redefined as socially excluded. These include young people under 18 who are not in education, employment or training (dubbed 'NEET'), those who are over 18 and unemployed, teenage parents, homeless young people and young offenders. These statuses may overlap into multiple disadvantage. It is curious that both NEET and its earlier incarnation, the concept of 'StatusZero' (Williamson, 1997), were applied to young people regardless of their other social roles (as parents, for example). Feminist concerns about defining social class according to economic status, and ignoring inequality as lived by young women, were clearly not seen as relevant to constructions of NEET, with the effect that the skills associated with young parenthood are devalued.

There are a number of other problems associated with the social exclusion agenda. Firstly, there is the problem of visibility. Those defined as socially excluded are in general fairly visible groups, easily targeted by policy and provision, but other less visible groups of young people may also experience or risk social exclusion and poverty. There are also dangers in blanket stereotyping of a community as disadvantaged: within any area there are likely to be pockets of affluence or some areas worse than others. This applies both to rural areas and to urban ones (Forsyth and Furlong, 2000; Pavis et al., 2000; Johnston et al., 2000). Communities can adopt a 'mask of similarity' (A. P. Cohen, 1985) which disguises the heterogeneity within.

Second, there is a contradiction between the notion of process, which lies at the heart of the concept of social exclusion, and the idea that vulnerable groups can be identified, categorized and targeted by interventions. Social exclusion thus becomes a crystallized and static concept. New vulnerable groups are simply identified as examples of social exclusion and added to the list, with little recognition of what links them. There is nevertheless an assumption implicit in the notion of social exclusion that marginalization is a progressive process, amenable to interruption by policy. In practice, marginalization can be seen more literally as being 'on the margins' with the result that there are periods of exclusion and periods of risk. Young people may move between temporary or casual jobs, inappropriate training and unemployment, along 'patchwork careers' (Bynner, 2005: 377). The result is that the boundaries between work and non-work become blurred (Johnston et al., 2000; Harris et al., 2003). Morris and Irwin (1992) have indicated the importance of recognizing 'broken employment' as well as secure employment and long-term unemployment. Similarly, 'rough sleepers' represent part of a wider 'career' of homelessness, as young people move between sleeping on friends' floors, staying in temporary hostels, returning to parents, and rough sleeping (Hutson and Liddiard, 1994; Jones, 1997). Young people may stray over the boundary, rather than suffer permanent exclusion (Johnston et al., 2000; Catan, 2004).

Thirdly, the concept of social exclusion as applied in the UK fails to take on board the question of the relationships between excluded and included groups and in particular whether those who are included serve their own interests by collaborating in the exclusion of others. For Savage (2000), social exclusion neither replaces social class nor presents an opportunity as intellectual space, but is produced uncritically as a fait accompli. At the time of writing, the concept of social exclusion is losing ground, and the policy focus is becoming concentrated on the most severely excluded who have not been helped by interventions so far. In order to understand why policies may fail to have their desired impact, a more coherent theoretical approach is needed. This must broaden out from the focus on the cultural and individual causes of disadvantage to address the problem of inequality. The bottom line is that political sensitivity has prevented attacking the root cause of working-class disadvantage: the interests of the more powerful middle classes.

The retreat from complexity

Understanding inequality even at national level has proved to be a challenge. Policy-makers and practitioners alike have retreated from the increasing complexity found through research and theorizing to focus on pieces of the jigsaw. Thus there has been a shift towards emphasizing rights, or giving young people a voice. There has also, as we have seen, been a history of subverting academic research on the nature of class identities and cultures and treating them as though they were the structures themselves. The problem is whether to focus in or widen out. It seems clear that a narrow approach to understanding inequality through the occupational class structure is not enough: not only is measurement problematic for adults, but it is doubly so for young people; further, it is necessary to take account of other dimensions of inequality to understand how they interact in the production and repro-duction of disadvantage; next, in order to understand the processes of social reproduction, we have to take account of how identities and cultures and interests act as mechanisms. This is a wide-ranging agenda.

It helps to apply this agenda to a specific problematic, and the study of youth contains this if we look more closely at the problem of dependence. It is essential to understanding inequality in youth to examine how young people can develop or acquire the resources they need to be able to engage in 'life politics' or life management. Young people's life chances vary considerably according to whether their parents can and will support them, and a supportive family is one of the keys to unlocking overall structures of opportunity (social inclusion in education, jobs or housing, for example). This is one of the ways that families are implicated in processes of social reproduction. The idea of a moral economy of class comes into play in the way values are constructed and/or adopted in different families. The mechanisms for family support can be seen as mechanisms of social reproduction – associated with the intergenerational transmission of capital – whether economic, social, cultural, symbolic or 'individual'. Family support can be theorized as social reproduction in practice, and family dynamics thus may constitute, to follow Savage (2000: 20), one of 'the systemic dynamics of contemporary capitalism'.

6
Youth and Dependence

It is impossible to understand the nature of youth without understanding its relationship to dependence, yet this has rarely been addressed in youth research. Sennett (2004) indicates how the liberal fathers drew a distinction between childhood and adulthood to show the passage from private to public definitions of dependency, reflected in legislative age structures. It is helpful to consider the transition to economic independence in these terms, as a transition from private family support to public state support.

The transition to independence creates difficulties for sociologists trying to apply social theories to it, for policy-makers trying to shape and encapsulate (or extend) it through age thresholds in legislation and provision and, not least, for those most directly involved in experiencing it – parents and young people themselves. However much policies may structure 'institutional biographies' for young people to lead, ultimately the transition from dependence is enacted in a family and generational context, where the mechanisms not only of support but also for the mediation of wider structural inequalities are generated and put into practice. The transition to economic independence is both a defining element in youth and reveals some of the mechanisms through which families act as conduits of structural advantage and disadvantage.

Conceptualizing transitions to independence

We have seen the significance of an independent wage for young people's feelings of autonomy and adulthood and speculated about the difficulties of deferred economic independence. The transition to economic independence underlies other strands of transition to adulthood (see chapter 4), affecting the source and level of resources that young people need to draw on in their decisions about education, employment, housing, partnership formation and having children of their own. Like other aspects of transition, it is a slow and complex process, rather than an event – for most young people at least – though there are event markers. The transition to economic independence from parents often starts when children begin to gain autonomy as consumers, so it begins (paradoxically) when their parents give them pocket money but then gains pace when they begin to earn their own wages through part-time or holiday jobs. The process continues at least until they are set up in independent homes with independent adult incomes, and often beyond this. Support is not one-way – as young people become older they begin to pay into the household budget as well as draw on it. There are levels of economic independence, but the process is not linear. There are also returns to dependence and, in such cases, there has to be a renegotiation of obligations and dependence status. So, for example, some young people whose pocket money was stopped when they started work may regain an allowance if they lose their jobs, though conversely young workers who had started paying board money are not necessarily let off the hook if they become unemployed. Individual transitions to economic independence thus involve a complex interweaving between relative dependence on parents/carers and relative independence from them, within a heavily structuring policy context. In these circumstances it becomes difficult to think in terms of 'biographies of choice'.

There is a strong impetus among young people to become economically independent of their parents because of its association with other forms of adult autonomy, even if this means transferring dependence elsewhere (for example onto the state or a partner). But independence involves particular risks (freedom being accompanied by new responsibilities and new perils) and so there is also some ambivalence about taking the first steps. Youth has been observed to be a period of experimentation when risks are assessed and negotiated. Some young people, taking a pragmatic approach to risk, reject it, finding the comforts of the parental home too seductive and the harsh alternative of independent living too un-appealing (Jones and Martin, 1999). Others are forced by family circumstances into risky and unplanned independence. Returning to dependence is not always an option and, since dependence is associated with childhood, not always desirable.

Dependence and social class

Long-standing social class differences in patterns of transition to independence are reflected in long-standing patterns of parental support (Jones and Wallace, 1992). In the past, middle-class families provided economic support for their children until well into adulthood (Bell, 1968), while working-class families indulged their children during adolescence but provided only material support once they started work (Leonard, 1980; Harris, 1983). The traditional working-class pattern, especially during periods of more stable employment, did not involve returns to *economic* dependence on parents, although working-class young people tended to continue to live in the parental home until they married. One reason why extended family support did not exist in working-class households may well have been that their working children did not need it (Galland, 1995; Jones, 1995). Though returns to dependence on parents have become more widespread, they remain contrary to the work ethic and notions of self-sufficiency which form part of working-class culture, and so a return to dependence is still regarded as a failure, especially if associated with unemployment (Sennett, 2004; Jones, forthcoming).

Once in employment, most young people in Britain supported themselves through their earnings, and, if they lived with their parents, paid them board money (Jones, 2005). Willis (1984) described the wage as the 'golden key' to adulthood but, with the loss of the better jobs in the youth labour market during the 1980s, manual work came to be seen instead as a mark of continued dependence (Savage, 2000). Youth incomes from whatever source (work, state benefits, student grants) have now reduced to 'component income' levels which require subsidizing, and make it more difficult for young people to support themselves. Whether staying on in education or entering the full-time labour market, young people can now neither be self-supporting nor gain adequate state help but need additional and extended help from their parents. For many young people and parents, this comes as a culture shock. Working-class families are now expected by policy-makers to function according to middle-class norms of extended support, despite differences in their economic and cultural resources (Jones et al., 2004, 2006). It comes as no surprise, therefore, that social class and family background remain critical factors in education and work outcomes, as the previous chapter showed. McKnight (2002: 49) suggests that the link between parental income and labour-market success may even have strengthened because of the increased cost of assisting young people into 'good jobs'.

Once dependence is put into the equation, it becomes a simplification to say that youth transitions have become polarized. In practice, there seem to be three broad groups: young people on extended transitions who are able to receive parental support; young people on extended transitions who are not able to receive parental support; and those on fast-track transitions who lack support (sometimes from both the family and the state). The first group is still dominated by the middle class. The second group contains upwardly mobile young people from working-class backgrounds among whom extended dependence is contrary to traditional class practices and for whom support may therefore be problematic. The third group represents attempts to continue 'traditional' working-class patterns of early independence in an un-welcoming and risky labour market where self-support has become unfeasible, family support inaccessible and state support inadequate.

Policy framework

There is a tension between the willingness of policy-makers to support and protect young people and their desire to support 'family values' by emphasizing that the primary responsibility for support lies with the family rather than with the state. As a result, the age threshold at which young people can begin to receive state support in their own right is continuinally rising; this involves a shift in responsibility onto the family for those below this age threshold. There are therefore two elements to the ideology underlying state policy, one concerning attitudes to young people and the other concerning attitudes to their families.

Age thresholds

Age thresholds determine young people's access to welfare citizenship (Jones and Wallace, 1992). Modern welfare capitalism was based on reciprocity, and citizenship involved a social contract between the individual adult and the state, set out in terms of rights and responsibilities on each side, but the position of young people in this construction has never been clear. There has been continued resistance to the idea that young people should be 'allowed' to live independently of their parents solely on state benefits (Finch, 1989), and state support for young people has tended to reflect this reluctance.

During the 1960s and 1970s, welfare policies were beginning to shift from treating young people as dependants of their parents towards treating them as individuals with welfare rights of their own (Marshall, 1952; Jones and Wallace, 1992). This trend was halted in the neo-liberal 1980s when the balance shifted to responsibilities rather than rights: welfare benefits for under-18s were stopped (with the 1989 Social Security Act), while other sources of state support for young people, such as board and lodging allowances, housing benefit and student grants, were withdrawn, leaving them dependent on parental support (Jones and Bell, 2000). According to neo-liberal political thinking in the 1980s, the welfare state (the 'nanny state') had spawned a 'culture of dependency' on the state, and a reduction of state benefits would both ease the burden on the taxpayer and strengthen the role of the family for both social protection and social control. The fear was that housing benefits could act as financial incentives (to a rationally acting individual) to leave the parental home 'prematurely'.[1] Instead, the removal of benefits from under-18s in 1989 resulted in heightened family conflicts and led to many young people leaving their parental homes. Policy-makers had failed to take family relationships into account. The unanticipated consequence of these policies – an increase in extreme destitution, including homelessness among young people – led to sticking-plaster provision, in the form of the Severe Hardship payments, for state support for those who could prove lack of access to parental support. In late modernity, the political rights of young people are emphasized over their welfare rights. Ideas about reducing the age of suffrage to 16, and giving young people a 'voice' through youth parliaments in the policies which affect them, underline the collapse of the concept of welfare citizenship. Young people who are economically dependent cannot be full citizens, however much they may be window-dressed as such, since full participation in society is dependent on individual resources and position in the social structure (Marshall, 1952; Lister, 1990).

The transition to economic independence from parents has to fit within a complex institutional framework of age thresholds constructed through policy legislation and is thus largely out of young people's control. Over the last century, different policies in different spheres have tried to anchor (in)dependence in age (see Jones and Bell, 2000). Policies fixing the ages at which young people can claim welfare benefits, or become eligible for housing benefit, or be protected by adult minimum wage legislation, all determine differing age thresholds between youth and adulthood, or private and public dependence. The most significant threshold is not necessarily the age of majority (18), which currently does little except allow access to the rights to vote and drink alcohol, the latter being more enthusiastically taken up than the former. In the past, the minimum school-leaving age provided a significant age marker, mainly because it allowed entry into the labour market. This rose to 14 in 1921, to 15 in 1947, to 16 in 1973, and the education/training leaving age will be formally increased again to 18 years in 2013. However, with the increasing complexity of school-to-work transitions and the greater likelihood of intermediate statuses in post-school education and training between leaving school and starting full-time jobs, this age marker has become less significant (Jones and Bell, 2000). The ages at which policy structures in other spheres (child protection, National Insurance, welfare and housing) treat young people as independent of their parents have also continued to rise. Young people receive different levels of benefit at different ages, kicking in for most with a 'transitional rate' at 18 and culminating in adult levels at 25 years. Wage protection through the National Minimum Wage (NMW) is also age-graded: the 16–17 rate (since 2005), the 'development' rate at 18–21, then adult rates at 22. Where young people have the right to claim state welfare, the level of their entitlement is set at a youth rate ('transitional' or 'development') so that they are expected to remain partially dependent on their parents (Finch, 1989; Jones and Bell, 2000). Youth incomes are thus at a level which requires subsidizing rather than one which covers the cost of living and can thus be described as 'component incomes'. A 'dependency assumption' (Harris, 1989) lay behind the policy changes in the 1980s, and has continued since. It assumes that parents are able and willing to subsidize young people's incomes until they reach the age threshold where full state support (at adult levels) takes over.

These age structures are markers of convenience and bear no relation to young people's lived experiences: it is not surprising therefore that, although they ensure some support for some young people, they put others at particular risk. Under-19s have been described as particularly at risk because of the dependency assumption (Masson, 1995). A government review of financial support for 16–19-year-olds (HM Treasury, DfES and DWP, 2004) sought to remedy this situation, and proposed a single unified system of financial support for 16–19-year-olds. This tried to deal with the age/dependence problem.[2] Though the review attempted to move beyond simple reliance on age thresholds by introducing the additional dimensions of employment status and household status, it still overlooked the complexity of family life, being based on the assumptions that unemployed young people can be dependent while in the family home and that young people are independent once they move out.

Independence from whom?

The boundary of responsibility between the family and the state is not only subject to changes in age thresholds but is continually redrawn according to different political agendas and changing socio-economic factors; it is thus both shifting and contested. Prior to the establishment of the welfare state, a policy idea had developed that working-class families in Britain, unlike those elsewhere, were neglecting their duties to their older adolescent children (Finch, 1989) who, as I have shown, were expected to be waged. The welfare state was therefore based on the premise that, in cases of need, the first port of call should be the family, with state welfare provision acting only as a back-up. There was however some ambivalence over whether the families were the 'natural' unit for support and therefore able to fulfil normative expectations of obligation on their own, or whether the state should legislate to ensure that they did so. Finch points out that the impact of family legislation on actual family practices can be contrary to policy expectations and policies aimed at 'supporting' family life can have the unanticipated impact of damaging it.[3]

Finch (1989) shows how, instead of legislation, a 'sense of obligation' in families has been manipulated by government policies. In practice, policies which have raised the age threshold for entry into independent adulthood have not been matched with legislation explicitly extending parental responsibility until that point. This is because governments tend to be reluctant to intervene directly and openly in family life (Jones and Bell, 2000). The result is that there are gaps in social protection but also some anomalies. For example, though parents in England and Wales have a legal responsibility for under-18s, they are not *required* by law to care for a child beyond the age of 16 years, the equivalent age in Scotland being 16 on both counts (Jones and Bell, 2000). This leaves young people aged between 16 and 18 without a legal basis for claiming parental support while at the same time lacking the right to support from the state (a problem which the review of their incomes tried to address).

The transfer of responsibility, since the 1980s, for the costs of education and welfare from the state onto families represented a shift by default (it was simply that state benefits were stopped) but it forms part of an ongoing wider trend. Welfare states worldwide are trying to find solutions to the looming demographic crisis of an ageing population and resulting imbalance in the 'dependency ratio'.[4] Demographic changes, especially greater longevity and a lower birth rate, are impacting on families both directly and indirectly. It is projected that, by 2014, there will be more over-65s than under-16s in the UK for the first time (ONS, 2000; Social Exclusion Unit, 2004). The change to the 'dependency ratio' across society has implications both for intergenerational solidarity and social welfare systems (European Commission, 2001). Policies are increasing the responsibility of families, providing back-up only where the primary support from the family has obviously failed.

From time to time politicians on all sides call for 'a return to traditional family values', based on hierarchical and gendered roles within the form of the nuclear family on which the welfare state was based (Smart, 1997; Finch, 1989). Parental support and control were seen to go hand in hand. Dependence of the child on the family was deemed necessary for primary socialization to occur, though the family had in time to 'help in emancipating the child from his dependency on the family' (Parsons and Bales, 1956: 19). Welfare reforms in the 1980s were based on a fear that the welfare system was undermining this particular model of 'the family'. One neo-liberal academic indicated: 'Young people need the support of their families and the family is seriously weakened as an institution if it loses its responsibility for young people. But genuine family responsibility for young people is make-believe unless at least some of the costs of their care are shifted back from the state to the family' (Marsland, 1986: 94). One flaw with this argument was that since 'youth' (as distinct from childhood and adulthood) did not exist as a welfare category when the welfare state was set up in post-war Britain, the care of young people could not be 'shifted back' from the state to their families (Dean, 1995).

There are, however, indications that family change is affecting access to parental support, thus highlighting the dangers of basing policy on outmoded models of the nuclear family or devising policies to bolster it up (Smart, 1997). Beck (1992) refers to the increased 'fragility' of family support as more marriages end in divorce, and youth research has shown that family breakdown or the death of a parent can affect levels of family support, as can the re-partnering of a parent (McDowell, 2001; Jones, 1995). Finch argues, however, that closeness in families is a more significant factor for family support than the structure of kin relationships, and that the failure of policy-makers to understand family relationships is reflected in dissonance between public and private discourse about 'family obligations' (Finch, 1989; Finch and Mason, 1993).

Parents in England were asked in a recent study (Jones, forthcoming) when they thought that their legal responsibilities for their children ended. Their responses reflect the ambiguity in the law: though many thought 18 was the age limit, some thought it was 16 years. The parental home is just that: 82 per cent of parents fairly accurately thought they had no legal responsibility to provide housing beyond eighteen years – and indeed over-18s in England and Wales (but over-16s in Scotland) can only stay in the parental home as licensees. Their parents can therefore evict them after these ages. Three-quarters of the parents thought they had no legal responsibility to subsidize young people's low wages, or (in a few cases) to provide food and clothing once young people start work – challenging therefore the dependency assumption underlying the age-grading of the NMW. In all, 37 per cent of parents thought they had no legal obligation to pay towards their children's education beyond the age of 18 years, despite the loss of state grants and the policy assumption that parents should subsidize the high costs. Young people too are unclear about the legal responsibility of their parents and, because of this, they lack a solid legal or normative basis for claiming support (Finch, 1989). Most young people in a recent study did not think that the answer was statutory enforcement of parental responsibility, and suggested instead that young people had a responsibility to support themselves through work if they could, especially if their parents could not afford to support them (Jones, forthcoming).

There is no European consensus on the legal obligations of parents. In northern European countries, the welfare state plays a more significant role, and in Mediterranean countries families continue to offer the main support (IARD, 2001; Jones, 2005; Holdsworth and Morgan, 2005). Some countries apply an age threshold when parental support can be replaced by state support: these include Norway (at 18 years), the Netherlands (21 years), Italy (26 years) and Germany (27 years). In other countries, such as Austria and Hungary, parental responsibilities legally end with the completion of a young person's education or training. Dependence in Mediterranean countries, where family support plays a far more significant role, is typically extended until the late 20s. This creates a new crisis in these countries, as parents are increasingly feeling the strain. There have been legal battles over parental responsibility in recent years in Italy and Spain. In one recent case (*The Guardian*, 6 April 2002), the Court of Cassation in Italy ordered an estranged father to continue paying maintenance to his 30-year-old son. The ruling placed responsibility firmly with the parents in indicating that a parent's duty of maintenance did not expire when children reached adulthood, but continued unchanged until the parents were able to prove that their children had either reached economic independence or had failed to do so through 'culpable inertia'. The media described the ruling as a 'loafer's charter'.

Sociology of dependence

Dependency forms part of the structure of the 'ties that bind', or social connectedness. Durkheim (1984), though he associated dependence with incompleteness, saw it as a source of social cohesion, and suggested that, since everyone has something to contribute, the net result will be interdependence. In contrast, for Bauman (1995), the real novelty of the postmodern world is there is no longer a social unity of mutual dependence, or interdependence, as the rich no longer need the poor.

This idea of interdependence is critical to understanding the situation of young people. Anthropological theories of gift exchange illuminate the problem. The gift implies asymmetry and inequality. The functionalist anthropologist Malinowski's (1922) work on the Trobriand Islanders pointed to the mutual respect involved in ritual gift behaviour which emphasized the modesty of the giver and the reluctance of the receiver. Mauss (1990 [1954]), from a neo-Marxist perspective, indicated however that it was the asymmetry of ritual gift exchanges, based on unequal resources, which created the social bond between giver and receiver. Mary Douglas (1990), seeing that it was the unrequited gift which had the power to humiliate, argued instead that mutual respect derived from reciprocity rather than one-way giving. Lévi-Strauss (1969) developed the idea of cycles of reciprocity over a longer term, an idea which allows reciprocity between children and parents to be acknowledged over the duration of their relationships, to include reciprocal care of older parents by their middle-aged children. Sahlins (1965) distinguished between 'balanced' reciprocity, which is more immediate and based on equivalence, and 'generalized' reciprocity which can be in the longer term.

This anthropological work sets the scene for understanding the relationships between young people and their parents during transitions to economic independence. There is a shift from unreciprocated support during childhood (forming an asymmetric bond of dependence) to increasingly mutual support as young people gain independent incomes and the power relationship between them and their parents becomes more equal. The idea that young people are dependent because they are receiving support from their parents ignores the possibility that there may be a degree of reciprocity and mutual dependence (with new bonds developing out of this mutuality). This is a point to be further discussed below, but in the meantime it is worth noting that young people have limited and indeed diminishing scope for short-term balanced reciprocity (Jones, 1992). The division assumed by welfare policy structures of young people into dependants and non-dependants based on their age thus bears no relation to the complex reality of contemporary life – but this is not just a measurement problem which can be resolved by shifting an age threshold.

Dependence and shame

The principle of reciprocity also underlies the welfare state, which is based on contributing and benefiting over the life course. Despite this, the stigma associated with claiming welfare benefits leads to the under-claiming of entitlements. This stigma goes back to the distinction between the deserving and undeserving poor of the Poor Law around the construction of the 'work ethic'. It relates also to the Freudian belief that the superego, operating through guilt, provides a moral curb on individual action. Sennett (2004) comments on the demeaning effect that a hatred of 'parasitism' in modern society has on welfare dependency. He argues that there are three modern codes of respect: self-development (developing abilities and skills), self-sufficiency (rather than being a burden on others), and reciprocity (giving back to others according to the social principle of exchange). While respect is accorded to those who follow these three codes, resources and opportunities are withdrawn from those who do not. Dependency is thus juxtaposed to the work ethic, which Sennett calls a perversion of liberal values, driving people to prove their worth through work. According to this ethic, education has to be useful and becomes preparation for productive work rather than for life (the working-class approach to post-school education still reflects this).

Sennett argues (2004: 103) that an 'infantilization thesis' makes childhood and adulthood, immaturity and maturity, into political categories, divided by the phenomenon of dependency. Sennett concludes that the shame and guilt commonly attached to dependency are misplaced, and he therefore suggests that the tarnish of dependency could be removed by admitting the just claims of *adult* dependency, so that autonomy is reconstructed as the acceptance of mutual and interdependent relationships. However, he sees a distinction between public dependence, where the need for others is shaming, and private dependence, where it appears to be dignified. This point is debatable. Youth research suggests that private dependence is equally shaming and policy structures extending dependence mean that young people cannot easily escape this shame.

Shame has been described as a response to the contempt of others whose values are respected, but it also depends on the loss of self-respect. Sayer (2005) describes shame as an emotion which leads to social conformity and social order, and it therefore has value for social control, but he points out that it can also lead to resistance. Young people, especially working-class ones, are faced with a choice between gaining the respect associated with implementing the work ethic (or alternatively the norms of their peer group) and the possibly shaming effect of dependence resulting from staying in education and training. Are they likely to 'choose' dependence?

Dependence in the private sphere

Both Beck and Giddens acknowledge the need to recognize mutuality and reciprocity in social bonds but admit that theories of reflexivity and individualization are hard to apply to younger people because of their dependence. Beck and Beck-Gernsheim (2002: xxi) describe late modern society as 'a paradoxical collectivity of reciprocal individualization'. They trace a shift from traditional families which operated as communities of need, to industrial-age families in which new forms of dependency developed, from the mutual obligation which forms the basis of the welfare state, to the neo-liberal notion of the self-sufficient individual. Like Sennett, Beck and Beck-Gernsheim (2002: 160) refer to the erroneous distinction between helpers and needy, pointing out that it tends to be forgotten that those who provide help also need it, and that 'the enrichment might lie precisely in the experience of "mutual helplessness".'

Giddens (1992) similarly develops the notion of 'co-dependence'. He suggests that, as young people move towards adulthood, their relationship with their parents becomes more similar to a 'pure relationship', a new stage in intimate relationships between adults, in which there is co-dependence and expectations of contributions and benefits are shared.

Thus parents increasingly see themselves in a more companionate relationship with their children, rather than in an authoritarian one. Giddens acknowledges that there are difficulties applying these ideas to parent–child relations which, however amicable, are necessarily based on a 'pregiven social obligation of a binding kind' on both sides, the responsibility of parents to care and the right of children to be cared for.

For Giddens (1992, following Finch, 1989), kin relations are becoming subject to greater negotiation than ever before, partly because external criteria such as social duty or traditional obligation are becoming less significant, and partly because of the new diversity of kinship ties resulting from 'recombinant families'. Rather than implement received ideologies, people have to work out the proper thing to do (Finch, 1989), reconstructing the ethics of family life through everyday experiments. Giddens (1992: 98) considers the implications for the quality of parent–child relations, given the imbalance of power, and concludes, still drawing on Finch's analysis, that 'it is the quality of the relationship which comes to the fore, with a stress on intimacy replacing that of parental authoritativeness.' This, he argues, sets the stage for a further transformation: the translation of the parent–child relationship into a relationship in the contemporary sense of that term. Giddens describes a gradual shift from the 'male doctrine' of authoritarian fatherhood, the basis for the transmission of traditional ideologies through dogmatic assertion, to an emphasis on mothering which opened up new possibilities for more democratic parenting practices, but this shift is not universal. Movement of parent–child relations closer to the pure relationship does not result in the loss of parental authority: 'A liberalising of the personal sphere would not mean the disappearance of authority; rather, coercive power gives way to authority relations which can be defended in a principled fashion' (Giddens, 1992: 109). This takes us back to Habermas's (1984) theory of communicative rationality, referring to action which can be defended through argumentation – a means of developing consensus over what is justifiable.

The suggestion that parent–child relations are changing in this way is challenged by Lynn Jamieson (1998) who suggests that, while the public face of parent–child relationships may be moving in the direction proposed by Giddens, quite different relationships are acted out in private. For Jamieson, middle-class parents in particular may disguise their power through a relationship which, though publicly companionate, remains unequal in the private sphere of family life. In recent research, parents have been found to contrast favourably their open relationships with their children with those they had with their own parents, but this apparently greater democracy in families may represent a 'subtle form' of parental control in Giddens's (1992) terms because it facilitates parental surveillance of their children (Brannen et al., 1994; Jamieson, 1998; Jones et al., 2006).

Parental support for young people is seen by policy-makers as socially desirable, especially when there is concern about youth offending rates, because an association is made between dependency and parental control.

The central paradox of parental support

The fostering of *in*dependence and responsibility is central to parent–child relations (Hutson and Jenkins, 1989; Allatt and Yeandle, 1992; Jones and Wallace, 1992). The continued extension of the period of dependent youth therefore creates a dilemma for parents who see their role as enabling social and economic independence, as well as for young people who are seeking autonomy. Although Sennett distinguishes between perceptions of public and private dependence, in practice most young people define dependence in relation to their parents rather than vis-à-vis the state, sometimes seeing state support as a means of achieving independence rather than as an end in itself. The impetus to become independent from parents is very strong, and the failure to do so may induce shame and guilt.

Both generations are ambivalent about dependence and independence. Finch (1989: 169) describes the difficulty in achieving 'the desired blend of dependence and independence'. Allatt and Yeandle (1992: 123) indicate that parents 'tread a tightrope between compulsion and protectiveness'.

Parents in a recent study (Jones et al., 2006) indicate the importance of 'being there', treading the fine line between support and interference (often muddied because of the very close link between support and control). It should not be forgotten that parents are often vulnerable, too, and afraid of losing their children. Family disagreements over money and the expected level of dependence can lead to young people leaving home precipitously (Smith et al., 1998).

Young people are ambivalent about seeking support and may be resistant to asking for help, even when they need it. Though Sennett has suggested that shame is associated with dependence in the public sector, young people clearly find asking their parents for help shaming. A 24-year-old (see Jones, forthcoming), Carol, thought the idea of returning to dependence shameful, saying that, if she had gone back to her parents, 'I'd have been a failure, wouldn't I, with my tail between my legs.' A young woman in a Scottish study of family support said she would not ask for help even when she needed it because her parents would never let her forget it (Jones, 1995). In the same study, Patricia and Denise, both aged around 22 years, also preferred to deny that they needed help, Patricia linking support with control, and Denise linking it with shame:

> *Patricia*: They always wanted to know what I was doing and if I had enough money. And I had, like, no money at all and I hadn't eaten for two days, and I'm saying, 'Of course I've eaten; of course I'm getting on fine'. You know, I wouldn't say 'I'm really starving.'

> *Denise*: See if I've nae money, absolutely really skint, I'll no go near him. It feels like begging even when you're going to your ain faither, ken. I dinnae like going and saying 'I've nae money, I need food, ken.'

Young people reluctant to ask their parents for help, whether through shame or through fear of loss of autonomy or rejection, are dependent on it being offered. The result is that the initiative for support often rests with the parent (Finch and Mason, 1993; Jones, 1995; Jones et al., 2006). Some parents diminish the risks for young people leaving the parental home by stressing that they can return if they need to (Jones, 1995). Without this guarantee, it is far more difficult for them to do so. The result in one case was a stand-off between a mother and son, both sides being inhibited about making the first move, whether asking or offering, until one of them gave way (Jones, 1995).

Traditional and experimental parenting

In a post-traditional society, though tradition continues to have some hold, it is more likely to be adapted to modern conditions through 'everyday experiments' (Giddens, 1994: 60). Parental obligations are (still) constructed within families, partly according to the prevailing ethos within the family or community, drawing on precedent and history, and partly on the quality of family relationships (Allatt and Yeandle, 1992). A recent study of parenting (Jones et al., 2006) found two types of parents. Some parents were inflexible and resistant to social change, constructing the parenting they had received when young as the traditional and right way to do things. This suggests that, in contrast to Giddens's (1992) view, some parenting is still of the authoritarian type which uses dogmatic assertion as a means of transmitting traditional ideology. In these families, there was more likely to be generational conflict over values. Other parents operated in a more flexible way, trying to accommodate social change and respond to need, rather than drawing on habit and precedent. In these families, there was discussion and negotiation, and even scope for developing cooperative strategy (Jones et al., 2006).

Although belief systems act as a resource to help families negotiate matters of dependence and support, Finch (1989: 242) concludes that the 'sense of obligation' which distinguishes kin relationships 'derives from commitments built up between real people over many years' rather than from an abstract set of moral values. Nevertheless, it is largely through negotiation that obligations are defined and redefined. Pre-existing notions of reciprocity, fairness and legitimacy guide family members in their everyday constructions and reconstructions of dependence and obligation.

Reciprocity, or mutual obligation, is a fundamental normative belief underlying family support (Finch, 1989) and is one way that young people attempt to equalize their power relationship with their parents. There are many examples of mutuality of need and support in families (Jones, 1992). Young people may help in a family business or be involved in caring for a parent or sibling. Nearly all young people who have left full-time education but live in the parental home pay board money to their parents (Allatt and Yeandle, 1992; Jones, 1992, 1995; Hutton and Seavers, 2002). Young people see this as a form of reciprocity which helps to mitigate the shame of dependence, making it easier for them to ask for help if they need it. As they get older, they see the board payments as the proper thing to do because it is what their friends do. Not paying board can be demeaning and shameful. Although board money is sometimes seen as a purely symbolic payment, it is important to recognize the impact on some family budgets when young people cannot contribute to their keep. The reduction of state support for education and training mean that students and trainees often have to live with their parents, but not being able to pay board can result in both eviction from the family home and drop-out from education (Smith et al., 1998; Jones et al., 2004). One implication of extended dependence is therefore that opportunities for this form of reciprocity have been withdrawn, and this can exacerbate the shame associated with dependence.

The concept of fairness provides another guiding principle of family support (Finch, 1989; Allatt and Yeandle, 1992), allowing parents to moderate competing demands and also allowing young people to see their own needs in a broader family context. Middle-aged parents may be trying to make arrangements for the care of older relatives, for their own pension schemes, or for the various needs of their different children. Young people may also apply a notion of fairness and moderate their demands, not asking 'too much' of their parents (Jones et al., 2006). Thus, some young people recognize that support for them would have to reduce because there were other siblings 'coming up' and needing support through higher education, or because their parents were saving for their retirement and had needs of their own. Competing obligations must be juggled and the complexity and size of a family – including the number of children – can be critical. Attias-Donfut and Wolff (2000), describing the parent generation as 'the pivot generation' (because they are expected to shoulder responsibilities for generations above them as well as the younger generations below them), found that parents with more children were less likely to provide care for their own parents.

Parents need to be able to prioritize but they need also to be *seen* to be fair. Bryan Turner (1986: 31) suggests that a 'conflict between our sense of fairness and the reality of mundane inequality shapes the elementary forms of our social world'. He argues that everyday life is made up of a myriad of reciprocities based on fairness and egalitarianism. Allatt and Yeandle (1992: 125) draw a useful distinction between equality and equity in the distribution of resources among children, indicating circumstances where parents may justify differential treatment of their children. Parents can pigeonhole their children in terms of their academic ability and support them accordingly – thus one child may 'deserve' support for extended education while another may not (Jones et al., 2004). An important point here is that this distinction between deserving and undeserving children overrides parents' views about the legitimacy of the need itself.

Legitimacy and cultural capital

Parental support depends on the parents' constructions of a request for help as legitimate or 'right' (Allatt and Yeandle, 1992; Jones, 1995) and thus whether support is the 'proper' thing to do. Young people are also very aware that they have to prove their case for support. There are many examples in both generations where Habermas's (1984) theory of communicative rationality is seen in practice. By subjecting their claims to scrutiny, some young adults may be able to prove their value and elicit parental support. For example, a young couple living with in-laws can prove the value of the partnership and be better placed to receive help with setting up a partnership home, or young people who have shown their commitment to education are better placed to have support to extend it. Parents may equally need to be able to justify support which they deem to have broken normative rules. Parents in our study who were supporting children who had become lone parents were able to deny personal agency, saying that they helped their children because 'fate' had intervened in the form of a redundancy payment or inheritance (Jones et al., 2004, 2006).

Individuals have to justify their behaviour in the light of prevailing neighbourhood values in order to receive or give support (Jones et al., 2006). Informal networks of parents reach consensus about desirable behaviour (Seaman and Sweeting, 2004) in approaches to education, teenage parenthood, amounts of board money, eviction from parental home, and so on. It is important that young people's own life plans reflect the ethos prevailing in their families and communities. Where a strong work ethic prevails, parents may not be willing to take on the expense of extended education and training. Young mothers may need their families around them for support with informal child care (Webster et al., 2004), so it is not surprising that the expectation of parental support plays an important part in young women's decisions whether to continue with a pregnancy (Tabberer, 2000).

The decision to defer independence for the sake of qualifications requires not only the prospect of support, but also more evidence that it works. Where there is agreement that post-school education has instrumental value and is worth the cost, young people and their parents draw on their own and each other's resources in order to pay. The fear of failure – failing to capitalize on education and training in a way which would justify the cost (including the emotional cost of asking for support) – becomes acute, not least because this is likely to involve a double humiliation. Several research studies have identified the problems for poorer students who are caught in a clash of cultural values. Extending the tradition that working-class young people support their own transitions, many students now take on part-time work, but this can adversely affect their academic work and jeopardize the whole justification for the sacrifice they (and/or their parents) are making in going to university (Forsyth and Furlong, 2000, 2001; Christie et al., 2002; Jones et al., 2004).

Family support strategies

In the extension of dependence by policy-makers, none of these factors is taken into account. There is no recognition that family resources are not equally distributed, or that cultural beliefs affect the legitimacy of claims for support, or that family bonds could be strengthened by supporting a reciprocal relationship between young people and their parents rather than one based on one-sided dependence. The age thresholds, imposed in policy structures and determining when young people can be deemed welfare citizens, take no account of these everyday realities affecting the willingness of young people to remain dependent or the willingness of their parents to support them. Even if both sides are willing to defer independence, they may not be able to.

If all the cultural, moral and emotional hurdles can be overcome, the next question is financial resources. At the very least, staying on in education means the loss to family budgets of contributions to board. 'Strategies' used by parents to find the resources to put children through university include parents doing overtime, taking on second jobs, selling shares, or cashing in savings (Jones et al., 2004, 2006).

The problems of treating young people's actions as strategic were examined in chapter 2. It is equally debatable whether family strategies are really involved in support practices since the term not only implies collective rationality but fails to take account of internal power structures (Wallace, 2002). Thompson (1997) suggests that 'family strategies', far from being collective, are overlapping individual strategies drawing on a family culture which is also only partly shared. Savage (2000) questions whether collective actions, such as instrumental family strategies, are feasible when there is a clash of individual interests. The aspirations of young adults and their parents (for them) may be different, as they may weigh up the costs and benefits of different education strategies differently (Marshall et al., 1997). Thus, in relation to parental support for education, Savage asks: 'What instrumental reasons might parents have for sacrificing their own well-being (in terms of childrearing work, financial support, etc.) to their children's disposal? Would parents in a rationally acting household choose to devote all resources towards one child's education, so minimizing the chances of other children in the household, or share the risk?' (Savage, 2000: 86).

One answer is that their actions could derive from value instrumentality: Leonard (1980) argues that parents are rewarded for their financial support with continued closeness to their adult child and the prospect of the support being reciprocated; Harris (1983) suggests that parents are judged by the quality of their products and rewarded with social respect if their children are deemed to have been successfully reared. The question of fairness raised by Savage has already been answered, although as we have seen there is a difference between equity and fairness in resource distribution.

It seems, though, that family support practices do not necessarily reflect strategy. In practice, young people describe three forms of parental support (Jones, forthcoming): *basic maintenance*, ending with full-time work or age (usually at 18 or 21); *one-off large-scale support* for specific needs, such as a flat, car or baby; and *safety-net support* in emergencies, expected to be available over a longer term. Few parents in the UK give regular financial support to 16–25-year olds – these are mainly middle-class parents supporting students, acting in a class-traditional manner. More common are irregular payments and help in kind, including letting children live at home (Hutton and Seavers, 2002; Jones, 1995). This leads Holdsworth and Morgan (2005) to describe most parental support as crisis management rather than as strategic practice. They distinguish between 'help up' as a support strategy, aimed at helping young people become independent, and 'handout' which is more associated with maintaining dependence, applying this distinction to support both from the family and from the state. The implication is that strategic 'help up' might be less shameful than a handout, possibly because, as Sennett suggests, respect is associated with self-improvement.

Precarious freedom?

Young people, as others, are constrained by their dependence on their families, which limits their ability to construct their own biographies, induces shame and guilt, and makes them less able to ask for help and more vulnerable to risks and 'moral panics'. This vicious circle could be seen as an external manipulation of youth, a point to which I shall return in the final chapter. As Giddens suggests, this creates a problem for theories of reflexivity.

The dependence and support beliefs described here create a social division between young people with and without parental support. This division arises because young people have differential access to normative constructions of family life as well as differential access to economic resources. Young people are not only unsupported by their parents in circumstances where they are estranged from them. Even in intact families, parents may not be willing to support young people and may instead expect them to support themselves. There are many cases where parents and their children have such a poor relationship that there is no question of support beyond the minimum, however they construct that (Smith et al., 1998; Jones et al., 2004). Many young people do, however, totally lack access to family life and are forced to cope alone, individualized in the most extreme sense. These include some who have been in care, who are homeless and, increasingly, young asylum seekers who may be geographically distanced from their families. Policies aimed at reducing social exclusion among young people must therefore not only be focused on young people themselves but ensure that their family circumstances are addressed.

Ironically, this is at a time when intergenerational cohesion is considered increasingly important if older generations are to be supported by younger ones. It is a time when the social obligations of young people should be supported rather than subjected to stress. There is a greater need than ever to understand the ways in which intergenerational social obligations and transitions between dependence and independence are constructed across the entire life course.

7
Youth in Society

If we want to understand youth and engage in debates about young people, we need to build a new conceptual framework from the ashes of old ones. This is not the most obvious solution because the grand narratives that gave rise at various times to various partial understandings of youth appear to have less and less relevance in the present age. Many of the debates outlined in chapter 1 were based on dichotomies and absolutes which have since been resolved or broken down. The answer nevertheless lies in theoretical synthesis, or *bricolage*, where youth studies might have to reconsider previously rejected theories and recombine and reconstruct them into a new theoretical framework which both reflects the real lives of real young people and can be intellectually defended in late modernity. This involves drawing on disciplines other than sociology – psychology and economics – but it also means stressing the *social* which must by definition be at the heart of any sociological account. Though youth can be characterized as a process of transition to adulthood, its context shifts from private to public worlds, and it is therefore important to consider these worlds, and the part played by young people's families and peers, and institutions, rather than focusing too exclusively on young people themselves.

Rather than review the story of this book, I want in this chapter to examine more closely the social connectedness of young people in late modernity – the theme which has been present throughout. I shall show how youth is connected both structurally and culturally with the wider society and is never 'outside' it. Youth in the modern age can be seen as a transition from private to public spheres, and from ascription to achievement in terms of identity, values and social status. It has been argued (Giddens, 1991) that among adults *ascribed* characteristics have become less significant and that individuals are freer of their history in reflexive late modernity. The extension and expansion of education intended as a means of escape has resulted in the extension of dependence and restrictions on autonomy in youth. At times, it therefore also acts as a *restraint* on young people's ability to escape their histories and forge their own biographies, identities and values. The extension of dependence means the extension of primary socialization in the family. Even when young people appear to be acting as autonomous individuals, this may be the result of individualization by others and not an individual achievement. It may seem that this extension of dependence involving the continuation of an unequal parent–child power relationship runs contrary to ideas about the reflexive individualization of young people. I will argue however that youth in late modernity is characterized by a tension between forced dependence and 'forced emancipation', and that it is this tension which individualizes young people during their youth and makes them vulnerable.

From pluralism to the individual

Youth as a social concept, freed from its basis in biological determinism, was a product of the modern age. Despite this, youth has never been adequately conceptualized, partly because it is constantly changing. The concept emerged as part of an Enlightenment project concerned with understanding, categorizing and above all *controlling* nature, with education put forward as having a civilizing agenda. Industrialization and urbanization in the nineteenth century set up a saint/ sinner dichotomy and a tension between the needs to protect young people from exploitation by adults and to control those whose activities threatened social stability.

The sociological construction of youth which developed in the twentieth century was largely concerned with social location – whether young people were structurally connected with the wider society through their age cohort or through their kin-generation structure, with young people seen in either case as social beings in waiting, on the fringes of society, rather than integrated with it. This was not a sterile exercise but concerned with understanding the processes of social reproduction and social stability. Gradually, theories shifted to a more inclusive construction which attempted to locate youth within the structures of 'mainstream' society. This increasingly pluralist formulation, built up layer by layer out of the social structures of modernity (class, gender and ethnicity), was thought by some to obscure the central concept of youth as a *process*. However, with the increasing instability of many certainties and social structures in late modernity, this new pluralist construction of youth itself becomes increasingly unstable, being based on unsteady foundations.

One of the debates between functionalists and subcultural theorists had been over process versus structure, acted out in terms of age versus class – a war in which the most recent battle has been won by age. If young people were only integrated with the social structure through their biological age, it would not matter to the integrity of the concept of youth that the social edifice was crumbling. But they are not, and so the concept of youth as structurally connected *is* challenged and, through a process of reductionism and manipulation, has been returned to its positivist age-generation origins. This process has been facilitated and confirmed by welfare-driven age structures in policy frameworks of protection and control which, however inconsistent, now determine biographies in youth. These age structures are trying to grasp hold of a sense of *process*, with age as an inadequate indicator, but the process has been taken out of its social context. Bourdieu (1978) argues that these arbitrary age constructions can be seen as manipulations. Once age becomes the main explanatory variable for youth, the social connectedness of the concept is threatened. A focus on age is therefore a step towards individualizing young people.

Individualized and found wanting

Youth has been seen as a period during which young people are neither children (deserving care and compassion) nor adults (worthy of respect for their self-sufficiency and responsibility), but 'unfinished' individuals, and therefore innately flawed. This has been described as the 'deficit model' (Cohen, 1997).

Psychoanalysts argue that young people are in the throes of psychological development from the egoistic narcissism of the baby to the rational altruism of the adult, but have also shown that their behaviour can swing between the two. Altruism involves self-restraint for the common good, the latter being defined according to a social consensus of values. Sigmund Freud suggested that the individual superego acted as a self-restraining mechanism in moral development, operating through guilt. Theories of developmental psychology, proposing a linear framework of tasks for individuals to master before adulthood can be achieved, furthered the idea of incompleteness, in terms of rationality and cognitive ability (Piaget) or identity and ego development (Erikson). Young people who have not reached these stages are deemed to have failed to gain mastery of the conscious (and rational and moral) mind. These theories present an ideal type as universal. Young people do become, in general, increasingly able objectively to assess their relationship with the world around them, but there is both individual and cultural variation from this linear universal model. The developmental model, though once again neglecting the social, was at least trying to get at the processes at the heart of youth but ended up with perceptions of youth as a period of moratorium and structured irresponsibility (before a mythical state of adulthood is achieved). When extended to transitions to social adulthood, this perspective leads some commentators to refer to individual 'failure' to achieve normative (white, male and middle-class) life stages, and youth, in these circumstances, as a limbo state.

Though individuals make these developmental journeys, they are not expected by sociologists to do so on their own but through 'civilizing' social processes including socialization, through which they will learn the 'adult' characteristics of rationality and altruism, essential for social cohesion, and normative patterns of behaviour. Commentators vary, however, in whether they see the development of moral values as individually or socially achieved. Foucault (1988) suggests a combination of individual self-regulation and external social control; Habermas (1984) suggests that the consensus changes socially through argumentation; Symbolic Interactionists went even further in proposing that values were negotiated *in situ*, attracting the criticism that they were describing an amoral society. Some suggest that morality has become more individual and localized in late modernity: according to Urry (1995), morality is now less to do with social roles and responsibilities and is more individually achieved; Bauman (1995) similarly suggests that morality has become a matter of individual loyalty acts. There seems to be concern among some current generation theorists that young people are more egoistic than the previous generation, but lack of altruism, if it exists, could be as much a failure of society as a 'generational' one.

Primary socialization in late modernity

The deficit state of immaturity in youth was to be rectified through primary socialization in the family, which, following Parsons, is the principal means through which the norms and values of altruism and morality are handed down from parent to child, ensuring some conformity across the generations and thus social cohesion. Because the capacity of parents to prepare their children for their adult lives was becoming increasingly restricted, secondary socialization through education would give access to knowledge, the prerequisite of a rational mind freed from myth and prejudice (including the prejudice instilled in them by their parents). This sets up a tension between parents and education, especially where there is a conflict of values between the two. But it also promotes the idea of young people as passive recipients of socialization – rather than as actively engaging in it – and emphasizes their dependence which according to Parsons is essential for the socialization process. (Thus, totalitarian regimes treated young people as empty vessels and sought to remove them from the influence of their parents in order to be able to indoctrinate them more effectively.) Although in some cases the aspirations of parents, policy-makers and young people themselves converge, in other cases young people are faced with conflicting pressures. It is typically when young people are caught between competing values of their parents and the state that anomie – which can lead to deviant behaviour – has been found to occur.

There are many reasons why this perception of socialization should be reappraised in late modernity. The extension of their dependence puts young people under the socializing influence of their parents for a longer period. This might be seen by some policy-makers as desirable because of greater prospects for parental control, but there are risks involved if the family culture is likely to support behaviour that policy-makers would like to prevent (teenage pregnancy or early entry into the labour market, for example). The process of socialization in the family may be weakened by a lack of the expert knowledge now needed and adversely affected by family breakdown. Generational changes result in lack of consensus between young people and their parents not only over educational aspirations but also over beliefs about obligation and support.

All these problems affect the type of cultural capital held in families. Families vary in their ability to pass on to their children any beneficial ('bridging') cultural capital held. But even more significantly, perhaps, family functioning varies from authoritarian parenting, based on inequality of power, in which habitual but unrealistic patterns of behaviour in the younger generation are not only encouraged but sometimes enforced, to more open and democratic parenting (Giddens, 1992), based on a more equal parent–child relationship, where family norms and values are changing in response to wider social change, in part through family argumentation and discussion (Habermas, 1984) between young people and their parents – and where the process of socialization is thus being not only extended but *transformed*.

Peer groups in late modernity

Whether in the form of middle-class student 'counter-cultural' demonstrations in the 1960s, or working-class sub-cultural gatherings in the 1970s, peer groups of young people have tended to attract a negative press, being seen as promoting alternative values and threatening social cohesion. The fear is that secondary socialization by peers threatens both primary socialization in their families and their secondary socialization in schools.

Peer groups provided transitional opportunities for young people to escape the identity and status and values ascribed from their families of origin, and develop *transitional* identities and statuses and values (Brake, 1980). Peer groups therefore had a role within what Bauman refers to as the 'modernist pilgrimage of the self', offering transitional opportunities within a development progression towards the achievement of adult identity. Bauman (1995) argues that this whole notion of modernist 'pilgrimage' was based on an illusion that mastery was possible, and indeed he argues that the 'self' was also an illusion. There may have been no modernist 'golden age' of the peer group, therefore, and its significance in this respect – as a transitional 'vehicle' – may have been overstressed.

In late modernity, working-class culture is still strong, though not as collective. Though anti-school working-class peer groups still exist, they have lost their authenticity, according to poststructuralist accounts. Instead of subcultures, we see 'style groups'. For Baudrillard, and Lasch before him, the consumer ideology has taken over the individual and everything is *simulacra*, or simulation. Transitoriness has become dominant in current youth styles, and Baudrillard (1993) suggests that we are in love with this transitoriness and seduced by the superficiality. Bauman (1995) comments on a 'fear of being fixed'. Current 'neo-tribes' (Maffesoli, 1996) may no longer provide opportunities for identity construction in youth, being too fluid and ephemeral. Melucci (1992) comments that there are now too many symbolic possibilities and too many memberships to allow identity-building. Being free-floating and concerned with style and self-referencing self-authentication, youth styles are market-ing 'consumer identity'. Žižek (1989) argues that popular culture merely screens the void of the Lacanian fragmented self, reflecting the dominant consumer ideology rather than offering any resistance to it.

Some commentators are anxious to show that youth styles still have cultural elements and still have both transitional identity potential and subversive potential. Thus, they are shown to maintain boundaries of membership, regulate inter-nal social control through values, rules, language and their own status system, and generally act in cultural (if not sub-cultural) ways. In a society in which uncertainty and risk have been individualized, acceptance into a style group with its badges of membership may be seen as offering collective security and protection, and even transitional identity (although such groups can be internally divided into core and periphery). Bauman (1995) suggests however that, in their attempts to appear less arbitrary, neo-tribes, whatever their internal structure, can become aggressive and intolerant of outsiders; unstable collective identities are therefore as prob-lematic as unstable individual ones for the development of positive social relationships. The 'subcultural capital' (Thorn-ton, 1995) held in peer groups – like other forms of cultural capital – may be bonding rather than bridging, and thus fail to provide transitional opportunities. It is possible that in late modernity the peer group may have less value as a transi-tional space, either because it has lost its ability to fulfil this function or because it is no longer needed in this way.

In late modernity, there has been a shift from the modern-ist pilgrimage of the self (Bauman, 1995) to self-identity as reflexively constructed over the life course, rather than mas-tered and fixed (Giddens, 1991). Constructed in this way, self-identity is not reliant on self-image or therefore prone to the misrepresentations of the Lacanian mirror. It is argued that individuals are increasingly freed from their referents and that both ascribed identity and transitional collective identi-ties (like other forms of collectivity) have become less signifi-cant. If the extension of dependence on parents increases the scope of parents in the socialization process, this does at the very least challenge modernist constructions of the role of the peer group in youth. The result may be that young people seeking support through their peer groups may be less likely to find it.

Social respect is afforded to success and blame to failure, based on a set of normative middle-class values which may not be shared by family and peers. The school system is studded with markers of 'success', even to the detriment of learning. By opting to adopt its values, young people (especially in working-class communities) may therefore be setting themselves up as different – standing out from the crowd. This may attract disapproval in working-class communities where respectability involves an ethic of work and self-sufficiency, and so acceptance of the norms of the school can be individualizing. In contrast, it is those whom the education system has labelled as 'failures' that are likely to form oppositional anti-school peer groups, less able to provide transitional solutions, and more prone to defensive distrust of outsiders (including not just other gangs but also individual 'swots') and thus aggression towards them. Young people who have signed up to the education ethic, sometimes in opposition to the values held in their families as well as that of their anti-school peers, may therefore be doubly individualized.

Individual agents or cultural dupes?

Young people are blamed for many things, which is why I have not succumbed to the prevailing political correctness of stressing young people's agency but instead questioned the extent to which they can, as individual or collectives, be held responsible for their actions by reviewing theories which consider action as conscious or unconscious, premeditated or impulsive, individual or collective. The main criticism of these theories has been that, like developmental theories, they fail to recognize cultural and structural diversity, but there is also the question of whether and how they can be applied to young people and especially the problem of how dependence affects action.

Rational action may be seen as an individual achievement, the result of education freeing young people from the possibly negative influence of their families. Rational action theories have been criticized for being over-focused on economic motivation when applied to adults, but rational action is also known to depend on resources to which young people may well not have access – and indeed, with extended dependence, may have diminishing access. However, for action to be deemed rational, it is likely that it has to conform to normative expectations, and thus young people who sign up to the goals set out in policy initiatives are more likely to be seen as rational actors than those who take alternative routes. Adults are believed to be more likely in late modernity to take a rational and calculative approach to life management, but is this because they are also more likely to be in a position to determine the normative goals?

Habitual or traditional action has (according to Giddens) become less significant in modern societies and adults are less likely to act in ways which merely repeat family or cultural tradition, thus making it more possible to escape their 'fate'. This idea is not easily applied to the actions of young people because their increasing dependence on their parents for all forms of resources, including cultural capital, strengthens the effects of socialization and gives parents the power to encourage the replication of patterns of behaviour which are deemed to represent the traditional. Habitual action by young people can therefore be the result of 'negative' socialization by their parents (failing to socialize their children according to middle-class norms), where resistance to parental pressure to conform to cultural practices would be futile because of their dependent status. In the case of both habitual and rational action, then, it seems that it is adults who determine what is rational and what is traditional, rather than young people themselves.

Subcultural theorists replaced rational explanations with cultural ones, based on the peer group, and opened up the idea of collective action. However, accounts of deviance and, later, working-class subcultures, presented these neither as outcomes of conscious and rational strategy nor as habitual/ traditional action, but as defensive and unconscious (though 'problem-solving') cultural responses to anomie and hegemonic power. The resistance was symbolic: ultimately, young people's attempts at subcultural 'resistance' reinforced the hegemonic capitalist and patriarchal structures which oppressed them. Effectively, then, the balance shifted from trying to present young people as individual failed rational actors or path-following traditional actors to implicitly presenting them (working-class young people, at any rate) as collectively acting *cultural dupes*. This represented a significant shift to cultural determinism. Subcultural theories which held good for the 1960s and 1970s are more questionable in a late modern era. According to Lash (2007), power is now 'post-hegemonic' and real. There is therefore no need for ideology to support it and no place for subcultural and symbolic – but also ultimately self-defeating – resistance to it. The notion of hegemonic resistance has thus been replaced in postmodern accounts with that of meaningless subversive anarchy and, in theories of reflexivity, by the idea of rational but constrained engagement between adult individuals and institutional structures. Some youth transition studies in late modernity are trying to synthesize developmental and reflexive approaches. The aim, following Bourdieu, is to understand how values and aspirations develop (individually, through family socialization, or culturally). The concept of identity capital, drawing broadly on Bourdieu's concept of *habitus* or disposition, is part of this project. It is variously suggested that identity capital in youth may be the product of socialization processes and thus largely ascribed, or achieved as a result of changing social relationships and social roles, or indeed the product of a young person's reflexive understanding of their place in the social structure. The point, though, is that it is always socially embedded. Like the concept of *habitus* it cannot be seen as an individual resource or as part of a linear progression from aspiration to action (Bourdieu, 1987).

Explanations of new social movements have similarly broadened out to merge psychological and economic theories into sociological accounts which reject the idea of linearity and shift towards understanding individual actions as socially as well as individually produced. Melucci showed how involvement in new social movements could fulfil personal psychological needs, while elements of instrumentalism and value rationality appear in recruitment to extreme organizations to this day. Rational action theory cannot therefore be rejected, though its basis can be questioned. If value rationality can be reincorporated with cultural explanations, and indeed with psychoanalytic ones, to explain recruitment to social movements and terrorist organizations, then youth studies could follow suit. Explanations now need to account for different levels of action – collective and individual (and public and private) – and also, following Habermas and Bourdieu, for example, take account of their cultural context. This confirms that individuals should be seen as 'social agents'.

Institutionally individualized biographies

Young people's transitions to adulthood take them from the private sphere of their families to the public sphere of 'adult' institutions such as the housing market and labour market, possibly via transitional opportunities in the peer group. They form part of a lifelong biographical project. In recent decades they have become more extended and their linearity has given way to complexity, comprising different and reversible strands of transition. Furthermore, adulthood has become less easy to define in terms of secure social destinations against which failure or success can be defined. Transitions to adulthood in late modernity therefore bear little resemblance either to the culturally varied patterns of transition or the 'normative timetables' on which some parents still draw for reference, even though some elements of the latter still form the basis of policy assumptions (doing things at the 'wrong age' or in the 'wrong order' is thus constructed according to these outdated normative beliefs).

Transitions appear to be more fluid, simply because they are more complex and less linear, but are actually more constrained by a complex set of institutional structures. The question is whether young people now have the power to shape their transitions to adulthood as personal biographical projects (sometimes referred to as 'biographies of choice') or whether they are only able to act within (or resist) the parameters of standardized 'institutional biographies' (Beck, 1992) or cultural pathways which have been mapped out for them. Welfare and education policies and institutional frameworks determine when they can become economically independent through their own employment and when they can receive social protection, if they need it, from the state. Parents determine whether to support institutional biographies which follow policy expectations or 'traditional' cultural patterns which aim to replicate their own transitions of two or three decades ago. In some families, as well as individuals, there is resistance to imposed change, especially change that they do not understand. Young people have to try to negotiate a passage between the two institutional structures of the state and the family, with their competing norms and values, neither of which may represent their personal aspirations. The result once again could be anomie. Social policy structures change without regard for non-normative cultural beliefs or whether there is a social consensus about their defined objectives (and without necessarily providing justifying evidence). The flexibility needed in order to negotiate risky transitions is in opposition to the rigidity of the policy structures themselves. When young people 'fail' to reach the destinations on the routes mapped out for them, this might therefore be the outcome of institutional failure – the result of policies which fail to recognize the differing and sometimes competing cultural values which contribute to the dispositions and actions of young people and their parents.

The question of biographies of 'choice' is complex. Young people develop values through the socializing influences of their families and schools, and also their peers, but their aspirations (*habitus*) form reflexively through an appraisal of an external structure of opportunities and constraints, and their control beliefs about their own power vis-à-vis that structure. They may be faced with a myriad of choices but their decisions are structured for them and may be beyond their control (as Giddens and Bourdieu both suggest). Ultimately, their power to act according to their aspirations and values depends on their access to individual and external resources. If we follow Bourdieu's theory of practice, then we must see reflexivity rather than causal linearity within this process.

Côté (2002) distinguishes between the passivity associated with 'default individualization', caused by institutional factors, and 'developmental individualization' which allows young people an active and strategic approach to life projects, suggesting that for some young people individualization can be positive. It is this last group which can follow biographies of choice, if they also have access to external resources. Other young people are individualized in a less benign way: they cannot follow established cultural normative practices because the structures needed (such as a youth labour market) no longer exist but must try to follow institutional paths in an individualized way (sometimes without family support). Like adults, they face enormous risks, including the risk of being blamed for the consequences whatever they do (Beck and Beck-Gernsheim, 2002), and yet an illusory belief in their own power to act renders them willing to offer themselves up for this blame (Evans, 2002). Young people have no power or influence over the policies and structures which determine their lives. In many respects, then, institutional individualization puts them more at risk than adults.

Structural inequality in late modernity

Although transitions to adulthood are in general more extended, they have been observed to be more polarized, so that, while the majority of young people are following extended paths, a minority continue to follow the faster routes reminiscent of traditional working-class patterns. In order to understand why this polarization is occurring, we have to move beyond explanations of action as rational or habitual but ultimately individual. Structural and cultural explanations are needed, not just to understand polarized transitions but also to identify the reasons for inequalities which can lead to absolute poverty in youth.

Social class is the main axis of inequality in youth in Britain, cross-cut by gender, ethnicity and, some have argued, age. The multidimensional nature of social structures creates problems for the study of inequalities, but the particular circumstances of young people embarking on a class career which leads from their class of origin to a supposed 'destination' class in adulthood create particular problems. This transition is effectively from ascribed to achieved social class.

Although ascribed class – like other forms of ascription – apparently has less significance in late modernity, it is not at all clear from structural analysis that either intragenerational or intergenerational upward social mobility has really increased in relative terms. This is not just a measurement problem. Young people's class careers have been delayed with the extension of education, and so they remain under the influence of their class of origin for longer, but although education is seen as a route to upward social mobility, it is a route which remains inaccessible to many, and the alternative work route has more or less collapsed with the demise of the youth labour market.

Despite undeniable evidence that social class inequalities persist, it seems that people do not realize this and do not therefore blame the social class structure for social inequality. In a social climate which valorizes wealth accumulation rather than wealth distribution, welfare policies for more than two decades have neglected the structural inequality which produces poverty, side-tracked, according to France (2007: 154) by a 'moralizing agenda' which blamed working-class young people for not acting according to middle-class values.

Both structural and cultural dynamics of social class are needed in a theory of inequality in youth but, given the difficulties in researching structural inequality, the cultural element may still be the most fruitful. The concept of cultural capital is one way of showing *how* structural inequalities affect young people's access to education and begins to explain how class cultures mediated by parents and peers contribute to the reproduction of social advantage and disadvantage. Cultural capital (like identity capital) is not a resource in the same sense as economic capital and can take forms which are disadvantageous (bonding) rather than helping mobility (bridging). Social and cultural capital are, *in conjunction with economic capital*, principal elements of the mechanisms for social reproduction in the family. Understanding the causes of social inequality in youth involves discovering how these mechanisms work in everyday life. This is not just a question of socialization. The focus on education has diverted attention from the way families transmit cultural values such as the work ethic and self-sufficiency and obligation to support. It is the continuing strength of class cultures and the power of family processes in transmitting these which cause the continuation of intergenerational patterns and social reproduction, despite family breakdown. Inequalities in youth can only be understood by examining patterns of family support and dependence and therefore whether young people have access to supportive family life. Murdock and McCron (1976) were wrong; it is dependence, rather than age, that acts as a mediator of class in youth.

Dependence and constraint

Youth transitions involve an age-structured shift from private dependence to public dependence on the state, but I take issue with Sennett's (2004) view that the former is less problematic because it is experienced as less shameful. It has become more difficult for young people to escape dependence on their families because the age of independence is rising, affecting the boundary of responsibility between the state and the family, making private dependence the main 'safety net', and parental support the main source of income for many. The policies which structure parental responsibility and extended dependence in youth should be questioning whether it is realistic to assume that parents will accept an extension of their responsibilities and that young people will accept an extension of their dependence and postpone their autonomy. Does an extension of their responsibility really strengthen the family as neo-liberal commentators have argued? Or rather does it weaken it? The problem is exacerbated with the demographic of an ageing population also needing care: how is social care and support to be apportioned between the state and the family, and how is it to be rationed out between potentially competing groups? The evidence suggests that it can put considerable strain on parent–child relationships, leading in some cases to their breakdown.

The impetus to become independent is strong. Many working-class young people still associate dependence with personal failure and blame themselves, seeing it as contrary to the cultural expectations into which they have been socialized. The reality that their dependence is structured by, and supposedly sanctioned by, government policies does not mitigate these feelings of failure and guilt, which may be exacerbated by negative labelling by peers. Just as forced emancipation leads to increasing individual responsibility and blame (according to Beck and Beck-Gernsheim, 2002), so structured dependence is individualized and responsibility for it laid at the feet of the individual. 'Private' dependence on the family reflects elements of public dependence on the state. Support must similarly be argued for and justified in the family (following Habermas, 1984).

It is only when research gets beneath the surface of family life that a very clear picture emerges of the way that relationships in families are based on mutual obligation and *inter*-dependence. Youth studies had for example been conducted for many decades before research discovered the particular situations of young carers, or young people working in family businesses, by entering into their private domestic worlds. The emphasis on the public side of young people's lives in their leisure styles and their school-to-work transitions has indeed continued to mask the private domestic lives of young people, particularly young men. Parsons referred to youth as a period of irresponsibility; recent research suggests that this is not the case.

In considering young people's relationships with their parents, one could question whether reciprocity and mutual obligation constitute the main social bond (following Douglas), or whether it is unreciprocated dependence which holds the family together through an unequal power relationship (the latter construction on which policies seem to be based, drawing on the functionalist anthropology of Malinowski). Reciprocity, unlike dependence, is associated with mature social relations and mutual respect, potentially freeing young people not only from shame but also from the socializing influence of their parents. The problem for young people wanting to develop mutually dependent and more equal relationships with their parents is that they are no longer able to earn the resources to reciprocate. I would argue that the ability to reciprocate is critical, especially in working-class families where it forms part of a cultural tradition, and where failure to do so is incapacitating and indeed sometimes punished – when for example parents evict their children for not paying board – as research has found.

Individualized generationally

Dependence in youth – whether partial or not – makes it difficult to construct a general social theory which works for young people, but this is precisely why it has to be incorporated into a theory of youth. The problem is that, in youth, social connectedness is needed for the reflexive development of identity and the construction of individual biographies, but scope for reflexivity is limited according to the degree of dependence. Individualization thesis is perhaps easier to understand when applied to adults who are more able to be in a reflexive relationship with the policy structures that affect their lives, or in 'pure relationships' with each other, as described by Giddens. Giddens himself acknowledged that his theories were harder to apply to young people because of socialization. This is why we have to understand the link between structured dependence and forced emancipation, seemingly a contradiction in terms but actually, when family functioning is taken into account, explaining why some young people forced into dependence on unsupporting families become instead forcibly emancipated – and at very great risk.

Structured dependence theoretically puts young people under the control of their parents and paradoxically puts them at risk of 'forced emancipation' at the whim of their parents. In other words, it individualizes them. This forced emancipation – forced because it is the product of the institutional biographies described by Beck – has led to a conception of youth as socially disconnected or disembedded. This construction is the outcome of the way in which the concept of youth has been treated in theory and in practice over the last hundred years. Young people are segregated into age-specific institutions and at times actively excluded from supposedly public spaces. When some form their own defensive social groupings, they merely reinforce a public perception that young people represent a threat to mainstream society.

The emphasis has shifted from local moral panics about specific phenomena or social groups to a generalized panic about young people as a whole (France, 2007). The 'youth question' becomes a matter of public concern. Why? One answer could be in the way that young people have been seen as a social barometer, as indicators of the state of the society they live in, rather than of the state of youth itself. This distinction is important if we are to understand why adults are so suspicious of young people. Is it because young people represent not only a collective future but also, for every adult individual, a projection of their fear of their own imagined and uncertain futures? The scapegoating of young people might thus be seen as a means of gaining control over the future.

Concerns about a lack of social cohesion and the breaking down of generational and other social bonds focus on the part supposedly played by young people. Young people do not have the monopoly on economic dependence or supposed 'structured irresponsibility'. There are many circumstances when individuals may make a transition between dependence and independence, between being a contributor and being a dependant. Demographic changes leading to ageing societies set up a generational divide between the increasing numbers of older people who will need care and the reducing numbers of younger ones who will be expected to care for them. There is fear that young people lack a sense of social obligation (because there is an assumption that responsibility is the prerogative of older age groups). While the mainstream society dreads a future in which older people will lack care, or panics about rising crime, their concerns are largely about themselves. In reality, it is young people who might lack care, or at least compassion, and who might be at greater and more immediate risk. The blame culture – also the prerogative of adults – tends to forget this. The individualization of young people results in their isolation.

The concept of youth may be a shifting social construction rather than an 'absolute', but this does not imply that it lacks authenticity or that it has become distanced from young people. A sound and workable theory of youth can evolve out of the foundations laid in the past so that, as is the practice in science, we can (like Isaac Newton) 'stand on the shoulders of giants' rather than abandon theoretical work which still has relevance. However, we also need to move from applying piecemeal elements of more recent theories appropriate to late or postmodernity to a greater understanding of how young people fit into the whole theory rather than politically acceptable bits of it. It is critical to identify the nature and sources of cultural differences and of the differential impacts of public and private institutions. By doing all of this, we can begin to understand local and global variation in young people's lives. Most importantly, though, we must accommodate in any theory of youth key features which make this theorizing difficult and which have been explored throughout this book – firstly, the changes in the social context of youth, affecting the societies and social institutions which frame young people's lives; second, the multiplicity of transitions from private to public spheres which take place during this part of the life course; and thirdly, the relationship of independence to these. When 'youth' is taken to mean age, then it really is 'just a word'.

Notes

Chapter 1   What is 'Youth'?

1   The concept of *Sturm und Drang* (storm and stress) developed through an eighteenth-century German romantic literary move-ment to denote youthful genius in rebellion against accepted standards.

2   Shakespeare, *The Winter's Tale*, Act III, Scene III; Socrates, cited in Brake (1980).

3   In Lincoln Barnett's *The Universe and Dr Einstein* (New York: W. Sloane, 1950).

4   The idea that youth is on a threshold between statuses rather than a status in itself is picked up again in the use of the label 'thresholders' to describe those experiencing extended depen-dence (chapter 4).

5   Norbert Elias (1982) and Habermas (1984) both paralleled the development of societies and that of young people, sometimes using youth as a metaphor for society.

6   In Eastern Europe, postmodern can imply post-Soviet rather than poststructural in a wider sociological sense.

Chapter 2   Youth as Action

1   A clear example of this emerged when the announcement of the raising of the age of compulsory education or training to 17 years by 2013 and 18 years by 2015 was accompanied by the

announcement that there would be *penalties* for those who do not comply.

2 The influence of the deep ideological divisions between fascism and communism is very apparent in the development of post-war structuralism. Many of the writers were themselves involved in the war, interned or imprisoned (such as Althusser and Gramsci) or fleeing fascism and Nazism (such as Mannheim). Edmunds and Turner (2002: 49) comment on these groups as 'intellectual generations'. Similarly, a generation of social scientists was greatly affected by the radical changes of the 1960s in technology, gender and race relations, collapse of imperialism, etc.

3 The CCCS, set up in 1964 (and controversially closed in 2002), was key to the development of cultural studies in the UK and was arguably the most influential centre there has ever been for youth studies in the UK.

4 Claude Lévi-Strauss saw cultures as systems of symbolic communication for which myth had social value and thus distanced himself from the functionalism of Malinowski who suggested that magical beliefs – myths – arise as a means of gaining a sense of individual control over the unpredictable, rather than to fulfil the needs of society as a whole.

5 Game theory similarly suggests that even where mutual benefit would be gained through collaboration, rational action is still more likely to be driven by individual self-interest, despite greater risk of failure.

6 Policy constructions of responsibility and age are confusing (Jones and Bell, 2000). For example, the age of criminal responsibility is currently ten years in England and Wales, and eight years in Scotland. There was, however, in England and Wales a common law *doli incapax* presumption that a child under 14 does not know the difference between right and wrong; this was abolished in 1998.

Chapter 3   Youth as Identity

1 Georg Simmel (2004 [1900]) saw economic exchange as a social fact from which money derives meaning. Mary Douglas (1990) developed the idea of goods and commodities as symbols. Roland Barthes (1983) studied ways that bourgeois society asserted its values by manipulating signs, for example through fashion – fashion being a badge of inclusion and confirmation of identity and, because of its transitory nature, also a means of

organizing time. These ideas were later developed in the work of Baudrillard.

Chapter 4   Youth as Transition

1   The National Child Development Study (NCDS) and the Birth Cohort Study (BCS70) are birth cohorts of young people born in 1958 and 1970 respectively. Each study has involved longitudinal tracking over time.

2   The anthropologist Mary Douglas developed a cultural theory of risk (1980, with Wildavsky). She argued that social structures generate 'cultural biases', similar to dispositions, which help maintain the social structure, differentiated by social status (grid) and social attachment (group). The principal dispositions are: *individualist* (low grid, low group – unconstrained by social ties, valuing individual initiative and willing to take risks); *egalitarian* (low grid, high group – clinging to traditional ways of life and unwilling to take risks); *hierarchist* (high grid, high group – needing rules and fearing deviance); and *fatalist* (high grid, low group – isolated and passive). Applied to young people, this would suggest that those most likely to take risks would be young people of working-class origin without social responsibilities, while those least likely to take risks would be socially integrated and conformist middle-class young people, or socially integrated working class (who cling to tradition).

3   Andy Furlong, personal communication, 14 March 2005.

4   Emler and McNamara (1996) comment that too little attention has been given to young people's social relationships during transitions to adulthood. Their study of 18–19-year-olds found that roles as family or household members, and in the institutions of education and work, provided young people with *almost all the basis for their informal social lives*. Lack of a formal role was not compensated for in other ways and meant lack of informal social contacts – thus unemployment could lead to social isolation.

Chapter 5   Youth and Inequality

1   Examples might include much of the debate on social class schemata between Goldthorpe and his Nuffield colleagues, and his Cambridge critics Blackburn and Prandy, during the 1980s and early 1990s.

2 The resulting typology comprised: intergenerationally 'stable' groups of middle class and of working class who from the start appeared to reproduce their class of origin in their own careers; intragenerationally mobile groups who improved on their class of origin (educationally mobile working class and work-route working class); and two groups of downwardly mobile middle class, one of which regained their class of origin through 'counter-mobility', while the other remained in a lower class position (Jones, 1987).

3 This description appears in the European Commission's call for research on social exclusion under the *Sixth Framework Programme*.

4 Though prospects for joined-up UK policy-making will reduce as devolution takes increasing effect in Scotland and Wales.

Chapter 6   Youth and Dependence

1 Similarly, public sector housing has never really catered for single young people unless they were specifically identified as 'at risk' (Jones, 1995; Jones and Bell, 2000; Ford et al., 2002).

2 Thus, all under-18s living in the parental home were to be treated as dependent unless they had full-time jobs, and support would be paid to their parents/carers who would be 'compensated' for the extension of their parental responsibility through Child Benefit and Child Tax Credit. Welfare support was to be paid direct to young people if they were living independently. There was some further recognition of young people's individual needs in the extension of the NMW to cover 16–17-year-olds, who had previously been excluded, and in the payment of financial 'learning incentives' to them.

3 According to the regulations governing the Household Means Test in the 1930s, employed young adults living with unemployed parents were expected to support them. In many families this was seen as contrary to their own constructions of family responsibility, with the result that many employed young people left their parental homes so that their parents received state support (an action unanticipated by policy-makers and regarded by the authorities as 'collusive desertion') (Finch, 1989).

4 This is currently important in Japan where there is concern that family members will not care for the increasing proportion of older people, but it is also a concern in countries with more developed welfare states where there is a diminishing pool of contributors.

References

Abrams, P. (1961). *The Teenage Consumer*. London: London Press Exchange.

Allatt, P. and Dixon, C. (2000/2001). 'From "work, rest and play" to "work, work, work": understanding the new A-level constituency', Newsletter, Youth Citizenship and Social Change, An ESRC Research Programme, Winter/Spring, pp. 9–10.

Allatt, P. and Yeandle, S. (1992). *Youth Unemployment and the Family: Voices of Disordered Times*. London: Routledge.

Allen, S. (1973). 'Some theoretical problems in the study of youth', in H. Silverstein (ed.), *The Sociology of Youth: Evolution and Revolution*. New York: Macmillan.

Althusser, L. (1965). *For Marx* (trans. B. Brewster). London: Verso.

— (1971). 'Ideology and ideological state apparatuses', in *Lenin and Philosophy and Other Essays*, London: New Left Books.

Anderson, M., Bechhofer, F. and Gershuny, J. (eds) (1994). *The Social and Political Economy of the Household*. Oxford: Oxford University Press.

Anderson, M., Bechhofer, F., McCrone, D., Jamieson, L., Li, Y. and Stewart, R. (2005). 'Timespans and plans among young adults', *Sociology* 39(1): 139–55.

Apter, T. (2001). *The Myth of Maturity*. New York: W. W. Norton.

Ariès, P. (1962). *Centuries of Childhood* (trans. R. Baldick). New York: Vintage Books.

Arnett, J. (2004). *Emerging Adulthood: The Winding Road from Late Teens through the Twenties*. Oxford: Oxford University Press.

Attias-Donfut, C. and Wolff, F.-C. (2000). 'Complementarity between public and private transfers', in S. Arber and C. Attias-Donfut (eds), *The Myth of Generational Conflict: Family and State in Ageing Societies*. London: Routledge.

Bancroft, A., Wilson, S., Cunningham-Burley, S., Backet-Milburn, K. and Masters, H. (2004). *Parental Drug and Alcohol Misuse: Resilience and Transition among Young People*. York: Joseph Rowntree Foundation.

Bandura, A. (1959). 'The stormy decade: fact or fiction?' in D. Rogers (ed.), *Issues in Adolescent Psychology*. New York: Appleton-Century-Crofts.

Banks, M., Bates, I., Breakwell, G., Bynner, J., Emler, N., Jamieson, L. and Roberts, K. (1992). *Careers and Identities*. Buckingham: Open University Press.

Barthes, R. (1983). *The Fashion System* (trans. M. Ward and R. Howard). Berkeley: University of California Press.

Bates, I. and Riseborough, G. (eds) (1993). *Youth and Inequality*. Buckingham: Open University Press.

Baudrillard, J. (1983). *Simulation* (trans. P. Foss et al.). New York: Semiotext(e).

— (1988). *The Ecstasy of Communication*. New York Semiotext(e).

— (1990 [1983]). *Fatal Strategies*. New York: Semiotext(e).

— (1993). *Symbolic Exchange and Death* (trans. I. Hamilton Grant). London: Sage.

— (1998 [1970]). *The Consumer Society: Myths and Structures*. London: Sage.

— (2002) 'Requiem for the Twin Towers', in *The Spirit of Terrorism and Other Essays* (trans. C. Turner). London: Verso.

Bauman, Z. (1995). *Life in Fragments: Essays in Postmodern Morality*. Oxford: Blackwell.

— (2001). *Community: Seeking Safety in an Insecure World*. Cambridge: Polity.

Beck, U. (1992). *The Risk Society: Towards a New Modernity* (trans. M. Ritter). London: Sage.

Beck, U. and Beck-Gernsheim, E. (2002). *Individualization*. London: Sage.

Becker, H. (1963). *Outsiders: Studies in the Sociology of Deviance*. New York: Free Press.

Behrens, M. and Evans, K. (2002). 'Taking control of their lives? A comparison of the experiences of unemployed young adults (18–25) in England and the new Germany', *Comparative Education* 38(1): 2–28.

Bell, C. (1968). *Middle Class Families*. London: Routledge and Kegan Paul.

Bell, R. and Jones, G. (2002). *Youth Policies in the UK: A Chronological Map* (2nd edn.). http://www.keele.ac.uk/depts/so/youthchron/index.htm

Bennett, A. (1999). 'Subcultures or Neo-Tribes: rethinking the relationship between youth, style and musical taste', *Sociology* 33(3): 599–617.

— (2006). 'Punk's not dead: the continuing significance of Punk Rock for an older generation of fans', *Sociology* 40(2): 219–35.

Bensman, J. (1973). 'American youth and the class structure', in H. Silverstein (ed.), *The Sociology of Youth: Evolution and Revolution*. New York: Macmillan.

Berger, B. (1963). 'Adolescence and beyond', *Social Problems* 10: 394–408.

Bertaux, D. (1981). 'From the life history approach to the transformation of sociological practice', in D. Bertaux (ed.), *Biography and Society*. London: Sage.

Bertaux, D. and Thompson, P. (eds) (1997). *Pathways to Social Class: A Qualitative Approach to Social Mobility*. Oxford: Clarendon Press.

Berthoud, R. (1999). *Young Caribbean Men and the Labour Market: A Comparison with Other Ethnic Groups*. York: York Publishing Services.

Biggart, A. and Furlong, A. (1996). 'Educating "discouraged workers": cultural diversity in the upper secondary school', *British Journal of Sociology of Education* 17(3): 253–66.

Bignall, T. and Butt, J. (2000). *Between Ambition and Achievement: Young Black Disabled People's Views and Experiences of Independence and Independent Living*. Bristol: Policy Press and the Joseph Rowntree Foundation.

Blackman, S. (2005). 'Youth subcultural theory: a critical engagement with the concepts, its origins and politics, from the Chicago School to postmodernism', *Journal of Youth Studies* 8(1): 1–20.

Boeck, T., Fleming, J. and Kemshall, H. (2005). 'The role of social capital in young people's navigation of risk pathways.' Paper presented to the BSA Annual Conference, *Life Course: Fragmentation, Diversity and Risk*. University of York (March).

Bourdieu, P. (1977). *Outline of a Theory of Practice* (trans. R. Nice). Cambridge: Cambridge University Press.

— (1978). 'La jeunesse n'est qu'un mot.' Interview with Anne-Marie Métailié, reprinted in *Les jeunes et le premier emploi*. Paris: Association des Ages, pp. 520–30.

— (1984). *Distinction: A Social Critique of the Judgement of Taste* (trans. R. Nice). London: Routledge.

— (1986). 'The forms of capital', in J. Richardson (ed.), *Handbook of Theory and Research for the Sociology of Education*, pp. 241–58. New York: Greenwood Press.

— (1987). *Choses Dites*. Paris: Editions de Minuit.

Bourdieu, P. and Passeron, J.-C. (1973). 'Cultural reproduction and social reproduction', in R. Brown (ed.), *Knowledge, Education and Cultural Change*. London: Tavistock.

— (1977). *Reproduction in Education, Society and Culture*. London: Sage.

Bourdieu, P. and Wacquant, L. J. D. (1992). *An Invitation to Reflexive Sociology*. Cambridge: Polity.

Bowlby, J. (1953). *Child Care and the Growth of Love*. Harmondsworth: Penguin Books.

Bradley, H. (1996). *Fractured Identities: Changing Patterns of Inequality*. Cambridge: Polity.

Bradley, H. and van Hoof, J. (eds) (2005). *Young People in Europe: Labour Markets and Citizenship*. Bristol: Policy Press.

Brake, M. (1980). *The Sociology of Youth Culture and Youth Subcultures*. London: Routledge and Kegan Paul.

— (1985). *Comparative Youth Culture: The Sociology of Youth Cultures and Youth in America, Britain and Canada*. London: Routledge and Kegan Paul.

Brannen, J. and Nilson, A. (2002). 'Young people's time perspectives: from youth to adulthood', *Sociology* 36(3): 513–36.

Brannen, J. and Wilson, G. (eds) (1987). *Give and Take in Families*. London: Allen and Unwin.

Brannen, J., Dodd, K., Oakley, A. and Storey, P. (1994). *Young People, Health and Family Life*. Buckingham: Open University Press.

Briggs, A. and Cobbley, B. (1999) ' "I like my shit sagged": youth, black musics and fashion', *Journal of Youth Studies* 2(3): 337–52.

Britton, L., Chatrik, B., Coles, B., Craig, G., Hylton, C. and Mumtaz, S. (2002). *Missing ConneXions: The Career Dynamics and Welfare Needs of Black and Minority Ethnic Young People at the Margins*. Bristol: Policy Press.

Brown, P. (1987). *Schooling Ordinary Kids*. London: Tavistock.

— (1996) 'Cultural capital and social exclusion: some observations on recent trends in education, employment and the labour market', in H. Helve and J. Bynner (eds), *Youth and Life Management: Research Perspectives*. Helsinki: Helsinki University Press.

Bühler, C. (1933). *Der Menschliche Lebenslauf als Psychologisches Problem (The Course of Human Life as a Psychological Problem)*. Leipzig: Hirzel.

Bulmer, M. (1978). 'Social structure and social change in the twentieth century', in M. Bulmer (ed.), *Mining and Social Change: Durham County in the Twentieth Century*. London: Croom Helm.

Bynner. J. (2005). 'Rethinking the youth phase of the life-course: the case for emerging adulthood?' *Journal of Youth Studies* 8(4): 367–84.

Bynner, J., Elias, P., McKnight, A., Pan, H. and Pierre, G. (2002). *Young People's Changing Routes to Independence*. York: Joseph Rowntree Foundation.

Bynner, J., Londra, M. and Jones, G. (2004). *The Impact of Government Policy on Social Exclusion among Young People: A Review of the Literature for the Social Exclusion Unit in the Breaking the Cycle Series*. London: Office of the Deputy Prime Minister.

Campbell, A. (1981). *Girl Delinquents*. Oxford: Blackwell.

Carter, M. P. (1975). 'Teenage workers: a second chance at eighteen?' in Brannen, P. (ed.), *Entering the World of Work: Some Sociological Perspectives*. London: Department of Employment.

Catan, L. (2004). 'Changing youth transitions in the 21st century: a synthesis of findings from the ESRC research programme', *Youth Citizenship and Social Change*. Brighton: TSA.

Chaney, D. (1996). *Lifestyles*. London: Routledge.

Christie, H., Munro, M. and Rettig, H. (2002). 'Making ends meet: student incomes and debt', *Studies in Higher Education* 26(3): 363–83.

Cieslik, M. and Simpson, D. (2005). 'The role of basic skills in transitions to adulthood.' Paper presented to the BSA Annual Conference (March) *Life Course: Fragmentation, Diversity and Risk*. University of York.

Clarke, J., Hall, S., Jefferson, T. and Roberts, B. (1976). 'Subcultures, cultures and class: a theoretical overview', in S. Hall and T. Jefferson (eds), *Resistance Through Rituals*. London: Hutchinson.

Coffield, F., Borrill, C. and Marshall, S. (1986). *Growing Up at the Margins*. Milton Keynes: Open University Press.

Cohen, A. K. (1955). *Delinquent Boys: The Subculture of the Gang*. London: Collier-Macmillan.

Cohen, A. P. (1985). *The Symbolic Construction of Community*. London: Routledge.

Cohen, P. (1997). *Rethinking the Youth Question: Education, Labour and Cultural Studies*, 2nd edn. Basingstoke: Macmillan.

Cohen, S. (1973). *Folk Devils and Moral Panics*. St Albans: Paladin.

Coleman, J. C. (1974). *Relationships in Adolescence*. London: Routledge and Kegan Paul.

Coleman, J. S. (1961). *The Adolescent Society*. New York: Free Press.

— (1988). 'Social capital in the creation of human capital', *American Journal of Sociology* 94: S95–S120.

— (1990). *Foundations of Social Theory*. Cambridge, Mass.: Belknap Press.

Comte, A. (2003 [1855]) *Positive Philosophy of Auguste Comte, Part I* (trans. H. Martineau). Whitefish, MT: Kessinger Publishing.

Corrigan, P. (1979). *Schooling the Smash Street Kids*. London: Macmillan.

Côté, J. E. (2000). *Arrested Adulthood: The Changing Nature of Identity and Maturity in the Late-Modern World*. New York: New York University Press.

— (2002). 'The role of identity capital in the transition to adulthood: the individualisation thesis examined', *Journal of Youth Studies* 5(2): 117–34.

Croghan, R., Griffin, C., Hunter, J. and Phoenix, A. (2006). 'Style failure: consumption, identity and social exclusion', *Journal of Youth Studies* 9(4): 463–78.

Crow, G. (1989). 'The use of the concept of "strategy" in recent sociological literature', *Sociology* 23(1): 1–24.

Dean, H. (1995). 'Paying for children', in H. Dean (ed.), *Parents' Duties, Children's Debts*. Aldershot: Arena.

Dearden, C. and Becker, S. (2000). *Growing Up Caring: Vulnerability and Transition to Adulthood – Young Carers' Experiences*. Leicester: Youth Work Press and the Joseph Rowntree Foundation.

de Certau, M. (1988). *The Practice of Everyday Life*. Berkeley: University of California Press.

Dennis, N. and Erdos, G. (1992). *Families without Fatherhood*. Choice in Welfare Series No. 12. London: Institute of Economic Affairs, Health and Welfare Unit.

Devine, F. (1998). 'Class analysis and the stability of class relations', *Sociology* 32(1): 23–41.

Dolton, P. (2002). 'Routes: a comparative and holistic study of youth transitions in the North-East of England.' End-of-award report to the ESRC (L234251001). www.regard.ac.uk.

Dolton, P., Makepeace, G., Sutton, S. and Audas, R. (1999). *Making the Grade: Education, the Labour Market and Young People*. Work and Opportunity Series No 15. York: York Publishing and the Joseph Rowntree Foundation.

Douglas, M. (with A. Wildavsky) (1982 [1980]). *Risk and Culture*. Berkeley, CA: University of California Press.

— (1990). 'No free gifts', foreword to M. Mauss, *The Gift*. London: Routledge.

Downes, D. (1966). *The Delinquent Solution*. London: Routledge and Kegan Paul.

Downes, D. and Rock, P. (1982). *Understanding Deviance*. Oxford: Clarendon Press.

du Bois-Reymond, M. (1998). 'I don't want to commit myself yet', *Journal of Youth Studies* 1(1): 63–79.

Durkheim, E. (1951 [1897]). *Suicide: A Study in Sociology* (trans. J. A. Spaulding and G. Simpson). New York: Free Press.

— (1984). *The Division of Labor in Society* (trans. W. D. Halls). New York: Free Press.

Edmunds, J. and Turner, B. (2002). *Generations, Culture and Society*. Buckingham: Open University Press.

Eisenstadt, S. N. (1973 [1956]). 'From generation to generation', reprinted in H. Silverstein (ed.), *The Sociology of Youth: Evolution and Revolution*. New York: Macmillan.

Elias, N. (1982 [1939]). *The Civilizing Process, Vol. 2: State Formation and Civilization*. Oxford: Blackwell.

Elliott, A. (2001). *Concepts of the Self*. Cambridge: Polity.

Elliott, B. (1997). 'Migration, mobility and social processes: Scottish migrants in Canada', in D. Bertaux and P. Thompson (eds), *Pathways to Social Class: A Qualitative Approach to Social Mobility*. Oxford: Clarendon Press.

Emler, N. (2001). *Self-Esteem: The Costs and Causes of Low Self-Worth*. York: Joseph Rowntree Foundation.

Emler, N. and McNamara, S. (1996). 'The social contact patterns of young people: effects of participation in the social institutions of family, education and work', in H. Helve and J. Bynner (eds), *Youth and Life Management: Research Perspectives*. Helsinki: Helsinki University Press.

Erikson, E. H. (1965). *Childhood and Society*. Harmondsworth: Penguin Books.

— (1968). *Identity: Youth and Crisis*. New York: W. W. Norton.

European Commission (2001). *A New Impetus for European Youth*. White Paper, COM(2001)681, Brussels: Commission of the European Communities.

Evans, K. (2002). 'Taking control of their lives? Agency in young adult transitions in England and the New Germany', *Journal of Youth Studies* 5(3): 245–70.

Evans, K. and Furlong, A. (1997). 'Metaphors of youth transitions: niches, pathways, trajectories or navigations', in J. Bynner, L.

Chisholm and A. Furlong (eds), *Youth, Citizenship and Social Change in a European Context*. Aldershot: Ashgate.

Evans, K. and Heinz, W. R. (1994). *Becoming Adults in England and Germany*. London: Anglo-German Foundation.

Evans, K., Rudd, P., Behrens, M., Kaluza, J. and Woolley, C. (2001). 'Reconstructing fate as choice? Initial findings from the comparative study "Taking Control: personal agency and social structures in young adult transitions in England and the new Germany",' *Young* 9(3): 2–9.

Evans-Pritchard, E. E. (1951). *Kinship and Marriage among the Nuer*. Oxford: Oxford University Press.

Ferri, E., Bynner, J. and Wadsworth, M. (2003). *Changing Britain: Changing Lives: Three Generations at the Turn of the Century*. Bedford Way Papers. London: University of London, Institute of Education.

Ferri, E. and Smith, K. (2003). 'Partnerships and parenthood', in E. Ferri, J. Bynner and M. Wadsworth (eds), *Changing Britain, Changing Lives: Three Generations at the Turn of the Century*. London: University of London, Institute of Education.

Feuer, L. S. (1969). *The Conflict of Generations*. London: Heinemann.

Finch, J. (1989). *Family Obligations and Social Change*. Cambridge: Polity.

Finch, J. and Mason, J. (1993). *Negotiating Family Responsibilities*. London: Routledge.

Flammer, A. (1997). 'Developmental analysis of control beliefs', in A. Bandura (ed.), *Self-Efficacy in Changing Societies*. Cambridge: Cambridge University Press.

Ford, J., Rugg, J. and Burrows, R. (2002). *Young People, Housing, and the Transition to Adult Life*. ESRC End-of-award report. www.regard.ac.uk

Forsyth, A. and Furlong, A. (2000). *Socio-Economic Disadvantage and Access to Higher Education*. Bristol: Policy Press and the Joseph Rowntree Foundation.

— (2001). *Socio-Economic Disadvantage and Experience in Further and Higher Education*. Bristol: Policy Press and the Joseph Rowntree Foundation.

Foucault, M. (1978). *The History of Sexuality. Volume I: An Introduction* (trans. R. Hurley). London: Penguin Books.

— (1988). 'Technologies of the self', in L. H. Martin, H. Gutman and P. H. Hutton (eds), *Technologies of the Self*. London: Tavistock.

— (1995 [1977]). *Discipline and Punish: The Birth of the Prison* (trans. A. Sheridan). New York: Vintage Books.

France, A. (2007). *Understanding Youth in Late Modernity.* Buckingham: Open University Press.

Freud, A. (1937). *The Ego and the Mechanisms of Defence.* London: Hogarth Press.

Freud, S. (1953–1974). 'An outline of psychoanalysis', in J. Strachey (ed.), *Standard Edition of the Complete Psychological Works,* Vol. 23. London: Hogarth.

Friedenberg, E. Z. (1963). *Coming of Age in America.* New York: Vintage Books.

— (1973). 'The vanishing adolescent', in H. Silverstein (ed.), *The Sociology of Youth: Evolution and Revolution.* New York: Macmillan.

Frith, S. (1978). *The Sociology of Rock.* London: Constable.

Furlong, A. (1992). *Growing Up in a Classless Society? School to Work Transitions.* Edinburgh: Edinburgh University Press.

Furlong, A. and Cartmel, F. (1997). *Young People and Social Change.* Buckingham: Open University Press.

— (2004). *Vulnerable Young Men in Fragile Labour Markets: Employment, Unemployment and the Search for Long-term Security.* York: Joseph Rowntree Foundation.

Furlong, A., Cartmel, F., Biggart, A., Sweeting, H. and West, P. (2003). *Youth Transitions: Patterns of Vulnerability and Processes of Social Inclusion.* Edinburgh: Scottish Executive, Social Research.

Galland, O. (1984). 'Précarité et entrées dans la vie', *Revue Française de Sociologie,* 25(1): 49–66.

— (1990). 'Un nouvel âge de la vie', *Revue Française de Sociologie,* 31(4): 529–51.

— (1995). 'Changing family transitions: young people and new ways of life in France', in L. Chisholm, P. Büchner, H.-H. Krüger and M. du-Bois Reymond (eds), *Growing Up in Europe.* Berlin/ New York: de Gruyter.

— (2001). 'Adolescence, post-adolescence, jeunesse: retour sur quelques interprétations', *Revue Française de Sociologie* 42(4): 611–40.

Gallie, D. (1994). 'Are the unemployed an underclass? Some evidence from the Social Change and Economic Life Initiative', *Sociology* 28(3): 737–57.

Ghate, D. and Hazel, N. (2004). *Parenting in Poor Environments: Stress, Support and Coping.* London: Policy Research Bureau.

Giddens, A. (1984). *The Constitution of Society.* Cambridge: Polity.

— (1991). *Modernity and Self-Identity: Self and Society in the Late Modern Age.* Cambridge: Polity.

— (1992). *The Transformation of Intimacy*. Cambridge: Polity.

— (1994). 'Living in a post-traditional society', in U. Beck, A. Giddens and S. Lash, *Reflexive Modernization: Politics, Tradition and Aesthetics in the Modern Social Order*. Cambridge: Polity.

— (1996). 'Reason without revolution: Habermas's *Theory of Communicative Action*', in *In Defence of Sociology*. Cambridge: Polity.

Gillies, V. (2005). 'Raising the "meritocracy": parenting and the individualization of social class', *Sociology* 39(5): 838–53.

Gillies, V., Ribbens McCarthy, J. and Holland, J. (2001). *'Pulling Together, Pulling Apart': The Family Lives of Young People*. London: Family Policy Studies Centre and the Joseph Rowntree Foundation.

Gillis, J. R. (1981). *Youth and History: Tradition and Change in Age Relations, 1770–Present*. New York: Academic Press.

Goffman, E. (1956). *The Presentation of Self in Everyday Life*. Harmondsworth: Penguin Books.

Goldscheider, F. K. and Goldscheider, K. (1999). *The Changing Transition to Adulthood*. London: Sage.

Goldthorpe, J. H. (1980). *Social Mobility and Class Structure in Modern Britain*. Oxford: Clarendon Press.

— (1988). 'The intellectuals and the working class', in D. Rose (ed.), *Social Stratification and Economic Change*. London: Hutchinson.

— (1996). 'Class analysis and the reorientation of class theory: the case of persisting differences in educational attainment', *British Journal of Sociology* 47(3): 481–505.

— (1998). 'Rational action theory for sociology', *British Journal of Sociology* 49(2): 167–92.

Goldthorpe, J. H., Lockwood, D., Beckhofer, F. and Platt, J. (1969). *The Affluent Worker in the Class Structure*. Cambridge: Cambridge University Press.

Goodey, J. (2001). 'The criminalization of British Asian youth: research from Bradford and Sheffield', *Journal of Youth Studies* 4(4): 429–50.

Graham, J. and Bowling, B. (1995). *Young People and Crime*. Research Study 145. London: Home Office.

Gramsci, A. (1971). *Selections from the Prison Notebooks* (ed. and trans. Q. Hoare and G. N. Smith). London: Lawrence and Wishart.

Greener, T. and Hollands, R. (2006). 'Beyond subculture and post-subculture? The case of virtual psytrance', *Journal of Youth Studies* 9(4): 393–418.

Grieco, M. (1987). *Keeping it in the Family: Social Networks and Employment Change*. London: Tavistock.

Griffin, C. (1985). *Typical Girls?* London: Routledge and Kegan Paul.

— (1993). *Representations of Youth: The Study of Youth and Adolescence in Britain and America*. Cambridge: Polity.

— (1997). 'Youth research in the 1990s: time for (another) rethink', *Sociological Research Online*, www.socresonline.org.uk/2/4/griffin.html. Accessed 19.08.08.

Guillemard, A.-M. (2000). *Aging and the Welfare State Crisis*. Cranbury, NJ: Delaware University Press.

Habermas, J. (1984). *The Theory of Communicative Action*, Vol. 1. London: Heinemann.

Hall, G. Stanley (1904). *Adolescence*. New York: Appleton.

Hall, S. (1980). 'Cultural studies and the centre: some problematics and perspectives', in S. Hall, D. Hobson, A. Lowe and P. Willis (eds), *Culture, Media, Language*. London: Routledge.

Hall, S. and Jefferson, T. (eds) (1976). *Resistance through Rituals*. London: Hutchinson.

Hall, S. et al. (1976). 'Youth: a stage in life?' *Youth in Society* 17: 17–19 [co-authors not known].

Halsey, A. H., Heath, A. F. and Ridge, J. M. (1980). *Origins and Destinations: Family, Class and Education in Modern Britain*. Oxford: Clarendon Press.

Hareven, T. K. (1982). *Family Time and Industrial Time*. Cambridge: Cambridge University Press.

Harris, C. C. (1983). *The Family and Industrial Society*. London: George Allen and Unwin.

— (1987). 'The individual and society: a processual approach', in A. Bryman, B. Bytheway, P. Allatt and T. Keil (eds), *Rethinking the Life Cycle*. London: Macmillan.

Harris, C., Roach, P., Behrens, M., Amory, D. and Yusuf, R. (2003). *Emergent Citizens? African-Caribbean and Pakistani Young People in Birmingham and Bradford*. Leicester: Youth Work Press.

Harris, N. S. (1989). *Social Security for Young People*. Aldershot: Avebury.

Hatcher, R. (1988). 'Class differentiation in education: rational choices?', *British Journal of Sociology of Education* 19(1): 5–24.

Havighurst, R. J. and Dreyer, P. H. (eds) (1975). *Youth*. Chicago: National Society for the Study of Education.

Heath, S. and Cleaver, E. (2003). *Young, Free and Single: Twenty-Somethings and Household Change*. Basingstoke: Palgrave Macmillan.

Heath, S. and Kenyon, L. (2001). 'Young single professionals and shared household living', *Journal of Youth Studies* 4(1): 83–100.

Hebdige, D. (1976). 'The Meaning of Mod', in S. Hall and T. Jefferson (eds), *Resistance Through Rituals: Youth Subcultures in Post-War Britain*. London: Hutchinson.

— (1979). *Subculture: The Meaning of Style*. London: Methuen.

— (1999). 'The function of subculture', in S. During (ed.), *The Cultural Studies Reader*, 2nd edn. New York, Routledge, pp. 441–50.

Heinz, W. (2002). 'Self-socialisation and post-traditional society', *Advances in Life Course Research* 7: 41–64.

Henderson, S. J., Holland, J., McGrellis, S., Sharpe, S. and Thomson, R. (2006). *Inventing Adulthoods: A Biographical Approach to Youth Transitions*. London: Sage.

Hesmondhalgh, D. (2005). 'Subcultures, scenes or tribes? None of the above', *Journal of Youth Studies* 8(1): 21–40.

HM Treasury, DfES and DWP (2004). *Supporting Young People to Achieve: Towards a New Deal for Skills. Inter-departmental Review of Financial Support for 16–19-Year Olds*. London: HMSO.

Hoggart, R. (1958). *The Uses of Literacy*. Harmondsworth: Pelican Books.

Holdsworth, C. and Morgan, D. (2005). *Transitions in Context: Independence, Adulthood and Home*. Buckingham: Open University Press.

Howe, N. and Strauss, W. (2000). *Millennials Rising*. New York: Vintage Books.

Hussain, Y. and Bagguley, P. (2005). 'Citizenship, ethnicity and identity: British Pakistanis after the 2001 "Riots"', *Sociology* 39(3): 407–25.

Hutson, S. and Jenkins, R. (1989). *Taking the Strain: Families, Unemployment and the Transition to Adulthood*. Milton Keynes: Open University Press.

Hutson, S. and Liddiard, M. (1994). *Youth Homelessness: The Construction of a Social Issue*. Basingstoke: Macmillan.

Hutton, S. and Seavers, J. (2002). 'How young people use, understand and manage money', Research Briefing No. 10, ESRC Youth Citizenship and Social Change research programme.

Iacovou, M. and Berthoud, R. (2001). *Young People's Lives: A Map of Europe*. Colchester: University of Essex, Institute for Social and Economic Research.

IARD (2001). *Study on the State of Young People and Youth Policy in Europe*. Report for the European Commission DG for Education and Culture. Contract n. 1999–1734/001-001. Mimeo. Milan: IARD.

Irwin, S. (1995). *Rights of Passage: Social Change and the Transition from Youth to Adulthood*. London: UCL Press.

Jackson, S., Ajayi, S. and Quigley, M. (2005). *Going to University from Care*. London: University of London, Institute of Education.

Jahoda, M. and Warren, N. (1965). 'The myths of youth', *Sociology of Education* 38(2): 138–49.

Jamieson, L. (1998). *Intimacy: Personal Relationships in Modern Society*. Cambridge: Polity.

— (2000). 'Migration, place and class: youth in a rural area', *Sociological Review* 48: 203–23.

Jamieson, L., Stewart, R., Li, Y., Anderson, M., Bechhofer, F. and McCrone, D. (2003). 'Single, 20-something and seeking?' in G. Allan and G. Jones (eds), *Social Relations and the Life Course*. London: Palgrave.

Jefferson, T. (1976). 'Cultural responses of the Teds: the defence of space and status', in S. Hall and T. Jefferson (eds), *Resistance Through Rituals: Youth Subcultures in Post-War Britain*. London: Hutchinson.

Jenkins, R. (1983). *Lads, Citizens and Ordinary Kids*. London: Routledge and Kegan Paul.

— (1992). *Pierre Bourdieu*. London: Routledge.

— (1996). *Social Identity*. London: Routledge.

Jenks, C. (1996). *Childhood*. London: Routledge.

Johnston, L., MacDonald, R., Mason, P., Ridley, L. and Webster, C. (2000). *Snakes and Ladders: Young People, Transitions and Alternative Careers*. Bristol: Policy Press and the Joseph Rowntree Foundation.

Jones, G. (1987). 'Young workers in the class structure', *Work, Employment and Society* 1(4): 486–507.

— (1988). 'Integrating process and structure in the concept of youth', *Sociological Review* 36(4): 706–31.

— (1992). 'Short-term reciprocity in parent–child economic relations', in C. Marsh and S. Arber (eds), *Families and Households: Divisions and Change*. Basingstoke: Macmillan.

— (1995). *Leaving Home*. Buckingham: Open University Press.

— (1997). 'Youth homelessness and the underclass', in R. Macdonald (ed.), *Youth, the 'Underclass' and Exclusion*. London: Routledge.

— (1999). 'The same people in the same places? Socio-spatial identities and migration in youth', *Sociology* 33(1): 1–22.

— (2000). 'Trail-blazers and path-followers: social reproduction and geographical mobility in youth', in S. Arber and C. Attias-Donfut (eds), *The Myth of Generational Conflict: Family and State in Ageing Societies*. London: Routledge.

— (2001). 'Fitting homes? Young people's housing and household strategies in rural Scotland', *Journal of Youth Studies* 4(1): 41–62.

— (2002). *The Youth Divide: Diverging Paths to Adulthood*. York: Joseph Rowntree Foundation.

— (2004). *The Parenting of Youth: Economic Dependence and Social Protection*. R000238379. End-of-award report to the ESRC. www.esrcsocietytoday.co.uk. Accessed 19.08.08.

— (2005). 'Social protection policies for young people: a cross-national comparison', in H. Bradley and J. van Hoof (eds), *Young People in Europe: Labour Markets and Citizenship*. Bristol: Policy Press, pp. 41–62.

— (forthcoming). 'Support for extended transitions: resolving the paradox', in I. Schoon and and R. K. Silbereisen (eds), *Transition from School to Work*. Jacobs Foundation Series on Adolescence. Cambridge: Cambridge University Press.

Jones, G. and Bell, R. (2000). *Balancing Acts? Youth, Parenting and Public Policy*. York: York Publishing.

Jones, G. and Martin, C. D. (1999). 'The "Young Consumer" at home: dependence, resistance and autonomy', in J. Hearn and S. Roseneil (eds), *Consuming Cultures: Power and Resistance*. Basingstoke: Macmillan.

Jones, G. and Wallace, C. (1990). 'Beyond individualisation', in L. Chisholm, P. Buchner, H.-H. Kruger and P. Brown (eds), *Childhood, Youth and Social Change: A Comparative Perspective*. London: Falmer Press.

— (1992). *Youth, Family and Citizenship*. Basingstoke: Open University Press.

Jones, G., O'Sullivan, A. and Rouse, J. (2004). ' "Because it's worth it"? Education beliefs among young people and their parents in the UK', *Youth and Society* 36(2): 203–26.

— (2006). 'Young adults, partners and parents: individual agency and the problem of support', *Journal of Youth Studies* 9(4): 375–92.

Kawasaki, K. (1994). 'Youth culture in Japan. (Japan enters the 21st Century)'. *Social Justice*. East Asian News File. Center for East Asian Studies, UCLA. www.isop.ucla.edu/eas/NewsFile/jpnyouth/94summer-sj1.htm. Accessed 19.08.08.

Kiernan, K. (1992). 'The impact of family disruption in childhood on transitions made in young adult life', *Population Studies* 46: 213–24.

Kohli, M. (1999). 'Private and public transfers between generations: linking the family and the state', *European Societies* 1(1): 81–104.

Kosugi, R. (2002). 'Increase in the numbers of young non-regular workers: situation and problems', *Japan Labour Bulletin* (1 July): 7–13.

Lacan, J. (2002 [1949]). *Ecrits: A Selection* (trans. A. Sheridan). Revised edn. New York: W. W. Norton.

Lasch, C. (1980). *The Culture of Narcissism*. London: Abacus.

Lash, S. (1994). 'Reflexivity and its doubles: structure, aesthetics, community', in U. Beck, A. Giddens and S. Lash (eds), *Reflexive Modernization: Politics, Tradition and Aesthetics in the Modern Social Order*. Cambridge: Polity.

— (2007). 'Power after hegemony: cultural studies in mutation?' *Theory, Culture and Society* 24(3): 55–78.

Lash, S. and Wynne, B. (1992). 'Introduction', in U. Beck (ed.), *Risk Society: Towards a New Modernity*. London: Sage.

Lawler, S. (2000). *Mothering the Self: Mothers, Daughters, Subjects*. London: Routledge.

Lee, N. (2001). *Children and Society: Growing Up in an Age of Uncertainty*. Buckingham: Open University Press.

Lehmann, W. (2004). ' "For some reason, I get a little scared": structure, agency, and risk in school–work transitions', *Journal of Youth Studies* 7(4): 379–96.

Lemert, C. (1997). *Postmodernism is Not What You Think*. Oxford: Blackwell.

Leonard, D. (1980). *Sex and Generation: A Study of Courtship and Weddings*. London: Tavistock.

Leonard, M. (2004). 'Bonding and bridging social capital: reflections from Belfast', *Sociology* 38(5): 927–44.

Leong, L. W. (1992). 'Cultural resistance: the cultural terrorism of British male working class youth', *Social Theory* 12: 29–58.

Lévi-Strauss, C. (1966 [1962]) *The Savage Mind*. London: Weidenfeld and Nicolson.

— (1969). *The Elementary Structure of Kinship*. Boston: Beacon Press.

Lewis, O. (1959). *Five Families: Mexican Case Studies in the Culture of Poverty*. New York: Basic Books.

Lister, R. (1990). 'Women, economic dependency and citizenship', *Journal of Social Policy* 19(4): 445–67.

Mac an Ghaill, M. (1994). *The Making of Men: Masculinities, Sexualities and Schooling*. Buckingham: Open University Press.

— (1999). *Contemporary Racisms and Ethnicities: Social and Cultural Transformations*. Buckingham: Open University Press.

MacDonald, R. (ed.) (1997). *Youth, the 'Underclass' and Social Exclusion*. London: Routledge.

MacDonald, R. and Marsh, J. (2001). 'Disconnected youth?' *Journal of Youth Studies* 4(4): 373–91.

— (2004). 'Missing school: educational engagement, youth transitions and social exclusion', *Youth and Society* 36(2): 143–62.

MacDonald, R., Shildrick, T., Webster, C. and Simpson, D. (2005). 'The significance of class and place in the extended transitions of "socially excluded" young adults', *Sociology* 39(5): 873–91.

Maffesoli, M. (1996). *The Time of the Tribes: The Decline of Individualism in Mass Society*. London: Sage.

Makeham, P. (1980). 'Youth unemployment: an examination of the evidence on youth unemployment using national statistics', Research Paper No. 10. London: Dept. of Employment.

Malinowski, B. (1922). *Argonauts of the Western Pacific*. London: Routledge and Kegan Paul.

Mannheim, K. (1952 [1927]). 'The problem of generations', in P. Kecskemeti (ed. and trans.), *Essays on the Sociology of Knowledge*. London: Routledge and Kegan Paul.

Mansfield, P. and Collard, J. (1988). *The Beginning of the Rest of Your Life? A Portrait of Newly-wed Marriage*. Basingstoke: Macmillan.

Marcuse, H. (1987 [1955]). *Eros and Civilization: A Philosophical Inquiry into Freud*, 2nd edn. London: Routledge and Kegan Paul.

Marini, M. M. (1984). 'The order of events in the transition to adulthood', *Sociology of Education* 57: 63–84.

Marsh, C. and Arber, S. (1992). 'Research on families and households in modern Britain: an introductory essay', in C. Marsh and S. Arber (eds), *Families and Households: Divisions and Change*. Basingstoke: Macmillan.

Marshall, G., Swift, A. and Roberts, S. (1997). *Against the Odds? Social Class and Social Justice in Industrial Societies*. Oxford: Clarendon Press.

Marshall, T. H. (1952). *Citizenship and Social Class*. Cambridge: Cambridge University Press.

Marsland, D. (1986). 'Young people, the family and the state', in D. Anderson and G. Dawson (eds), *Family Portraits*. London: Social Affairs Unit.

Marsland, D. and Hunter, P. (1976). 'Youth: a real force and essential concept?' *Youth in Society* 18: 10–11.

Masson, J. (1995). 'The Children Act 1989 and young people: dependence and rights to independence', in J. Brannen and M. O'Brien (eds), *Childhood and Parenthood, Part 1: Parents and Children*. London: University of London, Institute of Education.

Mauss, M. (1990 [1954]). *The Gift* (trans. W. D. Halls). London: Routledge.

Mays, J. B. (1954). *Juvenile Delinquency*. London: Cape.

McCall, G. J. and Simmons, J. L. (1971 [1966]). 'The dynamics of interactions', in K. Thompson and J. Tunstall (eds), *Sociological Perspectives*. Harmondsworth: Penguin.

McDowell, L. (2001). *Young Men Leaving School: White Working Class Masculinity*. Leicester: Youth Work Press and the Joseph Rowntree Foundation.

McKnight, A. (2002). 'From childhood poverty to labour market disadvantage', in J. Bynner, P. Elias, A. McKnight, H. Pan and G. Pierre, *Young People's Changing Routes to Independence*. York: Joseph Rowntree Foundation.

McRobbie, A. (1978). 'Working-class girls and the culture of femininity', in *Women Take Issue*, Women's Study Group. London: Hutchinson.

— (1980). 'Settling accounts with subcultures: a feminist critique', *Screen Education* 34: 37–49.

— (1994). *Postmodernism and Popular Culture*. London: Routledge.

McRobbie, A. and Garber, J. (1976). 'Girls and subcultures: an exploration', in S. Hall and T. Jefferson (eds), *Resistance through Rituals*. London: Hutchinson.

Mead, G. H. (1934 [1974]). *Mind, Self and Society*. Chicago: University of Chicago Press.

Mead, M. (1943). *Coming of Age in Samoa*. Harmondsworth: Penguin Books.

Melucci, A. (1989). 'New perspectives on social movements: an interview with Alberto Melucci', in J. Keane and P. Mier (eds), *Albert Melucci. Nomads of the Present: Social Movements and Individual Needs in Contemporary Society*. Philadelphia: Temple University Press.

— (1992). 'Youth silence and voice: selfhood and commitment in the everyday experience of adolescents', in J. Fornäs and G. Bolin (eds), *Moves in Modernity*. Stockholm: Almqvist and Wiksell International.

Merton, R. (1964). 'Anomie, anomia and social interaction', in M. Clinard (ed.), *Anomie and Deviant Behaviour*. New York: Free Press.

Miles, S. (2000). *Youth Lifestyles in a Changing World*. Buckingham: Open University Press.

Miles, S., Cliff, D. and Burr, V. (1998). 'Fitting in and sticking out: consumption, consumer meanings and the construction of young people's identities', *Journal of Youth Studies* 1(1): 81–96.

Mills, R. (1973). *Young Outsiders: A Study of Alternative Communities*. London: Routledge.

Mirza, M., Senthikumaran, A. and Ja'far, Z. (2007). *Living Together Apart: British Muslims and the Paradox of Multiculturalism*. London: Policy Exchange.

Miyamoto, M. (2001). 'Young people who don't grow up', *Japan Close-Up* (May): 12–19.

Modell, J. and Hareven, T. K. (1978). 'Transitions: patterns of timing', in T. Hareven (ed.), *Transitions: The Family and Life Course in Historical Perspective*. New York: Academy Press.

Morris, L. (1994). *Dangerous Classes: The Underclass and Social Citizenship*. London: Routledge.

Morris, L. and Irwin, S. (1992). 'Employment histories and the concept of the underclass', *Sociology* 26(3): 401–20.

Muggleton, D. (1997). 'The post-subculturalists', in S. Redhead (ed.), *The Club Culture Reader*. Oxford: Blackwell, pp. 185–203.

— (2000). *Inside Subcultures: The Postmodern Meaning of Style*. London: Berg.

Murdock, G. and McCron, R. (1976). 'Youth and class: the career of a confusion', in G. Mungham and G. Pearson (eds), *Working Class Youth Cultures*. London: Routledge and Kegan Paul.

Murray, C. (1990). *The Emerging British Underclass*. Choice in Welfare Series No. 2. London: IEA Health and Welfare Unit.

Musgrove, F. (1964). *Youth and the Social Order*. London: Routledge and Kegan Paul.

— (1969). 'The problems of youth and the social structure', *Youth and Society* 11: 35–58.

— (1974). *Ecstasy and Holiness: Counter Culture and the Open Society*. London: Methuen.

Olson, M. (1965). *The Logic of Collective Action*. Cambridge, Mass.: Harvard University Press.

ONS (2000). *Social Focus on Young People*. London: Office of National Statistics.

Ortega y Gasset, J. (1998 [1931]). *La Rebelión de las Masas* (ed. T. Mermall). Madrid: Castalia.

Pahl, R. M. E. (1984). *Divisions of Labour*. Oxford: Blackwell.

Park, A., Curtice, J., Thomson, K., Phillips, M. and Johnson, M. (eds) (2007). *British Social Attitudes Survey 23rd Report*. London: Sage.

Park, R. E., Burgess, E. W. and McKenzie, R. D. (1925). *The City*. Chicago: Chicago University Press.

Parker, I. (2004). *Slavoj Žižek: A Critical Introduction*. London: Pluto Press.

Parsons, T. (1940). 'An analytical approach to the theory of social stratification', reprinted in T. Parsons (1954), *Essays in Sociological Theory*. New York: Free Press.

— (1942). 'Age and sex in the social structure of the United States', *American Sociological Review* 7(5): 604–16.

— (1961). 'The school class as a social system,' in A. H. Halsey, Floud, J. and Anderson, C. Amold (eds), *Education, Economy and Society*. New York: Free Press Glencoe.

— (1973). 'Youth in the context of American society', in H. Silverstein (ed.), *The Sociology of Youth: Evolution and Revolution*. New York: Macmillan.

Parsons, T. and Bales, R. F. (1956). *Family: Socialization and Interaction Process*. London: Routledge and Kegan Paul.

Pascall, G. and Hendey, N. (2002). *Disability and Transition to Adulthood: Achieving Independent Living*. Brighton and York: Pavilion Publishing and the Joseph Rowntree Foundation.

Passeron, J.-C. (1990). 'Biographies, flux, itinéraires, trajectoires', *Revue Française de Sociologie* 31: 3–22.

Pavis, S., Platt, S. and Hubbard, G. (2000). *Young People in Rural Scotland: Pathways to Social Inclusion and Exclusion*. Work and Opportunity Series No. 17. York: York Publishing and the Joseph Rowntree Foundation.

Payne, J. (1987). 'Does unemployment run in families?' *Sociology* 21(2): 199–214.

Payne, J. and Payne, C. (1994). 'Recession, restructuring and the fate of the unemployed: evidence in the underclass debate', *Sociology* 28(1): 1–19.

Pearson, G. (1983). *Hooligan: A History of Respectable Fears*. Basingstoke: Macmillan.

Pedazhur, A. (2005). *Suicide Terrorism*. Cambridge: Polity.

Phoenix, A. (1991). *Young Mothers?* Cambridge: Polity.

Piaget, J. (1954). *The Construction of Reality in the Child*. New York: Basic Books.

— (1972). *Psychology and Epistemology* (trans. P. Wells). Harmondsworth: Penguin.

Pickvance, C. and Pickvance, K. (1995). 'The role of family help in the housing decisions of young people', *Sociological Review* 42: 123–49.

Pilkington, H. (1994). *Russia's Youth and Its Culture: A Nation's Constructors and Constructed*. London: Routledge.

— (ed.) (1996). *Gender, Generation and Identity in Contemporary Russia*. London: Routledge.

Platt, L. (2005). 'The intergenerational social mobility of minority ethnic groups', *Sociology* 39(3): 445–61.

— (2007). *Poverty and Ethnicity in the UK*. York: Joseph Rowntree Foundation.

Pollert, A. (1981). *Girls, Wives, Factory Lives*. London: Macmillan.

Putnam, R. D. (2000). *Bowling Alone*. New York: Simon and Schuster.

Raby, R. (2005). 'What is resistance?' *Journal of Youth Studies* 8(2): 151–71.

Raffe, D. (2003). 'Pathways linking education and work: a review of concepts, research and policy debates', *Journal of Youth Studies* 6(1): 3–20.

Reay, D. (1998). 'Rethinking social class: qualitative perspectives on class and gender', *Sociology* 32(2): 259–75.

— (2004). '"Mostly roughs and toughs": social class, race and representations in inner city schooling', *Sociology* 38(5): 1005–23.

— (2005). 'Beyond consciousness? The psychic landscape of social class', *Sociology* 39(5): 911–28.

Redhead, S. (ed.) (1993). *The End of the Century Party: Youth and Pop Towards 2000*. Manchester: University of Manchester Press.

— (1995). *Unpopular Cultures*. Manchester: Manchester University Press.

Reich, C. (1972). *The Greening of America*. Harmondsworth: Penguin.

Reich, W. (1970 [1933]). *The Mass Psychology of Fascism* (trans. V. Carfagno). New York: Farrar, Straus and Giroux.

Reuter, E. B. (1937). 'The sociology of adolescence', *American Journal of Sociology* 43: 414–27.

Rex, J. (1972). 'Power', *New Society*, 5 Oct.

Rich, A. (1981). *Compulsory Heterosexuality and Lesbian Experience*, London: Onlywomen Press.

Riesman, D. (1950). *The Lonely Crowd*. New Haven: Yale University Press.

Riley, A. (2005). 'The rebirth of tragedy out of the spirit of hip hop: a cultural sociology of gangsta rap music', *Journal of Youth Studies* 8(3): 297–311.

Riley, S. C. E. and Cahill, S. (2005). 'Managing meaning and belonging: young women's negotiation of authenticity in body art', *Journal of Youth Studies* 8(3): 261–79.

Riordan, J. (ed.) (1989). *Soviet Youth Culture*. Bloomington, IN: Indiana University Press.

Roberts, K. (1997). 'Structure and agency: the new youth research agenda', in J. Bynner, L. Chisholm and A. Furlong (eds), *Youth,*

Citizenship and Social Change in a European Context. Aldershot: Ashgate.

— (2003), 'Problems and priorities for the sociology of youth', in A. Bennett, M. Cieslik and S. Miles (eds), *Researching Youth*. Basingstoke: Palgrave Macmillan.

Rose, J. (2002). *The Intellectual Life of the British Working Class*. New Haven: Yale Nota Bene.

Rousseau, J.-J. (1911 [1762]). *Émile, or On Education*. London: Dent.

Rowntree, J. and Rowntree, M. (1968). 'The political economy of youth', *International Socialist Journal* (February): 25–58.

Rudd, P. and Evans, K. (1998). 'Structure and agency in youth transitions: student experiences of vocational further education', *Journal of Youth Studies* 1(1): 39–62.

Rugg, J. (ed.) (1999). *Young People, Housing and Social Policy*. London: Routledge.

Runciman, W. G. (1990). 'How many classes are there in contemporary British society?', *Sociology* 24: 377–96.

Rutter, M. and Madge, N. (1976). *Cycles of Disadvantage*. London: Heinemann.

Sahlins, M. (1965). 'On the sociology of primitive exchange', in M. Branton (ed.), *The Relevance of Models in Social Anthropology*. London: Tavistock.

Savage, M. (2000). *Class Analysis and Social Transformation*. Buckingham: Open University Press.

— (2005). 'Working class identities in the 1960s: revisiting the Affluent Worker Study', *Sociology* 39(5): 929–46.

Sayer, A. (2005). 'Class, moral worth and recognition', *Sociology* 39(5): 947–63.

Schoon, I. (2002). 'The accumulation of risk in the life course', YCSC Research Briefing No. 9. Brighton: ESRC/TSA.

Schoon, I. and Bynner, J. (2003). 'Risk and resilience in the life course: implications for interventions and social policies', *Journal of Youth Studies* 6(1): 21–31.

Schoon, I. and Parsons, S. (2003). 'Competence in the face of adversity: the impact of early family environment and long-term consequences', *Children and Society* 16: 260–72.

Scott, Jacqueline (2000). 'Is it a different world than when you were growing up? Generational effects on social representations and child-rearing values', *British Journal of Sociology* 51: 355–76.

Scott, Jacqueline and Chaudhary, C. (2003). *Beating the Odds: Youth and Family Disadvantage*. Leicester: Youth Work Press.

Scott, John (2000). 'Rational choice theory', in G. Browning, A. Halcli and F. Webster (eds), *Understanding Contemporary Society: Theories of the Present*. London: Sage.

Seaman, O. and Sweeting, H. (2004). 'Assisting young people's access to social capital in contemporary families: a qualitative study', *Journal of Youth Studies* 7(2): 173–90.

Sennett, R. (1998). *The Corrosion of Character: The Personal Consequences of Work in the New Capitalism*. London: Norton.

— (2004 [2003]). *Respect: The Formation of Character in an Age of Inequality*. Harmondsworth: Penguin.

Shanahan, M. J. and Longest, K. (2007). 'Thinking about the transition to adulthood: from grand theories to useful theories'. Paper presented at the Jacobs Foundation Conference *Transition from School to Work*, Marbach Castle, Germany (April).

Shields, R. (1992). 'Spaces for the study of consumption', in R. Shields (ed.), *Lifestyle Shopping: The Subject of Consumption*. London: Routledge.

Shildrick, T. and MacDonald, R. (2006). 'In defence of subculture: young people, leisure and social divisions', *Journal of Youth Studies* 9(2): 125–40.

SOED (1983). *Shorter Oxford English Dictionary on Historical Principles*, 3rd edn, ed. C. T. Onions. London: Guild Publishing.

Siegel, C. (2005). *Goth's Dark Empire*. Bloomington, IN: Indiana University Press.

Simmel, G. (1994 [1909]). 'The bridge and the door' (trans. M. Ritter), *Theory, Culture and Society* 11(1): 5–10.

— (2004 [1900]). *The Philosophy of Money* (trans. T. Bottomore and D. Frisby). London: Routledge.

Skeggs, B. (1997). *Formations of Class and Gender*. London: Sage.

— (2004). *Class, Self, Culture*. London: Routledge.

— (2005). 'The making of class and gender through visualizing moral subject formation', *Sociology* 39(5): 965–82.

Slater, D. (1997). *Consumer Culture and Modernity*. Cambridge: Polity.

Smart, C. (1997). 'Wishful thinking and harmful tinkering? Sociological reflections on family policy', *Journal of Social Policy* 26(3): 301–21.

Smith, D. (1981). 'New movements in the sociology of youth: a critique', *British Journal of Sociology* 32: 239–51.

— (1991). *Understanding the Underclass*. London: Policy Studies Institute.

Smith, J., Gilford, S. and O'Sullivan, A. (1998). *The Family Lives of Homeless Young People*. London: Family Policy Studies Centre.

Smith, R. J. and Maughan, T. (1998). 'Youth culture and the making of the post-Fordist economy: dance music in contemporary Britain', *Journal of Youth Studies* 1(2): 211–28.

Social Exclusion Unit (1998a). 'What is social exclusion?' at www.cabinet-office.gov.uk/seu/index/march

— (1998b). *Truancy and School Exclusion*, Cm 3957. London: Stationery Office.

— (1998c). *Rough Sleeping*, Cm 4008. London: Stationery Office.

— (1999a). *Teenage Pregnancy*, Cm 4342. London: Stationery Office.

— (1999b). *Bridging the Gap: New Opportunities for 16–18-year-olds Not in Education, Employment or Training*, Cm 4405. London: Stationery Office.

— (2000). *Young People: National Strategy for Neighbourhood Renewal*. Report of Policy Action Team 12. London: Stationery Office. http://www.cabinetoffice.gov.uk/seu/2000/pat12/htm

— (2001). *Preventing Social Exclusion*. London: Stationery Office.

— (2003). *A Better Education for Children in Care: The Issues*. www.socialexclusionunit.gov.uk/young_people/young_people/DissLeaflet.pdf

— (2005). *Transitions: Young Adults with Complex Needs*. SEU Final Report. London: ODPM.

Solomos, J. (1988). *Black Youth, Racism and the State: The Politics of Ideology and Policy*. Cambridge: Cambridge University Press.

Stafford, B., Heaver, C., Ashworth, K., Bates, C., Walker, R., McKay, S. and Trickey, H. (1999). *Work and Young Men*. Work and Opportunity Series No. 14. York: York Publishing and the Joseph Rowntree Foundation.

Stein, M. and Carey, K. (1986). *Leaving Care*. Oxford: Blackwell.

Tabberer, S. (2000). 'Teenage motherhood, decision-making and the transition to adulthood', *Youth and Policy* 67: 41–54.

Thatcher, M. (1987). Interview with Douglas Keay, *Woman's Own*, October 31: 8.

Thompson, E. P. (1968). *The Making of the English Working Class*. Harmondsworth: Pelican Books.

Thompson, P. (1997). 'Women, men and transgenerational family influences in social mobility', in D. Bertaux and P. Thompson (eds), *Pathways to Social Class: A Qualitative Approach to Social Mobility*. Oxford: Clarendon Press.

Thomson, R. and Taylor, R. (2005). 'Between cosmopolitanism and the locals: mobility as a resource in the transition to adulthood', *Young* 13: 327–42.

Thomson, R., Bell, R., Henderson, S., Holland, J., McCrellis, S. and Sharpe, S. (2002). 'Critical moments: choice, chance and opportunity in young people's narratives of transition to adulthood', *Sociology* 36(2): 335–54.

Thomson, R., Henderson, S. and Holland, J. (2003). 'Making the most of what you've got? Resources, values and inequalities in young women's transitions to adulthood', *Educational Review* 55(1): 33–46.

Thomson, R., Holland, J., McGrellis, S., Bell, R., Henderson, S. and Sharpe, S. (2004). 'Inventing adulthoods: a biographical approach to understanding youth citizenship', *Sociological Review* 52(2): 218–39.

Thornton, S. (1995). *Club Cultures: Music, Media and Subcultural Capital.* Cambridge: Polity.

Tomlinson, S. (2005). 'Race, ethnicity and education under New Labour', *Oxford Review of Education* 31(1): 153–71.

Tosini, D. (2007). 'Sociology of terrorism and counterterrorism: a social science understanding of terrorist threat'. *Sociology Compass* 1(2): 664–81.

Turner, B. (1986). *Equality.* London: Tavistock.

Turner, K. M. (2004). 'Young women's views on teenage motherhood: a possible explanation for the relationship between socio-economic background and teenage pregnancy outcome', *Journal of Youth Studies* 7(2): 221–38.

Turner, V. (1967). *The Forest of Symbols.* Ithaca, NY: Cornell University Press.

Twenge, J. M. (2006). *Generation Me.* New York: Free Press.

UN (1989). *Convention on the Rights of the Child.* UN Office of the High Commission for Human Rights. New York: United Nations.

— (2007). *Transitions to Adulthood: Progress and Challenges.* World Youth Report 2007. UN Department of Economic and Social Affairs. New York: United Nations.

Urry, J. (1995). *Consuming Places.* London: Routledge.

Valentine, G., Skelton, T. and Butler, R. (2003). *Towards Inclusive Youth Policies and Practices: Lessons Learned from Young Lesbians, Gay Men and D/deaf People.* Leicester: Youth Work Press.

Wacquant, L. J. D. (1989). 'Towards a reflexive sociology: a workshop with Pierre Bourdieu', *Sociological Theory* 7: 26–63.

— (1992). 'Towards a social praxeology: the structure and logic of Bourdieu's sociology', in P. Bourdieu and L. J. D. Wacquant (eds), *An Invitation to Reflexive Sociology*. Cambridge: Polity.

Walker, A. (1990). 'Blaming the victims', commentary in C. Murray (ed.), *The Emerging British Underclass*, Choice in Welfare Series No. 2. London: IEA Health and Welfare Unit.

Wallace, C. (1987). *For Richer, For Poorer: Growing Up in and out of Work*. London: Tavistock.

— (1993). 'Reflections on the concept of "strategy"', in D. Morgan and L. Stanley (eds), *Debates in Sociology*. Manchester: Manchester University Press.

— (2002). 'Household strategies: their conceptual relevance and analytical scope in social research', *Sociology* 36(2): 275–92.

Wallace, C. and Kovatcheva, S. (1998). *Youth in Society: The Construction and Deconstruction of Youth in East and West Europe*. Basingstoke: Macmillan.

Walther, A., Stauber, B. and Pohl, A. (2005). 'Informal networks in youth transitions in West Germany: biographical resource or reproduction of social inequality?' *Journal of Youth Studies* 8(2): 221–40.

Weber, M. (1961 [1923]). *General Economic History* (trans. F. Knight). New York: Collier Books.

— (1978 [1922]). *Economy and Society*. Berkeley: University of California Press.

Webster, C., Simpson, D., MacDonald, R., Abbas, A., Cieslik, M., Shildrick, T. and Simpson, M. (2004). *Poor Transitions: Social Exclusion and Young Adults*. Bristol: Policy Press.

West, A., Xavier, R. and Hind, A. (2002). *Evaluation of Excellence Challenge: Survey of Higher Education Providers*. DfES Research Report RR449. London: Department for Education and Science.

White, C., Bruce, S. and Ritchie, J. (2000). *Young People's Politics: Political Interest and Engagement amongst 14- to 24-year-olds*. York: Joseph Rowntree Foundation.

White, R. and Wyn, J. (2004). *Youth and Society: Exploring the Social Dynamics of Youth Experience*. Oxford: Oxford University Press.

Whyte, W. F. (1943). *Street Corner Society*. Chicago: University of Chicago Press.

Williamson, H. (1997). 'Status Zero youth and the "underclass": some considerations', in R. MacDonald (ed.), *Youth, the 'Underclass' and Social Exclusion*. London: Routledge.

Willis, P. (1977). *Learning to Labour: How Working Class Kids Get Working Class Jobs*. Farnborough: Saxon House.

— (1978). *Profane Culture*. London: Routledge and Kegan Paul.

— (1981). 'Cultural production is different from cultural reproduction is different from social reproduction is different from reproduction', *Interchange* 12(2–3): 48–67.

— (1984). 'Youth unemployment', *New Society*, 29 March, 5 April and 12 April.

— (1990). *Common Culture*. Milton Keynes: Open University Press.

Willmott, P. (1966). *Adolescent Boys of East London*. London: Routledge and Kegan Paul.

Wilson, B. R. (1970). *The Youth Culture and the Universities*. London: Faber.

Winnicott, D. W. (1964). *The Child, the Family, and the Outside World*. Harmondsworth: Penguin Books.

Women and Equality Unit (2002). *Key Indicators of Women's Position in Britain*. London: Department of Trade and Industry.

Wood, R. T. (1999). ' "Nailed to the X": a lyrical history of the straightedge youth subculture', *Journal of Youth Studies* 2(2): 133–51.

Wright, E. Olin (1978). *Class, Crisis and the State*, 2nd edn. London: Verso.

Wyn, J. (2004). 'Becoming adult in the 2000s: new transitions and new careers'. Australian Institute of Family Studies, *Family Matters* 68: 6–12.

Wyn, J. and Dwyer, P. (1999). 'New directions in research on youth in transition', *Journal of Youth Studies* 2(1): 5–21.

Wyn, J. and Harris, A. (2004). 'Youth research in Australia and New Zealand', *Young* 12(3): 271–89.

Young, C. M. (1987). *Young People Leaving Home in Australia: The Trend Towards Independence*. Australian Family Formation Project Monograph No. 9, Canberra.

Younge, G. (2006). 'Young people's protests are easy to mock. But ignore them at your peril', *The Guardian*, 12 June 2006, p. 29.

Žižek, S. (1989). *The Sublime Object of Ideology*. New York: Verso.

— (2007). 'Resistance is surrender', *London Review of Books*. www.lrb.co.uk/v29/n22/print/zize01_.html (downloaded 04-12-2007).

Zweig, F. (1963). *The Student in the Age of Anxiety*. London: Heinemann.

Index